Gustave Masson

Early Chroniclers of Europe : France

Gustave Masson

Early Chroniclers of Europe : France

ISBN/EAN: 9783742891679

Manufactured in Europe, USA, Canada, Australia, Japa

Cover: Foto ©ninafisch / pixelio.de

Manufactured and distributed by brebook publishing software (www.brebook.com)

Gustave Masson

Early Chroniclers of Europe : France

EARLY CHRONICLERS OF EUROPE.

FRANCE.

BY

GUSTAVE MASSON, B.A. Univ. Gallic.,

OFFICIER D'ACADÉMIE, ASSISTANT MASTER AND LIBRARIAN OF HARROW SCHOOL,
AND MEMBER OF THE SOCIÉTÉ DE L'HISTOIRE DE FRANCE.

PUBLISHED UNDER THE DIRECTION OF THE COMMITTEE
OF GENERAL LITERATURE AND EDUCATION APPOINTED BY THE
SOCIETY FOR PROMOTING CHRISTIAN KNOWLEDGE.

LONDON:
SOCIETY FOR PROMOTING CHRISTIAN KNOWLEDGE;
NORTHUMBERLAND AVENUE, CHARING CROSS;
4, ROYAL EXCHANGE; AND 48, PICCADILLY.
NEW YORK: POTT, YOUNG AND CO.

LONDON:
PRINTED BY WILLIAM CLOWES AND SONS,
STAMFORD STREET AND CHARING CROSS.

PREFACE.

THE object of this little book is to give, in a moderately small compass, an account of the sources available for the study of mediæval French history. In preparing the volume, I have made constant use of the prefaces, disquisitions, essays, and notices of every kind which accompany the best editions of the various chronicles, and which are likewise to be found in the *Bibliothèque de l'École des Chartes*, the *Histoire Littéraire de la France*, the *Journal des Savants*, and other similar works. The admirable history of French mediæval literature recently published by M. Aubertin (Paris, 2 vols. 8º.), and M. Gabriel Monod's exhaustive treatise on the sources of Merovingian history, have also been of the greatest assistance to me.

It is hoped that the following unpretending sketch, supplemented by chronological, biographical, and geographical indices, will be deemed useful. No pains have been spared to make it as complete as possible; and, in order to give to it additional literary interest, I have inserted short characteristic extracts from the leading French annalists, such as Villehardouin, Joinville, and Commines.

GUSTAVE MASSON.

CONTENTS.

PAGE

A CHRONOLOGICAL LIST OF THE PRINCIPAL FRENCH MEDIÆVAL MEMOIRS AND CHRONICLES ix

CHAPTER I.
EARLY ANNALISTS—EUSEBIUS—PROSPER OF AQUITAINE—"THE CHRONOGRAPHER FOR 534"—GREGORIUS TURONENSIS AND HIS CONTINUATORS 1

CHAPTER II.
SIDONIUS APOLLINARIS—CASSIODORUS—SAINT AVITUS—"LIVES OF THE SAINTS"—EGINHARD 13

CHAPTER III.
METRICAL CHRONICLES—CHANSONS DE GESTE—THE CARLOVINGIAN LEGEND—ROBERT WACE 35

CHAPTER IV.
LATIN ANNALISTS OF THE LATER CARLOVINGIAN AND THE CAPETIAN EPOCHS—GLABER—ANNALS OF SAINT BERTIN AND SAINT VAAST—SUGER—"L'YSTOIRE DE LI NORMANT" 50

CHAPTER V.

THE CRUSADES—FOULQUES DE CHARTRES—GUIBERT DE NOGENT—"GESTA FRANCORUM"—WILLIAM OF TYRE AND HIS CONTINUATORS 63

CHAPTER VI.

THE CRUSADES—"LA CHANSON D'ANTIOCHE"—CHRONICLE OF THE DUKES OF NORMANDY—"LE ROMAN DE HAM"—GARNIER DE PONT SAINT-MAXENCE AND HIS METRICAL LIFE OF THOMAS À BECKET ... 83

CHAPTER VII.

REIGN OF PHILIP AUGUSTUS—CRUSADE AGAINST THE ALBIGENSES—RIGORD—GULIELMUS BRITO ... 101

CHAPTER VIII.

SAINT LOUIS—GUILLAUME DE NANGIS AND HIS CONTINUATORS—JEAN DE VENETTE 114

CHAPTER IX.

VILLEHARDOUIN—JOINVILLE—ROBERT DE CLARI ... 123

CHAPTER X.

SECOND CRUSADE OF SAINT LOUIS—GUILLAUME ANELIER—GRINGORE'S "VIE MONSEIGNEUR SAINT LOYS"—PHILIPPE MOUSKES—"RÉCITS DU MÉNESTREL DE REIMS" 146

CHAPTER XI.

THE "CHRONIQUES DE SAINT DENIS"—FROISSART ... 157

CHAPTER XII.

MONSTRELET AND HIS CONTINUATORS 177

CHAPTER XIII.

The Religieux de Saint Denis—The Chronicle of Du Guesclin—The Chronicles of Louis of Bourbon 198

CHAPTER XIV.

"Le Livre des Faictz de Boucicaut"—Jouvenel des Ursins—The Cousinots—Pierre Cochon and his "Chronique Normande" 213

CHAPTER XV.

The Maid of Orleans—"Mystère du Siège d'Orléans"—Jean de Wavrin—Christine de Pisan   233

CHAPTER XVI.

Thomas Basin — Philippe de Commines—Jean de Troyes and the "Chronique Scandaleuse" ... 248

CHAPTER XVII.

Molinet—Guillaume de Villeneuve—Bouchet—Jean Masselin 267

CHAPTER XVIII.

Legislative Monuments—Laws of the Barbarians—The Feudal System and the "Coutumes"—Publicists 279

CHAPTER XIX.

Chronicles of a Local Character—"Chronique des Comtes d'Anjou"—"Chronique des Églises d'Anjou"—"Chronique de Saint Martial de Limoges" — Sermon Literature — Political Preachers—Anecdotes of Etienne de Bourbon 292

CHAPTER XX.

THE DRAMA CONSIDERED AS A SOURCE OF HISTORICAL INFORMATION 318

CHAPTER XXI.

"LA GUERRE DE METZ"—BOURDIGNÉ—PARADIN—ALAIN BOUCHARD—CARTULARIES—POLITICAL SONGS—HISTORIANS—"CHRONIQUES MARTINIANES"—NICOLE GILLES—ROBERT GAGUIN 331

BIOGRAPHICAL INDEX 355

GEOGRAPHICAL INDEX 362

A CHRONOLOGICAL LIST

OF THE

PRINCIPAL FRENCH MEDIÆVAL MEMOIRS AND CHRONICLES.

N.B.—The figures on the left-hand side represent the extreme dates of the epoch covered by the work; those on the right indicate the birth and death of the authors.

S.H.F.—Publications of the *Société de l'Histoire de France*. 147 volumes are now edited.

D.—*Collection des Documents Inédits relatifs à l'Histoire de France*. 180 volumes, 4º, in progress.

G.—F. GUIZOT: *Collection de Mémoires relatifs à l'Histoire de France, depuis la Fondation de la Monarchie Française, jusqu'au 13ᵉ Siècle.* 31 vols. 8º.

Bu.—J. A. BUCHON: *Collection des Chroniques Nationales Françaises écrites en Langue Vulgaire, du 13ᵉ au 16ᵉ Siècle.* 47 vols. 8º.

Pet.—PETITOT (ET MONMERQUE): *Collection Complète des Mémoires relatifs à l'Histoire de France, depuis le Règne de Philippe Auguste, jusqu'à la Paix de Paris* (1763). 131 vols. 8º.

Mich.—MICHAUD ET POUJOULAT. *Nouvelle Collection de Mémoires pour servir à l'Histoire de France, depuis le 13ᵉ Siècle jusqu'à la Fin du 18ᵉ.* 32 vols. 8º.

C.B.—*Collection des Chroniques Belges Inédites.* 44 vols. 8º.

300–591	Histoire Ecclésiastique des Francs, par Grégoire de Tours. S.H.F., G. 1, 2	544–595
583–641	Chronique de Frédégaire. G. 2	–600?
600–651	Vie de Dagobert I., par un Moine de Saint Denis. G. 2.	
616–683	Vie de Saint Léger, par un Moine de Saint Symphorien d'Autun. G. 2.	
622–752	Vie de Pépin le Vieux, ou de Landen. G. 2.	

642–768	Continuateurs Anonymes de Frédégaire. G. 2.	
771–812	Des Faits et Gestes de Charles le Grand, par le Moine de Saint Gall. G. 3.	
740–814	Annales, et Vie de Charlemagne, par Eginhard. G. 3, S.H.F.	771–844
780–826	Faits et Gestes de Louis le Pieux, par Ermold le Noir. G. 4	9th cent.
813–835	Vie et Actes de Louis le Débonnaire. G. 3.	
768–840	Vie de Louis le Débonnaire, par l'Astronome. G. 3.	
814–843	Histoire des Dissensions des Fils de Louis le Débonnaire, par Nithard. G. 3 ...	–858 ?
830–882	Annales de Saint Bertin, et de Saint Waast. G. 4, S.H.F.	
885–896	Siège de Paris par les Normands ; poème d'Abbon. G. 6	945–1004
883–903	Annales de Metz. G. 4.	
290–940	Histoire de l'Église de Reims, par Flodoard. G. 5	894–966
877–978	Chronique de Flodoard. G. 6.	
888–999	Richer, Histoire de son Temps. S.H.F.	10th cent.
997–1031	Helgaud, Vie du Roi Robert. G. 6.	
–1035	Chronique des Ducs de Normandie. D.	
900–1044	Chronique de Raoul Glaber. G. 6 ...	–1050 ?
950–1058	Vie de Bouchard, Comte de Melun et de Corbeil, par Eudes. G. 7.	
1090–1100	Histoire des Croisades, par Guibert de Nogent. G. 9, 10	1053–1124
1096–1100	Histoire des Croisades, par Raimond d'Agiles. G. 21	11th cent.
949–1108	Chronicon Floriacense. G. 7.	
1053–1120	Vie de Guibert de Nogent. G. 9, 10.	
1095–1120	Histoire des Croisades, par Albert d'Aix. G. 20, 21.	12th cent.
1119–1127	Vie de Charles le Bon, Comte de Flandres, par Galbert. G. 8.	
1095–1127	Histoire des Croisades, par Foulcher de Chartres. G. 24	1059–1127
850–1137	Histoire des Normands, par Guillaume de Jumiège. G. 29	10th cent.
–1141	Histoire de Normandie, par Orderic Vital. G. 25–28	1075–1142
1146–1148	Histoire de la Croisade de Louis VII., par Odon de Deuil. G. 24	–1162
1098–1151	Œuvres de Suger. G. 8, S.H.F ...	1082–1152 ?
1091–1153	Vie de Saint Bernard. G. 10.	

1140–1167	Histoire du Monastère de Vézelay. G. 7.	
610–1184	Histoire des Croisades, par Guillaume de Tyr. G. 16, 18	?1130–1192?
–1204	Chronique des Comtes d'Anjou. S.H.F.	
1198–1207	La Conqueste de Constantinople, par Villehardouin, et Henri de Valenciennes. S.H.F., Pet. 1, Mich. 1, Bu. 3	?1155–1213
1165–1208	Vie de Philippe Auguste, par Rigord. G. 11	–1207
1165–1217	Vie de Philippe Auguste, par Guillaume le Breton. G. 11	–1227?
1203–1219	Histoire de l'Hérésie des Albigeois, par Pierre de Vaulx-Cernay. G. 14, 15 ...	–1218?
1204–1219	Chronique de la Croisade contre les Albigeois. S.H.F., D.	
1096–1220	Histoire des Croisades, par Jacques de Vitry. G. 22	–1240
–1220	Histoire des Ducs de Normandie. Roman de Ham. S.H.F.	
1183–1223	La Philippide. G. 12.	
1101–1231	Chronique d'Ernoul et de Bernard le Trésorier. G. 19, S.H.F.	
700–1242	Chronique de Philippe Mousket. C.B., Bu. 4.	
1187–1271	Histoire de Saint Louis, par Joinville. S.H.F., Pet. 2, Mich. 1	1224–1319
1200–1272	Histoire de l'Hérésie des Albigeois, par Guillaume de Puy-Laurens. G. 15.	
1276–1276	Histoire de la Guerre de Navarre, par Anelier. D.	
380–1282	Chroniques des Églises d'Anjou. S.H.F.	
–1282	L'Ystoire de Li Normant, et la Chronique de Robert Viscart. S.H.F.	
–1282	Chronique Métrique d'Adam de la Halle. Bu. 7	–1286?
1223–1292	Chronique de Saint Magloire. Bu. 7.	
1160–1306	Guillaume Guiart, La Branche des Royaux Lignages. Bu. 7, 8	13th cent.
1202–1311	Chronique de Simon de Montfort. G. 15.	
700–1315	Chronique de Saint Martial de Limoges. S.H.F.	
1306–1316	Chronique Métrique de Philippe le Bel, par Godefroy de Paris. Bu. 9.	
1113–1368	Chronique Latine de Guillaume de Nangis. S.H.F., G. 13 (up to 1327)	13th cent.
1336–1380	Livre des Faits et Gestes du Roi Charles V., par Christine de Pisan. Pet. 5, 6, Mich. 1, 2	?1363-1431?

376–1381	Grandes Chroniques de France.	
1324–1389	Chronique de Bertrand Duguesclin, par Cuvelier. D.	
1327–1393	Chronique des Quatre Premiers Valois. S.H.F.	
1307–1400	Chroniques de Froissart. Bu. 13–25, S.H.F.	?1337–1410?
1360–1410	Chronique du Bon Duc Louis de Bourbon. S.H.F.	
1407–1415	Chronique de Lefèvre de Saint Rémy. Bu. 32, 33, S.H.F.	?1394–1468
1364–1421	Le Livre des Faicts du Maréchal de Boucicaut. Pet. 6, 7, Mich. 2.	
1380–1422	Chronique des Religieux de Saint Denis. D.	
1380–1422	Histoire de Charles VI., par Juvenal des Ursins. Mich. 2	1388–1473
1407–1427	Mémoires de Pierre de Fénin. Pet. 7, Mich. 2, S.H.F.	15th cent.
1422–1429	Chronique de Charles VII., par Cousinot	15th cent.
1400–1444	Chronique d'Enguerrand de Monstrelet. Bu. 26–32, S.H.F.	1390–1453
1409–1449	Journal d'un Bourgeois de Paris. Bu. 40, Mich. 2, 3.	
1434–1449	Chroniques d'Olivier de la Marche. Pet. 9, 10, Mich. 3	?1426–1502
1430–1450	Procès de la Pucelle. Bu. 3, 4, Pet. 8, S.H.F.	
1444–1461	Chronique de Mathieu d'Escouchy. Bu. 34, 35, S.H.F.	15th cent.
1448–1462	Chronique de Jacques du Clercq. Bu. 37–40, Pet. 11, Mich. 3	1420–1468
1430–1470	Chronique de George Chastelain. Bu. 41–43	1403–1475
–1471	Anciennes Chroniques, par Jean de Wavrin. S.H.F.	–1472?
1460–1483	Chronique Scandaleuse, par Jean de Troyes. Pet. 13, 14, Mich. 4 ...	15th cent.
1400–1483	Histoire des Règnes de Charles VII. et de Louis XI., par Th. Basin. S.H.F. ...	1412–1491
1494–1497	Mémoires de Guillaume de Villeneuve. Pet. 14, Mich. 4.	
1464–1498	Mémoires de Philippe de Commines. Pet. 11 13, Mich. 4, S.H.F.	1445–1509
1474–1506	Chronique de Molinet. Bu. 43–47 ...	–1507
1460–1525	Panégyrique du Chevalier sans Reproche, par Jean Bouchet. Pet. 14, Mich. 4	1476–1550

EARLY CHRONICLERS OF EUROPE.

FRANCE.

CHAPTER I.

EARLY ANNALISTS — EUSEBIUS — PROSPER OF AQUITAINE — THE "CHRONOGRAPHER FOR 354" — GREGORIUS TURONENSIS AND HIS CONTINUATORS.

IT is a generally received fact that no European nation can bear comparison with France for the richness, the variety, and the interest of its memoir-writers and epistolographers. Beginning with Villehardouin, and ending with Count de Ségur, we have an unbroken series of autobiographies, in which it would be difficult indeed to say whether we should admire most the beauty of the style, the historical importance, or the sketches they give us of social and domestic life. The voluminous collections of Messrs. Michaud and Poujoulat, Petitot and Monmerqué, the publications of the *Société de l'Histoire de France*, are ample evidences of the fact we are now stating; and, to select only two illustrations, England, Germany, Spain, and Italy can be challenged to produce a gallery of pictures equalling in merit either Saint Simon's memoirs or the correspondence of Madame de Sévigné.

But we must not forget that the scope of the present volume is limited by the sixteenth century, and that the numerous crop of memoirs resulting from the religious wars of the Huguenot epoch does not fall within our province. Philippe de Commines, marking as he does the transition from mediæval to modern institutions, is the last figure we shall have to consider; he inaugurates history properly so called, and in his pages the *naïveté* of the old chroniclers has made room for a more elaborate and artificial style of composition.

The earliest specimens of historical writing, in France as elsewhere, must be sought in those dull, lifeless annals composed by monks, and in which the most barbarous Latin is made the vehicle for preserving the record of both physical phenomena and ecclesiastical or political events. The painstaking recluse, knowing the world only from the horizon of his *scriptorium*, registered with equal concision a solar eclipse, a supposed shower of stones or of blood, and the revolution which swept from the throne a dynasty of kings. He generally began with the creation of the world, and was extremely ingenious in tracing the origins of the French nation to Æneas and the Trojan fugitives. Most of these monuments of monkish industry have been handed down to us in the first place by Pithou, then by Duchesne, and finally by the Benedictines in the *Recueil des Historiens de France*, which they began in 1738, and which the *Académie des Inscriptions et Belles-lettres* continued when the Revolution broke up all the religious communities throughout the country, and dispersed the literary treasures they had perseveringly and laboriously accumulated.

The question, however, suggests itself, What was the origin of all these works? What authority did the annalists take as their guide? What pattern did they endeavour to imitate? In a very ingenious and remarkable essay on the sources for the history of the Merovingian epoch, M. Monod names Eusebius as *the* father of mediæval chroniclers. Born at Cæsarea, in Palestine, about the year 270, he died about 340, and has left, under the title Παντοδαπὴ ἱστορία Χρονικὰ συγγράμματα, a kind of comparative chronology of all the nations whose existence was then known. "It is in this work," says M. Monod, "that history appears to us for the first time as an *ensemble*, grouped around one centre; for the religious idea really lives under this seemingly dry chronology. The Bible becomes the rule for the computation of years;

Jewish history is the starting-point for the annals of all other nations; the Roman era, the dates of the emperors, even the era of Diocletian, are made subordinate to sacred chronology. Ecclesiastical events, the death of martyrs, the election of bishops, the various episodes in the history of the Church, are noted with as much care as the accession or deposition of emperors. During the eighth century a step forward is taken; regenerate humanity counts the dates from the incarnation of our Lord, and modern chronology is founded." *

The work of Eusebius, in its primitive form, does not go further than the year 329; Saint Jerome translated it into Latin, adding a continuation as far as 378. The chronicle thus completed and vulgarized became the great historical authority for the western world, side by side with the decidedly inferior compilation of Paulus Orosius (who died about 420), entitled *Historiarum Libri VII. adversus Paganos*. All those who aimed at the reputation of historians copied Eusebius, or rather Saint Jerome, tacking on to the original narrative the facts which had fallen under their own personal observation, the records of this or that monastery, the petty revolutions of this or that diocese. Amongst the numerous continuators of the Χρονικὰ συγγράματα, we may

---

* G. Monod, *Étude Critique sur les Sources de l'Histoire Mérovingienne*. 8°. Paris, 1872.

name Marcellinus, chancellor to the Emperor Justinian (died 534), author of a chronicle extending from 379 to 534; and Idatius, a Spanish bishop, who, describing the events between 379 and 468, deals especially with the history of the Visigoths and of Southern Gaul. Marius, Bishop of Avenche, Victor, Bishop of Tunis, John, Abbot of Biclar, at the foot of the Pyrenees, Cassiodorus, Isidorus Hispalensis, and finally the well-known Bede, all belong to the same group of writers, and lead us on by a kind of uninterrupted chain from the year 445 to the year 726, having, as historians, the common characteristic of extreme dulness.

It would be a waste of time to describe here the works which swell the collections of Duchesne and of the Benedictines, but two or three of the most important deserve a passing mention, and may be quoted as possessing a certain amount of historical value. Prosper of Aquitaine (403-463?), one of the most distinguished members of the clergy of Marseille, the friend and correspondent of Saint Augustine, should certainly not be forgotten. He discussed the origin of the French nation in a work extending down to the death of Valentinian III. and the taking of Rome by Genseric in the year 455. Written as an abridgment, it follows the chronicle, of Eusebius as far as the year 326, and for the subsequent events adheres to the text of Saint Jerome. With the year 379 Prosper starts a fresh work, giving us a brief history of the

Lombards, whom he describes as a nation coming from Scandinavia, on the extreme limits of the ocean. The chronicle of Prosper contains a list of the consuls beginning with L. Rubellius Geminus and C. Fufius Geminus, in the fifteenth year of the reign of Tiberius (A.D. 29). Cassiodorus, who flourished during the fifth century, and also wrote a *chronicon*, in obedience to the orders of Theodoric, borrowed from Prosper his list of consuls, transcribing it blindly with all its mistakes.

We must notice that Prosper composed, so to say, three different editions of his chronicle. The first one ended with the fourteenth consulate of the younger Theodosius and with that of Maximus (A.D. 433). In a subsequent revision the author added a supplemental narrative, extending over the space of twelve years, and taking us as far as A.D. 445, when Valentinian III. was consul for the sixth time, sharing his dignity with Nonius or Nono. Finally, the third *rédaction* brought Prosper's compilation down to the storming of Rome by the Vandals, as we have already said, when the same Valentinian, having Anthemius as his colleague, was in his eighth consulate.

The chronicle we are now describing is divided into two parts, the former beginning with the year 378, whilst the extreme date of the latter is 455. This half alone was known to the learned when Labbe published the entire work in 1657, ascribing it to Tiro Prosper. As a matter of course, ecclesiastical history has the lion's share in Prosper's chronicle, and more especially the events connected with the Pelagian controversy. However, we also find brief notices of political occurrences, accounts of the Roman emperors, bishops, etc. It is a singular circumstance, that whilst the first draft of the work follows the years of the consuls so far as the chronological arrangement is concerned, the second takes as its standard of computation the years of the emperors; hence the titles *Chronicon Consulare* and *Chronicon Imperiale* which they respectively bear. The distinctive feature of this work, nay, of all the collections of annals belonging to the Merovingian epoch, is that the influence of the Roman empire asserts itself strongly side by side with that of the Christian Church. The destinies of the spiritual power seem closely related to the traditions of the past; and even beyond the frontiers of Italy, and at a time when the imperial rule was, to all appearances, destroyed for ever, the clergy persistently and earnestly believed in the perpetuity of the empire.

The fact is that the great majority of the "clerics" belonged to races which had long since been incorporated in the Roman world, now conquered and trampled down by the barbarians. As late as the eighth century they retained with pride the name of Romans; and the ecclesiastical chroniclers, till the time of Marius, Bishop of Avenche (end of the sixth century), following the example set by Prosper of Aquitaine, count the years either in accordance with the reigns of the emperors or the names of the consuls. In all these works the affairs of Rome, or even of the East, absorb nearly the whole space, very little attention being paid to what was taking place in the various countries to which the writers belonged by birth. Throughout the whole of the mediæval period we constantly notice traces of this parallel movement; the Roman traditions and the interests of the Church exercise equal weight upon the mind of the annalists, and are held by them in equal respect. M. Gabriel Monod, from whom we have borrowed the above remarks, quotes, as an instance of this tendency, a book which enjoyed at one time very great popularity, and a copy of which is preserved in the public library at Vienna; it is entitled the *Chronographer for* 354, and gives us an official Roman calendar for that year. The following is a list of its contents :—1. A calendar of a purely secular (heathen) and Roman kind, with the indication of the public games, days of the meeting of the senate, etc. 2. A set of annals, beginning with Julius Cæsar, and going down to the year 539. 3. The Consular Fasti, to the year 354. 4. Easter tables from 312, and calculated for one hundred years. 5. A list of the prefects of Rome from 258 to 354. 6. A necrological table of the bishops of Rome and of the Christian martyrs. 7. A list of the popes from 352 to 369. 8. A second series of annals from Julius Cæsar to 403, and from 455 to 496. 9. A general chronicle (*Chronicon Horosii*). 10. A special chronicle of the city of Rome to the year 334. 11. A description of the regions and districts of Rome. The numbers 1, 9, and 10 of this remarkable work have been published by Mommsen in his treatise *Ueber den Chronograph des Jahres*, 354. Copies of the whole collection, or of portions of it, were of frequent occurrence; they served as a kind of common memorandum-book, to which additions were subsequently made, and many an important local chronicle was engrafted upon the *Chronograph* for the year 354. Thus, the Vienna manuscript gives us annals written at Ravenna, and known to antiquarians by the designation of the *Cuspinian anonym;* thus, again, the pontifical biographies ascribed to Anastasius have their origin in the list of the popes which forms number 7; finally, the necrological indications contained in number 6, expanded and completed, have formed the martyrologies so common during the mediæval epoch (*Martyr. Hieronymi, Gellonensis, Bedæ, Usuardi, Notkeri*). It is not too much to say that nearly all the historical literature of the Middle Ages is derived from this twofold source—Saint Prosper and the *Chronographer*. Even when, in the eighth and ninth centuries, the study of classical antiquity was partly revived, the most enthusiastic admirers of Cicero, Livy, and Tacitus copied over and over again the prose of the Aquitanian controversialist, and the dreary catalogues of the official calendar.

We need scarcely inform our readers that the only merit of such works consists in their being for a certain limited epoch the record of contemporary observers. Style is entirely out of the question in the writings of Prosper, as well as in those of Gregorius Turonensis (539–593), who, however, judged from the standpoint of historical importance alone, is immeasurably superior to all the Latin annalists of the early Middle Ages. The *Historia Francorum* of the Bishop of Tours, divided into sixteen books, covers the space of 174 years, from 417 to 591, and is of the highest value for the whole period of the Merovingian dynasty. No one has described with more picturesque truth that strange condition of a society still in a state of disorganization, where the work of conquest was not yet accomplished, and where a number of discordant elements had still to be welded together, so as to form one powerful nation. Romans, Gauls, Franks, Burgundians, contribute in equal proportion their share of interest to the dramatic narrative, and the contrast presented between the rudeness of the invaders and the comparative polish of Gallo-Roman society is extremely striking. M. Augustin Thierry has observed that Froissart alone equals Gregorius Turonensis in the talent of bringing out the individual character of his personages, and of making a dialogue the means of pictorial representation. The authority of our chronicler may, perhaps, be challenged on certain points,[1] and it would be a wonder if an annalist of the sixth century was always and uniformly accurate; but the Bishop of Tours must be judged less from the details of his work, than from the general view it gives us of the society amidst which he moved; and, besides, a duly qualified *savant* has recently proved that the frequent travels of Gregorius Turonensis throughout the length and breadth of Gaul gave him the means of forming a tolerable idea of the state of the people, and that the study of the *Historia Francorum*, by supplying us with minute information respecting the political subdivisions of France, can alone enable us to understand thoroughly the relative importance of the various kingdoms amongst which the country was split up during the time of the Merovingians.[2]

Fredegarius continued the history of Gregorius Turonensis to the year 641, giving us curious and valuable details on the reigns of Clotaire II., Dagobert I., and Clovis II. His compilation cannot, however, be named in the same breath as the more elaborate work of his predecessor. Four annalists took up in succession the thread of the

---

[1] See M. Lecoy de la Marche's essay, *De l'Autorité de Grégoire de Tours*. 8°. Paris, 1861; and, on the other side of the question, M. G. Monod's disquisition, already referred to.

[2] See M. A. Longnon's *Géographie de la Gaule au VI° Siècle*. 8°. Paris, 1878.

narrative where Fredegarius had left it, and the intolerable tediousness of these worthy personages seems to increase in the same proportion as the political wretchedness of the last days of the Merovingians. The *rois fainéants* deserved, to commemorate their insignificance, no better pens than those of dry, stupid chroniclers.

CHAPTER II.

SIDONIUS APOLLINARIS — CASSIODORUS — SAINT AVITUS — "LIVES OF THE SAINTS" — EGINHARD.

LITERATURE, strictly so called, contributes an abundant store of historical information on the events which took place in Gaul during the mediæval period. Sermons and homilies, letters, poetical effusions, had all for their groundwork certain events, and were suggested by the transactions of statesmen, generals, prelates, or other personages holding high offices in Church and State. Political revolutions, the movements of the hordes of barbarians, the vices or qualities of local administrators, the authority, either bad or good, of delegates from Rome, are the habitual theme of these compositions, and give to them an interest which amply makes up for their shortcomings in point of style and of literary merit. Let us name, in the first place, under this head, the correspondence of Sidonius Apollinaris, a new and excellent edition of which has just been published

(Eugène Baret, *C. Soll. Apollinaris Sidonii Opera.* 8°. Paris, 1879).

Born at Lyons in 430 or 431, Sidonius Apollinaris belonged to an ancient Gallo-Roman family, and married the daughter of Avitus, who having ascended the imperial throne in 456, named him to the post of senator and prefect of Rome. After the downfall of his father-in-law (457), Sidonius sent in his submission to Majorian, condescending even to celebrate him in a panegyric; he acknowledged with equal readiness the rule of the Emperor Anthemius, who rewarded him for his servility by the appointments of chief of the senate, *patrice*, and prefect of Rome. He had evidently no very strong political convictions, and unhesitatingly worshipped the powers that were, whatever might be their origin, for we find him celebrating the virtues of Euric, king of the Visigoths, although he had been sent to prison by him a short time before. He was then Bishop of Clermont; he died in 488. We need scarcely tell our readers that the literary productions of Sidonius Apollinaris consist chiefly of panegyrics, besides other short poetical effusions. As we have already stated, these pieces interest us exclusively by their historical importance, and in this respect they are quite equal to the bishop's correspondence, which consists of 147 letters addressed to various persons.

A modern French author, who has himself given in his writings the most perfect specimen of the picturesque style applied to history—M. Augustin Thierry—shows us to what use the letters and panegyrics of Sidonius Apollinaris can be put by those students who wish to know the state of Gallo-Roman society during the Merovingian times. The sixth *Lettre sur l'Histoire de France* is full of interesting details on this subject, and it would not be difficult to gather from the compositions of the Bishop of Clermont the elements of a striking and animated picture of the court held at Bordeaux by Euric, king of the Visigoths. The following may serve as a specimen :—

"I have seen the moon nearly run its race twice, and have been able to obtain only one single hearing. The master of this place can afford me little of his leisure, for the whole world is also asking for an answer to its requests, and awaits that answer with submission. Here we see the blue-eyed Saxon, intrepid enough when he ploughs the main, but ill at ease when he is on shore. Here the old Sicamber allows his hair to grow again, which he had been compelled to cut after his defeat. Here the Herulus stalks about; his cheeks are of a greenish colour, nearly approximating that of the ocean, the furthest banks of which he inhabits. Here the Burgundian, seven feet high, bends his knee and implores peace. Here the Ostrogoth claims the patronage which is the secret of his strength, and by means of which he strikes terror into the Huns; humble in one respect, proud in the other. And thou, O Roman, thou comest here thyself to sue for life; when the north threatens thee with any troubles, thou entreatest the help of Euric's arm against the hordes of Scythia; thou askest the powerful Garonne to lend its assistance to the weakened Tiber."[1]

The style of this extract indicates sufficiently the date of its composition. Sidonius Apollinaris was then under sentence of banishment from Auvergne as suspected of regretting the imperial *régime*, and he had come to Bordeaux for the purpose of obtaining from the king of the Visigoths the remission of the penalty.

"We all know," says M. Baret, "to what excellent profit talented men have turned the letters of Cicero, and those of Pliny; the collection of Sidonius Apollinaris corresponds, so far as the fifth century is concerned, to the voluminous *recueil* of the friend of Atticus. The light it casts upon that epoch reminds us of the information we derive from Madame de Sévigné's brilliant gossip towards an accurate knowledge of the court of Louis XIV."

No one has better related than our poet the particulars of Avitus's promotion to the imperial dignity; no one has given more precise and trustworthy details on the share which Theodoric II. had in that event. "Only assume the title of Augustus," says the king of the Visigoths. "Why dost

---

[1] Sidon. Apollin. *Epist.* lib. viii. ep. 9.

thou turn thine eyes away? It is a fine thing to spurn the empire of the world. We do not place any compulsion upon thee; we only exhort thee to accept. I am the friend of Rome, if thou becomest its chief; I shall fight on the side of Rome, if thou art emperor. Thou deprivest no one of the throne; no Augustus reigns within the walls of Rome. The empty palace belongs to thee."[1]

We shall now give another curious sketch, from which an historical painter could easily borrow hints on the costume and weapons of a Frankish chieftain. The personage introduced is a prince named Sigismer, who had come to Lyons in order to marry a daughter of the Burgundian king, Chilpéric.

"Sigismer was a man of lofty stature and of vigorous appearance; his features were ruddy, his red hair fell in golden locks on his shoulders. His dress consisted of a close-fitting tunic of white silk with a golden embroidery, over which was thrown a purple mantle; the trappings of his horse were resplendent with gold and precious stones. On entering the town, he jumped from his steed, and as a mark of honour to his father-in-law, he went on foot to the *prætorium*, where the king awaited him. The Frankish nobles thus marched through the streets of Lyons in complete war attire—a jacket of various colours just touching the

---

[1] *Paneg. Avito Augusto socero dictus.*

leg; over this, by way of a cloak, a green tunic edged with red fringe; leggings of undressed leather fixed below their knee, and leaving the calf of the leg bare. Their strong arms were also uncovered as high up as the elbow. In their right hand they carried a spear provided with hooks, and one of those double-edged battle-axes meant to be hurled from a distance, and which are the national weapons of the Franks. The other hand supported a golden shield with silver rim, protecting their left side; a long sword hung from their girdle; the whole air rang with the noise of their armour."[1]

The relations between the nobles and the inferior classes of society, those which existed between serfs and serfs, are admirably described by Sidonius Apollinaris; we are also indebted to him for literary facts and incidents which he alone has mentioned. But for him we should not know that Saint Remi composed several *declamations*, or speeches, and that Faustus, Bishop of Riez, wrote and sent off to Brittany a certain *opus operosissimum*, which must not be confounded with the two treatises on predestination and freewill we already possess from the pen of that celebrated divine.

If we now pass on to the consideration of events of a strictly historical character, a great many occur to us which Sidonius Apollinaris alone has described. No other writer, for instance, has

---

[1] *Epist.* iv. 7.

handed down to us either the name of Sigismer, the barbarian king alluded to above, or that of the Queen Ragnahild. The war carried on by Leo I. against the Huns is mentioned in the panegyric of Anthemius, and from the letters 9 and 11, Book IV. and 9, Book V., we see that Euric's attack upon Auvergne occurred in 470. The victory gained by Aetius and Majorian over Clovis has sometimes been questioned by critics; a passage in the panegyric of Majorian establishes it beyond a doubt. We find also in the letters of the Bishop of Clermont details of the most valuable kind on the character, the government, and the quarrels of the Burgundian kings, sons of Gundioc.

It is time, however, that we should turn our attention to another personage, whose works are full of information about the events of the Merovingian epoch, and who has thus helped in an indirect manner to confirm the statements made by professed annalists. We mean the poet Fortunatus (Venantius Honorius Clementianus). Born at Trevisa in Italy about the year 530, he died at Poitiers at the beginning of the sixth century. Having made a vow to visit the tomb of Saint Martin at Tours, he went to Gaul in 567, and repaired to the court of the Frankish chieftain Sigebert, whose marriage with Brunehaut he celebrated in a kind of *epithalamium*. M. Augustin Thierry has given (*Récits des Temps Mérovingiens*: 5° récit) very full and interesting details on

Fortunatus, and we shall borrow from him a few characteristic remarks. When he had accomplished his pilgrimage at Tours, the poet went on from town to town, greeted, entertained, sought after by men rich and of high rank, who prided themselves on their politeness and their elegance. From Mentz to Bordeaux, and from Toulouse to Cologne, he traversed the length and breadth of Gaul, visiting on his passage bishops, counts, dukes, whether they were Gauls or Franks by birth, and finding in most of them first kind hosts, then often real friends. Those whom he had just left, after a stay more or less prolonged in their episcopal palace, their country house, or their fortified residence, kept up with him a regular correspondence; he, in his turn, acknowledging their letters by elegiac poems, in which he related the incidents and reminiscences of his travels. He spoke to each of the natural scenery or the monuments of his country; described the picturesque sites, the rivers, the woods, the cultivation of the rural districts, the splendour of the ecclesiastical buildings, the agreeable character of the private residences. . . . If his correspondent happened to be a Frankish lord, he praised the good nature of his fellow-countrymen, their genuine hospitality, the ease with which they carried on a conversation in the Latin tongue; if, on the other hand, he addressed a Gallo-Roman, the merits described were political skill, cleverness, knowledge of business, deep acquaintance with the mysteries of legal science. In the case of a bishop, due praise was given to his piety, his zeal in building and consecrating new churches, his administrative energy in providing for the safety, the cleanliness, and the embellishment of the chief towns in his diocese. One man is eulogized for having restored ancient buildings which were falling in ruins—a prætorium, a portico, public baths; another for improving the drainage, digging canals, and encouraging agriculture; a third for erecting citadels, and strengthening posts till then easy of attack. It can easily be imagined that enumerations of this kind give plenty of scope for historical allusions, sketches of character, notice of important social and political events. In the course of his journeys, Fortunatus became acquainted with Saint Radegonde, daughter of Bertharius, King of Thuringia, and wife of Chilpéric, King of Soissons. This princess, struck with a violent desire of embracing a religious life, had fled to Poitiers (541), founded there the celebrated monastery of Sainte Croix, and assembled around herself a kind of community, to which she set the example of a life where the practice of strict religious duties was united to intellectual pursuits and a taste for literature. Fortunatus, settled in the midst of this attractive society, soon rose to be one of its chief ornaments; and the praises of Saint Radegonde and her companions occupy a large place in his poetry. As we have already said, however, the effusions of the Bishop of Poitiers have often the character and the importance of a chronicle; and M. Augustin Thierry has reprinted in the appendix to his *Récits des Temps Mérovingiens* a fragment of one hundred elegiac couplets supposed to be written by Saint Radegonde, and treating of the downfall of the Thuringian nation, and the marriage of King Chilpéric with Galeswinthe (vol. ii. Appendix, No. 6). The entire poem contains 372 lines, and is described by M. Guizot (*Histoire de la Civilisation*, leçon xviii.) as full of feeling, ingeniously and not infrequently well expressed.

Cassiodorus is a writer whom we must not forget in our gallery, and whose works claim a place amongst the historical monuments of the early Middle Ages. "His letters," says M. Gabriel Monod, "are a genuine historical collection, giving us royal despatches, diplomas, official documents of every kind, of the highest value for the history of the sixth century in Italy and in Southern Gaul." Born in 468, at Scylacium in Calabria, Magnus Aurelius Cassiodorus enjoyed the greatest favour at the court of Theodoric, king of the Ostrogoths, whose minister he became. After having tried in vain to protect Italy against the invasion of the Goths on the one side, and the pretensions of the Greeks on the other, he retired from public life in 538, settled on his estates in Calabria, and founded there a monastic establishment, the members of which studied sacred and profane literature, the liberal arts, and agriculture. He died after the year 563. The works of Cassiodorus which are interesting to the historian are the twelve books of letters, mentioned above, and an ecclesiastical chronicle which is both dry and inaccurate.

Although they discuss subjects closely connected with the history of France, both Fortunatus and Cassiodorus are foreigners. Avitus, on the other hand, with whom we have now to deal, is essentially a Frenchman, and therefore possesses a twofold claim upon our attention. Alcimus Ecdicius Avitus, born in Auvergne, about the middle of the fifth century, and who died in 522, belonged to an illustrious family, which had given, during the preceding century, the Emperor Avitus to the throne. He succeeded his father as Bishop of Vienne, and acquired great favour at the court of Gondebaud, king of the Burgundians. This prince was fond of making him dispute with Arian priests, and commissioned him to refute the doctrines of Nestorius, Eutychius, and Faustus, Bishop of Riez. Avitus failed, however, to convert Gondebaud to orthodox Christianity, and carried on a correspondence with Clovis, whom he is suspected of having excited to the conquest of Burgundy. Avitus has left numerous letters addressed to the bishops of Rome, Constantinople, and Jerusalem, as well as to several prelates in

Gaul, besides six poems on religious subjects. Three of these poems have formed the subject of an ingenious parallel, by M. Guizot, with Milton's *Paradise Lost*. For the history of the reigns of Gondebaud and Sigismond, the letters of Saint Avitus, the great Bishop of Vienne, are of the highest importance.

The celebrated Italian scholar Muratori, in the preface to his edition of the *Chronicon Farfense*, said one day, "It seems to me useless to insist with my readers on the value of monastic chronicles, as illustrating not only the ecclesiastical, but also the civil and political, history of a country. Even, if I left this truth to pass unnoticed, it would be manifest for the learned. It is sufficiently explained by the fact that the order of Saint Benedict, having for a long time spread itself far and wide, had acquired so much power and influence that the monks belonging to it had numerous relations both with temporal and ecclesiastical princes. Their abbots were obliged to frequent at intervals the courts of popes, emperors, and kings, and they had to give to this or that government the benefit of their advice and of their support." This remark of Muratori's can be extended and made applicable to all religious communities in France as elsewhere; and the abbeys of Marmoutier, Saint Bertin, Saint Denis, and Saint Germain des Prés—to name only these four—were centres from which proceeded some of the most precious contributions to the historical literature of the nation.

Together, therefore, with these memoirs, composed *ex professo*, if we may so say, and intended to hand down to posterity the record of events which were altering the face of society, let us reserve a place for the hagiographers whose praiseworthy labours have contributed so much to our knowledge of the Middle Ages. The *acta sanctorum*, which swell the folios of the Bollandists, originally written with a view to edification, are valuable sources of information on the history of Gallo-Roman civilization, and the pious legends they contain supply us with nearly all the knowledge we possess on those bygone times.

The editions of lives of the saints published by Mabillon are generally superior, so far as the text is concerned, to those of the Bollandists, but they are limited to members of the order of Saint Benedict, and lack the critical disquisitions which are so conspicuous a part of the great Jesuit collection. The old heathen schools of Lyons, Bordeaux, and Trèves had done excellent work, but they had given way to a new order of things, and the Church had inherited the traditions left by these once celebrated centres of learning. By a kind of natural transformation, history, like poetry and literature properly so called, became essentially and exclusively ecclesiastical; instead of dealing with political subjects, and describing events of what we may style a secular character, the annalists of the second, third, and fourth centuries devoted their attention to the interests of the Church, and the lives of saints and martyrs. The earliest specimen of that kind of literature is the epistle sent by the Christians of Vienne and of Lyons to their brethren in Asia, on the occasion of the martyrdom of Saint Pothinus and his forty-seven companions (A.D. 177). This document is not, strictly speaking, a biography, but rather a *pièce justificative;* if we wish to find the earliest biographical sketch of a Gallo-Roman saint, we must take up the memoir devoted to Saint Martin of Tours by his disciple and friend Sulpicius Severus (end of the fourth century). As time goes on, these monuments of hagiography become more and more numerous; during the fourth and fifth centuries they supply an abundant crop of the richest historical materials, and as the Church in those days was intimately and constantly mixed up with every event of a political character, it follows that the details these documents give us on the state of society, the dissolution of the old Roman civilization, and the progress of the barbarians, are both abundant and perfectly reliable. Thus, as M. G. Monod remarks, the life of Saint Severinus, the apostle of the Upper Danube (died in 482), written by the Abbot Eugippus, his pupil, who flourished at the end of the fifth century and at the beginning of the sixth, is one of the most curious documents for the history of Southern Germany at the time of the invasion of the barbarians. Later on, monks and priests became the confidential advisers of the Merovingian kings; they filled the highest offices at their court, and often ruled in their name. We find Saint Eligius, Saint Léger, Saint Ouen, and Saint Arnulphus, invested with almost regal powers; and at last the mayors of the palace openly assume the position of rivals of the *rois fainéants*, the military force of the Franks is placed at the service of Christian propagandism, and the destinies of the community, whether Austrasian or Neustrian, are in the hands of the clergy. Under such circumstances the monuments of biographical literature we have just been alluding to become increasingly valuable, and form the framework, so to say, of history, whether secular or ecclesiastical. Neander's *Kirchengeschichte* and Montalembert's *Moines d'Occident* are full of episodes which serve to illustrate the fact we are stating, and which can be recommended to those amongst our readers who have no time to study the folios of Mabillon, Ruinart, or the Bollandists. For instance, the biography of Saint Maur, although it has probably suffered some grievous interpolations (Mabillon, *Præf. in Sæc.* I. *Act. SS. O. S. B.*), gives us curious details on claustral life during the sixth century, and contains, at any rate, one of the first examples of the forms employed for donations made by kings and other chieftains to heads of ecclesiastical communities. Thus, again, the fact of the persistence of paganism in Gaul down to a comparatively late period is amply established by texts from the hagiographers. Saint Lupus, Bishop of Sens, exiled by Clotaire II. about 615, was intrusted to the care of a duke called Boson, who was still pagan, and who occupied the shores of the Oise (Bolland., *Act. SS.* tom. 1, sept. p. 859). The second successor of Saint Columba at Bobbio, the Abbot Bertulf, who died in 640, was of pagan birth, although a near relation of Saint Arnoul, Bishop of Metz (Montalembert, *Monks of the West*, ii. 226). Some persons have supposed that the ceremony of the tonsure always indicated, on the part of him who accepted it, the intention of taking holy orders. Now, it is, if not quite certain, at least extremely probable, that in the case of the children of Clodomir, the tonsure was merely a symbol of the renouncing the hereditary right to the position of chieftain, and to the *status* of a freeman. "A Merovingian prince," says M. Augustin Thierry, "could suffer this temporary humiliation in two different ways: either the hair was cut in the manner of the Franks—that is to say, to the top of the neck—or cut very short in the Roman fashion" (*Récits des Temps Mérovingiens*). This latter process, being used in connection with the ecclesiastical tonsure, was, of course, of a permanent character, whereas the former one had a temporary nature, and did not imply absolute and unconditional abdication of political rights and privileges. An example of this occurs in the biography of Saint Léger, where the person mentioned is Thierry III., King of Neustria, deposed in 670 by the great rebels against the tyranny of Ebroin, and succeeded by his brother Childeric II. His brother asked him what should be done with him; he answered, "What they will; unjustly deposed, I wait the judgment of the King of Heaven." He was shut up in the monastery of Saint Denis, till his hair had grown again to its usual length, and then the judgment of God, which he had appealed to, allowed him to reign happily afterwards (*Anon. Œduen. Vit. S. Leodegarii*, c. 3, quoted by Montalembert, ii. 256).

It is curious to notice the desponding tone in which the venerable annalists express themselves, and the gloomy hue which history assumes under their pen. As M. Guizot aptly remarks, from the tenth to the twelfth centuries the clergy alone cared for either the past or the future; they alone were invested with that power which is derived from moral and intellectual worth; they set the highest value on their recollections and on their hopes, and it is not surprising that the sight of the apparent triumph of brutal force, and of a world living exclusively for the present, should have wrung from them accents of despair.

"The cultivation of literature fades away, or rather disappears, in all the cities of Gaul. In the midst of good and of bad actions, whilst the fierceness of nations and the fury of kings were let loose; whilst the Church was attacked by heresy and defended by the faithful; whilst the belief in Christian truth, fervent in many hearts, was perishing in a few others; whilst churches were endowed by some pious men and robbed by the wicked;— no grammarian, accomplished in the science of dialectics, has undertaken to relate these events, either in prose or in verse. Many men, therefore, groaned, saying, 'Woe to our time! because the study of literature perishes from amongst us, and no one is able to commemorate in his writings the events of the present day.'"[1]

The powerful hand of Charlemagne, however, re-established order for a season, and if the new Empire of the West, constructed out of heterogeneous elements, did not last much longer than its founder, yet it was a grand attempt to restore the unity which the invasions of the barbarians seemed to have broken up for ever. If it be true that he who founds a dynasty is greater than the one who consolidates it, Charles Martel must be pronounced decidedly superior to Charlemagne, and yet it is the latter whom posterity has always regarded as *the* representative man of the Carlovingian race. This may be ascribed chiefly to two causes. First of all, the title of emperor carries along with it a

---

[1] Preface to the *Historia Francorum* of Gregorius Turonensis.

prestige which, to many, is overruling; and "The Hammerer," who never wore a crown, must needs yield to him who donned the imperial purple. But further, during the whole space of his forty years' reign, Charlemagne proved himself the generous and constant protector of the Church, whilst Charles Martel, on the contrary, was its spoliator; and as, at that time, "the pen of a ready writer" was exclusively held by ecclesiastics, we may imagine that the portrait they gave of the conqueror of the Saracens was not likely to be flattering.

The great historical authority for the reign of Charlemagne is Eginhard. A pupil of Alcuin's, and a friend of the emperor, Eginhard soon rose into great favour; he became the private secretary of Charlemagne, and having been honoured with the duty of bestowing upon the *literati* of the day the rewards, pensions, and dignities granted by his master, he thus found himself thrown into the society of men whose conversation enabled him to increase daily his own stock of knowledge. Amongst the members of what was known as the Palatine Academy, Eginhard appeared under the name of Beleseel. The story of his supposed marriage with Emma, the daughter of Charlemagne, is well known, but it has been preserved only in the chronicles of the monastery of Lauresheim, and is evidently apocryphal. Eginhard does not wish in the least to pass as a *littérateur*—he describes himself "a barbarian little accustomed to the language of the Romans;" at the same time we must acknowledge, in all fairness, that he underrates his talent, and, although his imitations of Suetonius are scarcely disguised, some credit must be allowed to the man who, in the ninth century, could say that he was acquainted with the writings of the Roman historians. Independently of his correspondence, Eginhard has left two works of a distinctly historical character—1. *The Life of Charlemagne;* 2. *The Annals of his Time.* We cannot do better than transcribe here M. Guizot's remarks on the former of these productions; they will show conclusively that, since the days of Gregorius Turonensis and of his continuators, the art of the historian had been making rapid progress, and that the ruggedness of the old annalists was softening down.

"*The Life of Charlemagne* is, without comparison, the most distinguished history from the sixth to the eighth century—indeed, the only one which can be called a history, for it is the only one in which we recognize any traces of composition, any political and literary pretension. . . . *The Life of Charlemagne* is not a chronicle; it is a genuine political biography, written by a man who was present at the events he narrates, and who understood them. Eginhard commences by describing the state of Frankish Gaul under the last Merovingians. We see that their dethronement by

Pepin was still a subject of discussion with a certain number of men, and caused some disquietude to the race of Charlemagne. Eginhard took care to show how it could not be otherwise. He minutely describes the humiliation and powerlessness into which the Merovingians had fallen; proceeds from this exposition to recount the natural accessions of the Carlovingians; adds a few words upon the reign of Pepin, upon the beginning of that of Charlemagne, and his relations with his brother Carloman; and enters at last into the account of the reign of Charlemagne alone. The first part of the account is devoted to the wars of that prince, and especially his wars against the Saxons. From wars and conquests, the author passes to the internal government, to the administration of Charlemagne; lastly, he comes to his domestic life, his personal character. Composed on so elaborate a plan, in so systematic a method, *The Life of Charlemagne* rises almost to the position of a work of art; it combines the importance of an excellent historical authority with the merits of a literary production, and if Eginhard's language is open to criticism, the plan of the work and the general harmony of its constituent part is, on the other hand, remarkable."[1]

With reference to *The Annals*, it may be noticed that several critics have denied that they are the

---

[1] *Histoire de la Civilisation en France*: leçon 23.

work of Eginhard, although there is no reason for this supposition. The difference between the artistic qualities of the biography and the dry, dull style of the other work, is certainly strong enough to have justified the opinion of those who could not see in both compositions signs of the same origin; but still the overwhelming evidence must be pronounced to be in the other direction. It is said that Eginhard composed also a detailed account of the wars against the Saxons. Nothing of it has come down to us. He died in 839, in the monastery of Sligestadt, which he had founded.

CHAPTER III.

METRICAL CHRONICLES—CHANSONS DE GESTE—
THE CARLOVINGIAN LEGEND—ROBERT WACE.

THE empire of Charlemagne was falling to pieces, and whilst Charles the Bald, Louis the Stammerer, and Charles the Simple allowed the crown to lose all its prestige in the face of growing feudalism, it seemed as if another invasion of barbarians was once more threatening the very existence of society. "One day," says an old annalist, "that Charlemagne had stopped in a city of Gallia Narbonnensis, a few Scandinavian boats came to plunder even within the limits of the harbour. Some thought that they were Jewish merchants; others believed them to be either Africans, or traders from Brittany. Charles, however, recognized them by the fleetness of their craft. 'They are not merchants,' he said, 'but cruel enemies.' Pursued, they speedily disappeared. Then the emperor, rising from the table, went to the window which looked towards the east, and remained there a long time, his face suffused with tears. As no one ventured to question him, he said to the nobles standing around: 'Do you know, my faithful friends, why I weep so bitterly? I certainly do not fear that they should annoy me by these wretched acts of piracy; but I am deeply afflicted because during my lifetime they have come so near these shores, and I am tormented by a violent grief, when I think of the woes they will inflict upon my successors and the whole nation."

The chronicler from whose pages the preceding extract is taken was a monk belonging to the abbey of Saint Gall, in Normandy. His biography of Charlemagne is printed in M. Guizot's collection. The pirates he alludes to are the Northmen, who, after some preliminary raids on the French coast, landed in Neustria, and, favoured by the weakness of Louis the Fat, laid siege to Paris. So important an event (886-887) deserved a Virgil or a Homer; it was celebrated by Abbo (Abbo Cernuus, died 923), a monk of the famous abbey of Saint Germain des Prés, who had witnessed the siege, and described it in a poem of more than twelve hundred lines, entitled *De Bello Parisiacæ urbis*. The author declares that he has taken the *Æneid* as his model, but the merest glance at the work shows that Eginhard was a much more successful imitator of Suetonius than Abbo was of Virgil. The historical particulars contained in the *De Bello*, have nevertheless contributed to make it live; for the would-be poet could honestly say, *Quæque ipse miserrima vidi*, and on the various incidents of the siege he deserves the fullest credence.

Before taking our leave of the Carlovingians, we must say a few words of a class of writings which, in times gone by, passed, in the opinion of many people, as historical productions, and were considered as embodying the history of Charlemagne and of his immediate successors. We allude to the metrical romances known by the name of *chansons de geste*, because they were composed for the purpose of commemorating the heroic deeds (*gesta*) of warriors, and which treated almost exclusively of Carlovingian glory and Carlovingian prowess. The question is whether these works have any authority whatever, or whether they must be dismissed altogether as fictions. If we open Eginhard's *Life of Charlemagne*, we find the following passage: "Charles invades Spain with as great a force as he is able to collect; the Pyrenees are crossed, and having received the surrender of all the towns and castles he had attacked, he returns with his army safe and sound, except that through the treachery of the Gascons he encounters a check in the very passes of the Pyrenees . . . then Egginard, the comptroller of the royal table, Count Anselm, Roland, warden of the marches of Brittany, and many others are slain."[1] Now, this

---

[1] "Hispaniam quam maximo poterat belli apparatu agreditur

passage from Eginhard represents nearly the whole amount of trustworthy information we possess on the episode which is the subject of the *Chanson de Roland*—the oldest of the *chansons de geste*. If, therefore, the name of historical poem is applied to that romance, we see at once to what extent the designation is justified. The event selected by the *trouvère* as the theme of his song is historical, and the various features of Teutonic civilization are abundantly illustrated in the details of the work, but that is all. Imagination has magnified the characters introduced, and misrepresented the facts, or thrown around them a dress which prevents us from distinguishing the reality. It would be absurd to suppose that all the *dramatis personæ* of the *Chanson de Roland* actually lived at some epoch or other of the reign of Charlemagne. M. Génin, for example, has taken a great deal of useless trouble to prove[1] that the traitor Ganelon was none other than Wenilo, Archbishop of Sens, who betrayed the cause of Charles the Bald, and was condemned, in the year 859, by the Council of Savonières. Ganelon is a fiction invented by the poet to personify the idea of tragedy, and it would

---

Karolus, saltuque Pyrinei superato, omnibus quæ adierat oppidis atque castellis in deditionem susceptis, salvo et incolumi exercitu revertitur, præter quod in ipso Pyrinei jugo Wasconicam perfidiam in redeundo contigit experiri. . . . in quo prælio Egginardus regiæ mensæ præpositus, Anselmus comes palatii, et Hruotlandus, Britannici limitis præfectus, cum aliis compluribus interficiuntur."

[1] In his edition of the *Chanson de Roland*. 8°. Paris, 1850.

be vain to try to identify him with any real individual who flourished during the ninth century.

What has just been said about the *Chanson de Roland* is exactly applicable to all the cycle of metrical romances we are now considering. Whether the *geste* bears upon the great emperor's exploits against his enemies in Germany, in Italy, or in Aquitaine, the process of composition is the same; a passage from some monkish chronicle has supplied the *trouvère* with his text, which he develops more or less minutely, according to the resources of his own imagination, and which he gives as a chapter in the eventful career of Charlemagne.

Next to the compositions bearing distinctly and professedly upon the emperor's life, another class of metrical romances must be named, not written at the same early period as those just alluded to, but still sufficiently ancient to have preserved many curious traces of historic truth. These romances, however, are not essentially connected with the life of Charlemagne, and it is very probable that, in the shape they first assumed, they had nothing to do with him. But the anxiety of late rhapsodists to secure popularity for certain tales, by making them cluster around the biography of the emperor, led them to give to these compositions what we may call an *air de famille*. A third group of *chansons de geste* includes several old romances describing the wars between Charlemagne and his vassals.

These productions belong to the epoch when the Carlovingian dynasty was dying away, and they express in a very naïve manner the feudal reaction against the monarchical principle. Thus, the *Chanson de Roland* alludes three times to a celebrated chieftain, Gérard de Roussillon, who was one of the hero's brethren-in-arms. Now, whilst a Provençal poem, which has been handed down to us, represents Gérard as carrying on for many years a terrible war against Charles Martel, the *trouvères* substituted Charlemagne instead of his grandfather, thus connecting the *geste* of the Duc de Roussillon with the Carlovingian legend.

One more remark will serve to show exactly how the authors of the old romances understood the manner of dealing with historical facts; it bears upon the central event of the *Chanson de Roland*, the battle of Roncevaux. According to the most trustworthy historians, the people who destroyed Charlemagne's rear-guard were, not Saracens, as the poem represents them, but Basque highlanders; in the passage quoted above, Eginhard distinctly says, "The Gascons ... throw the army into great confusion."[1] It is not strictly impossible that the Saracens should have taken part in this onslaught; but whether they did or not matters very little. Spain and Islam, during the ninth, tenth, and eleventh centuries, were for Northern

---

[1] "Wascones ... exercitum magno tumultu perturbant."

Europe identical terms, and any enemy of the
Christians of the Langue d'Oïl must necessarily
be a believer in Mahomet. We further notice that
a number of subsequent engagements with the
Basque mountaineers added, so to say, fresh
elements to the Roncevaux legend, with which
they became identified. In 792-793 the Saracens
invaded France, and were signally defeated at
Villedaigne, on the banks of the river Orbieux, by
Guillaume au Court-nez, Duke of Aquitaine. In 821
the Basques, "endeavouring to practise the deceit
which is characteristic of their native country, and
to which they are accustomed,"[1] did their best to
destroy the army of King Louis on its way back
from Pampeluna. Twelve years later, in 824, the
French troops were once more surprised in the
fastnesses of the Pyrenees by the treacherous
highlanders, and two of their principal leaders
perished. Now, it is very natural that a *trouvère*,
in composing his *chanson de geste*, should have
allowed his imagination to blend together the traditions bearing upon these successive events, so
as to make them the features of one grand striking
picture.

The metrical romances we have thus described
were based upon passages taken from the old
annalists. By a kind of reciprocal arrangement,
the poems, in their turn, led to the production of a

---

[1] "Nativum assuetumque fallendi morem exercere conati."

work which must be noticed here; we mean the well-known chronicle ascribed to Archbishop Turpin. A praiseworthy desire of exalting the character of Roland, Charlemagne's nephew, induced the author, or rather the authors, of this wretched trash to compose their narrative; but they completely altered the portrait of the hero, and made it a downright caricature. "Roland was a Christian," says M. Gautier; "the pseudo-Turpin transforms him into a schoolman. He argues, speechifies, symbolizes, and subtilizes; how much I preferred him when he was dealing with his sword those blows which were more opportune and more useful! He says off by heart the treatise *De Trinitate;* I like better to see him in the thick of the fight, his arms stained with blood. Then we find him offering a prayer which extends over two pages; he pleased me more when he prayed in two words, holding out naïvely to God the glove of his right hand. He was thus a soldier, a Christian soldier; the pseudo-Turpin has transformed him into a churchwarden."[1]

The favour with which this Latin composition was received appears from the fact that as many as fifty manuscript copies of it are enumerated by the Greek scholar, M. Potthast, in his *Bibliotheca Historica*. Twenty of these codices are preserved amongst the collections of the Paris National

---

[1] L. Gautier, *La Chanson de Roland*, vol. ii. p. 75.

Library. It is ascertained now that the chronicle is the work of two authors, the former of whom lived about the middle of the eleventh century, whilst the latter wrote his portion of the narrative between the years 1109 and 1119. In reading the first five chapters, we are struck by the circumstance that the anonymous author is thoroughly acquainted with Spain, and even with the history of the Saracens. The only French hero he introduces is Charlemagne; the sole object he has in view is the glory of the national saint of the Spaniards, St. James of Compostella. He never pretends to be the Archbishop Turpin, whom he names only once, and in the third person. The writer of the last twenty-seven chapters, on the contrary, is a Frenchman. He borrows largely from the old *chansons de geste* the absurd tales which he would fain make us accept as history, and his principal aim is evidently to amuse his readers.

The pseudo-Turpin is not the only author who has endeavoured to palm off fiction as truth, and to invest the old *chansons de geste* with the dignity of well-authenticated chronicles. In order to please their readers, and to render their own tedious compilations more attractive, the annalists of the twelfth and thirteenth centuries drew largely upon the legends which had immortalized Charlemagne and his twelve peers; and they have often transmitted down to us, if not by extracts, at any rate in substance, narratives which otherwise we should never have been acquainted with. The most valuable and most ancient of these chroniclers is the monk generally known as Albéric des Trois Fontaines, from the supposition that he belonged to a Cistercian monastery of that name in the district of Liège, but who really was an Augustinian monk of Neufmoutier, near Huy, in the same neighbourhood, and who died about 1246. M. Gaston Paris gives us an interesting account of him (*Histoire Poétique de Charlemagne*, livre i.), and describes him as a mere compiler. The chronicle, which bears his name, printed in the *Accessiones Historicæ* of Leibnitz, extends from the creation of the world to the year 1241, the account of the last quarter of a century alone being original, because Albéric there gave the description of contemporary events. He had with the utmost industry made extracts from fifty-six authors, transcribing these extracts in chronological order, and always trying to give for each year its history, beginning with the seventh century. Whenever the monk found any *chanson de geste* bearing upon a noteworthy event, he copied the appropriate passage, placing it sometimes on exactly the same line as the gravest historical composition, sometimes criticizing it with considerable ingenuity, not unfrequently repudiating it altogether. Thus he reproduces in one passage the fictitious genealogy of Garin de Monglane, without suspecting in the least its romantic character; in another, finding that truth and fancy do not agree about a chronological statement, or about the designation of a pope or a king, he hesitates. Either the same individual had two different names, or two individuals had the same name. He has a place in his chronicle for Huon de Bordeaux, but he takes care to add, "Wonders are related about him, whether true or fabulous." Talking of a certain Queen Sibylla, the heroine of a *chanson de geste* now lost, he says, "The French minstrels have made respecting that lady a very fine narrative . . . but although these tales please the hearers, moving them either to laughter or to tears, they depart too visibly from historic truth, and have been invented for the sake of gain."

Albéric had many imitators. M. Gaston Paris names two: a monk of Saintonge, who published an interpolation of Turpin; and an anonymous French annalist belonging to Northern France, and who avowedly drew from the *chansons de geste* the materials of his history of Charlemagne and of Louis le Débonnaire.

From the romances of the Carlovingian cycle, the transition to the compositions of Robert Wace is extremely easy. It was in 1155 that the French *chansons de geste* had reached their highest degree of glory, and had fairly taken possession of the poetical supremacy in France. All of a sudden, the appearance of the *Roman de Brut*, by Robert Wace, produced, especially in the western districts

of the country, a revolution which can easily be
understood by those who have taken the trouble to
compare the old romaunts about *France la garnie*
with the poems forming the Arthurian cycle. An
entirely new world of feelings, traditions, affec-
tions, and thoughts was opened up, and the mind
of the reader or listener was transported from the
Teutonic to the Celtic civilization. Was the *Brut*
a work of fiction, or a chronicle? No one could
decide; historic truth and romantic stories were
closely interwoven in the narrative of the Anglo-
Norman poet, and the attention was equally
arrested, whether the authentic annals of England
were unfolded, or the apocryphal adventures of
King Arthur and Merlin the enchanter were related in all their circumstantial details. The fact
is that the word *roman* must be understood, when
applied to the works of the early mediæval period,
in a far different meaning to the one which it
has now. The old *trouvères* would not have admitted that their productions were distinctly and
exclusively works of fiction; on the contrary, they
regarded them as containing a large admixture of
real fact, and the difference between one particular
roman and another consisted in the proportion
which the author allowed to well-authenticated
truth. Now, in the metrical compositions of Robert
Wace that proportion is by no means unimportant,
and it entitles the author to a distinguished place
amongst the chroniclers of his time. A modern

writer, whose opinion on questions of this kind cannot be impugned by the most daring critic, observes: "The name of Wace I can never utter without thankfulness, as that of one who has preserved to us the most minute, and, as I fully believe, next to the contemporary sketch-work, the most trustworthy narrative of the central scene of my history."[1]

Robert Wace (1112–1182) forms part of that band of Anglo-Norman poets who, like Geoffroy Gaimar, Benoit de Sainte-Maure, Jordan Fantosme, and many other inferior ones, belong to both nationalities, being English by the subjects they treat, and French by the language they made use of to express their thoughts. If, however, his *Roman de Brut*, describing as it does the origins of the Celtic nationality, and being chiefly derived from the *Origo et Gesta Regum Britanniæ* of Geoffrey of Monmouth, falls, strictly speaking, beyond the scope of our subject, the *Roman de Rou*, on the other hand, is, to all intents and purposes, a contribution to the history of France. Composed about the end of the twelfth century, it rises to the importance of a chronicle, and deserves a place amongst the monuments of mediæval history. The first part of the work contains the biographies of the early Dukes of Normandy, Rollo (*Rou*, hence the title of the work), William Longue-Epée, and Richard I. It

---

[1] Mr. Freeman.

appears to have been written in 1160, as "Master Robert" himself expressly declares—

> "One thousand one hundred and sixty years had elapsed
> Since God, by His grace, came into the Virgin,
> When a clerk of Caen, by name Wace,
> Busied himself with the history of Rollo and his race."[1]

Henry II., King of England, having rewarded Robert Wace with a canonry in the church of Bayeux, our annalist, thus encouraged, wrote a continuation of his work, taking the reader down to the reign of Henry I. (1106). The *Roman de Rou* stops there; but "Maistre" Robert bethought himself that, by starting with Rollo, he had neglected to relate the first incursions of the Normans under the Carlovingian dynasty. He therefore composed a kind of introduction to his poem, telling us all he knew about Hastings (*Hastainz*) and the other pirates, who, after a series of forays, ended by settling down at Chartres, with the consent of Charles the Bald. The *Roman de Rou*, comprising seventeen thousand lines, is, to a great extent, a translation of the chronicles of Dudo of Saint Quentin, and William of Jumièges, the two oldest Norman annalists. The first part of the poem, based chiefly upon Dudo's work, is mainly a farrago of the most absurd stories; the second, on the

---

[1] "Mil et cent et soixante ans eut de temps et d'espace,
Puis que Diex en la Vierge descendi par sa grace,
Quant un clerc de Caën, qui ot nom maistre Wace,
S'entremist de l'estoire de Rou et de sa race."

contrary, in which Robert Wace has taken William of Jumièges as his guide, is extremely valuable for the historical information it gives. As Mr. Freeman observes, it may be read by way of a commentary on the Bayeux tapestry. In point of fact, the Benedictine Dom Montfaucon, and Lancelot, his *collaborateur*, used it for that very purpose.

The very important chronicle of Ordericus Vitalis should be noticed here ; but it belongs rather to the history of England, and therefore we may dismiss it with just a passing allusion.

Benoit de Sainte-Maure, thus named from his native place in Touraine, had won for himself considerable reputation as a poet by his metrical romance on the Trojan war, when Henry II. ordered him to compose a history of the Dukes of Normandy. This work, comprising twenty-three thousand octosyllabic lines, extends from the invasions of the Northmen, under Hastings, to the reign of William the Conqueror. It is very inferior in point of historical merit to the *Roman de Rou ;* but the celebrity it obtained when it first appeared cast into the shade "Maistre Robert," who complained bitterly, in the concluding lines of his own poem, that the King of England had ungenerously given him a rival, and thus deprived him of the honour which he believed was his due. The work of Benoit de Sainte-Maure was, in all probability, written in the year 1170.

CHAPTER IV.

LATIN ANNALISTS OF THE LATER CARLOVINGIAN AND THE CAPETIAN EPOCHS—GLABER—ANNALS OF SAINT BERTIN AND SAINT VAAST—SUGER—"L'YSTOIRE DE LI NORMANT."

WE have been led to anticipate a little; and, taking leave for a season of metrical chronicles and histories written in the French language, we shall notice some of the principal Latin annalists belonging to the later Carlovingian and to the Capetian epochs. M. Guizot's collection introduces us to a number of ecclesiastics, who, although of not much importance taken separately, either as writers or as historians, give us a body of evidence which we cannot afford to neglect. Raoul or Radulphus Glaber may be mentioned amongst the most distinguished. Born in Burgundy towards the end of the tenth century, he led a rather dissolute life, wandering from convent to convent in order to escape from the punishment which he had incurred through his misdeeds. At last he accompanied to Italy William, Abbot of Saint Bénigne in Dijon, and, following this dignitary's advice, he composed a chronicle which is equalled by few in real interest; it extends from 900 to 1046, and was published for the first time in Pithou's collection. The authors of the *Histoire Littéraire de la France* have shown Glaber's defects as an historian, given instances of his inaccuracy, denounced his fondness for idle legends, and remarked on his utter want of judgment. Notwithstanding all these drawbacks, the work of Radulphus Glaber is extremely important, and it gives us many details which we would uselessly look for elsewhere.

One of the most valuable sources of information respecting the history of the later Carlovingians is to be found in a series of chronicles, known under the name of *Annales de Saint Bertin*, from the monastery where a Jesuit father, Herbert van Roswey, discovered the original manuscript, more than two hundred years ago. These annals are the work of three different authors. The first part, comprising the narrative of events from 830 till near the end of 853, is written by a staunch champion of Louis le Débonnaire. As the most recent editor (M. l'Abbé Dehaisnes) remarks, this portion of the annals is specially noteworthy, not in point of style, but on account of the uniform care with which the author confines himself to his subject. Most of his contemporaries were fond both of dwelling with considerable detail on natural phenomena, such as eclipses, storms, etc., and of devoting a large part of their work to the history of foreign nations. Here, on the contrary, the weak son of Charlemagne fills the canvas; and, although we are reduced to conjectures as to the identity of the author, we know thus much, that he took part as a dignitary of the Church in the events he relates, and that he inhabited the northern district of Gaul.

The second section of the annals of Saint Bertin (end of 855 to beginning of 861) is known to be the composition of Saint Prudentius, Bishop of Troyes (?–861), and is distinguished by characteristics diametrically contrary to those we have just enumerated as belonging to the first part. The *ensemble* of history here comes under consideration; Spain and Italy occupy about the same space as France and Germany; wars and invasions, treaties and councils, rejoicings and royal progresses, inundations, eclipses, comets, tempests, and natural prodigies of every kind are duly registered. As a writer, Saint Prudentius is not only far superior to his anonymous predecessor, but he affects an elegance which often amounts to pedantry.

The concluding portion of the annals of Saint Bertin, treating of the reign of Charles the Bald, was written by the famous Hincmar, Archbishop of Reims (? 806–882). Here, again, we have a style of narrative differing as much from that of Saint Prudentius as from that of the anonymous annalist. Hincmar relates, in great detail, the career of Charles the Bald; but at the same time he records, with equal minuteness, the acts of his own administration, and his work is a kind of journal of the see of Reims during his tenure of office. The affairs of the Church are of more importance in his eyes than physical phenomena, and he is fond of discussing points of canon law.

The annals of Saint Vaast form the natural sequel to those of the monastery of Saint Bertin. They were put together, between 1024 and 1054, by a monk of the abbey of Saint Vaast at Arras; and, beginning with the creation of the world, they take us down to the year 899. Superior both to Prudentius and to Hincmar as a writer, in spite of a few solecisms, the ecclesiastic we are now alluding to is especially remarkable for his clearness, the animation of his style, and the interest which he has contrived to throw upon the political and military events of the times. He traces the hand of God in the development of this world's history, but he notes also with care the action of secondary causes. He sympathizes deeply with the sufferings of the people, and deplores the endless horrors of public and private warfare. Favourable to King Eudes and to Baldwin, Count of Flanders, he nevertheless blames these two princes when they follow what seems to him a dangerous course of policy.

The annalist who can be named as the best authority on the origin of the Capetian dynasty is undoubtedly Richer, a monk of the abbey of Saint Rémy at Reims, and who flourished during the tenth century. Very little is known about his life; but the *Historia* which he has left behind him, and which, divided into four books, covered all the period included between 887 and 898, is a work of the greatest historical importance. We do not mean to quote it as either a model of style or a specimen of criticism; but Richer is well informed and honest, and it is not too much to say that no writer helps us more to understand the nature of the revolution which swept away the effete descendants of Charlemagne, and placed the sceptre in the hands of Hugh Capet. Duke of France and Count of Paris, Abbot of Saint Martin of Tours, Saint Denis, and Saint Germain des Prés—that is to say, having at his disposal the revenues of the three richest abbeys in France—the grandson of Duke Robert might well venture upon the attempt he had long meditated, of seizing the crown. The name of king conveyed, during the tenth century, very little power, and yet the accession of the founder of the Capetian dynasty was a momentous event, because, in the first place, it implied a rupture with Germany and with Teutonic traditions; and, in the second, the crown was thus transferred to the family of one of the greatest feudal princes. Hugh felt all the advantages of his new position, and by having his son immediately consecrated as king, he prevented the recurrence of those electoral assemblies which had, indeed, procured his own elevation to the throne, but which, if repeated, would have resulted in a sort of periodical anarchy.

It was two centuries before a monarch really deserving that title made his appearance, and the three first successors of Hugh Capet occupied the throne for 112 years (996–1108), without leaving in the pages of history anything beyond the bare mention of their names. This need not excite any astonishment; at the time we are treating of, the king had neither power nor influence to do more than exercise, within the limits of his own private domains, the same rights which devolved upon other feudal lords in the same capacity. The last capitulary—that is to say, the last law applying to the whole of the kingdom—belongs to the reign of Charles the Simple; and, subsequently to that time, we must come down as late as the year 1190 to find an enactment which is not of a local character.

In like manner the *catena* of French mediæval annalists does not present to us, after the disappearance of Richer, any name worth mentioning until we come to the reign of Louis VII. The policy of this monarch, like that of his father, was to curtail as much as possible the power of the feudal barons, and to favour the establishment of the *communes*. It was a scheme beset, as may be supposed, with many difficulties, and requiring all the prudence of a consummate statesman, as well as the courage of a soldier. Fortunately, the king enjoyed the privilege of having for his guide a personage of whom it has justly been said:

"A Cicero by his eloquence, a Cato by his virtues, and a Cæsar by his courage,
His advice ruled kings; his power ruled kingdoms."[1]

Suger, the celebrated adviser of Louis VII., and who took so important a part in the administration of France, is one of the noblest figures of the twelfth century. Born in 1087, and educated at Saint Denis with the young prince, he became afterwards his chief councillor. In the year 1122, he was made Abbot of Saint Denis, and applied his talents for government to the religious community over which he was appointed, as well as to the reformation of the abuses which had crept into the State. The works of Suger, lately published by the *Société de l'Histoire de France*, are of much interest towards an accurate knowledge of the time in which he lived; they comprise a biography of Louis the Fat (*Gesta Ludovici regis cognomento Grossi*), a memoir on his own abbatial administration, an account of the consecration of the church of Saint Denis, and a collection of letters.

---

[1] "Tullius ore, Cato meritis, et pectore Cæsar,
Consilio reges, regna regebat ope."

Of the first of these writings, we may observe that it is certainly more of a panegyric than of a real history; however, Suger is never carried away by his partiality to garble the truth, or to misrepresent facts. If he omits certain circumstances, it is not to the advantage of his hero. On the one hand, the differences between Louis VI. and Stephen, Bishop of Paris, are not recorded, and the king's line of action in the disturbances at Laon is not criticized with sufficient severity; but, on the other, Suger says nothing of the murder of the lord of Montlhéry by Hugh de Crécy, a crime which led to the confiscation by the State of the assassin's landed property. It is also worthy of notice that Suger speaks of the English with an impartiality which, as his latest editor observes, often amounts to positive kindness; we know that he frequently endeavoured, in his official capacity, to bring about peace between the two nations, and he never loses the opportunity of deploring the spirit of rivalry which was unfortunately to produce a long series of terrible wars. "The English," says he, "should not be submitted to the French, nor the French to the English." We must bear in mind that Suger had not the intention of composing a regular and detailed history of the reign—his object was merely to give the biography of his friend and master; therefore the narrative of political events is to be looked for in other chronicles. The *Gesta Ludovici Grossi* are also deficient in point of method, and the chronological order is not strictly adhered to; but no one can deny their high value as a document. Suger relates chiefly the circumstances in which he took a part, and his evidence is constantly supported by a declaration such as this: "*Et nos ipsi interfuimus.*"

The history of the abbey of Saint Denis under Suger's administration, and the account of the consecration of the church, have only a local interest, and we shall dismiss them without further mention. The epistles, on the other hand, are, as might be supposed, extremely curious, and it is a matter of regret that, out of a correspondence which could not but be very extensive, only twenty-six letters have been handed down to us. Fortunately they belong to the most important epoch in Suger's life (1146–1151), and they show in the clearest manner the anxiety with which he watched over the interests of the king, especially during the Crusade. Whether he addresses himself to the barons, the clergy, or the pope, he gives proof of the sincerest devotedness and patriotism, and when he writes to the son of the prince who had always been his friend, he expresses himself with the earnestness of almost paternal affection. The letter in which he urges Louis VII. to return to his kingdom is a model in that respect, only equalled by the one in which, from his deathbed, he gives to the monarch his last advice, recommending him to preserve always about his person the message containing the wholesome counsel of a faithful minister to a powerful monarch.

The style of Suger is not, we must acknowledge, on a level with the importance of his works. "His facts are valuable," says Sharon Turner, "his Latin execrable."[1] The careful reader cannot, at the same time, fail to observe that when some dramatic event, such as the description of a battle, presents itself, the language of the author becomes more coloured, and even rises to a certain kind of elegance. The episode of the murder of the lord of Laroche-Guyon is an instance in point; the account of the siege of Puiset is also a striking piece of composition, and as we read it, we can see at once, as we have already hinted, that Suger was an eye-witness of the events which he unfolds before us. The parallel between William Rufus and Louis, his adversary, which opens the *Gesta*, inspired as it seems to be by reminiscences of classical antiquity, and contrasting in point of vigour with the usual dry form of annals, should not be forgotten. Suger died in 1152.

The history of the Normans, their origin, their conquests, and their settlements in the various countries of Europe, was well calculated, by its romantic character, to engage the attention of chroniclers and annalists. Let us notice, amongst the works to which it has given rise, *L'Ystoire de*

---

[1] *History of England*, vol. i.

Li Normant and *La Chronique de Robert Viscart*, which were published more than forty years ago, under the auspices of the *Société de l'Histoire de France*. The author of these two compositions was a certain Amatus, Bishop of Nusco, a native of Italy, and who belonged to the regular clergy. He appears to have been distinguished by learning, and to have devoted a great deal of his time to intellectual pursuits; he flourished during the eleventh century, at the time when the Normans established themselves in Italy and in Sicily; he died at a very advanced age in 1093.

The two works we are now describing were originally written in Latin, and the French translation printed by the *Société* seems to have been done by an Italian scholar, or a Norman who was more thoroughly acquainted with the Italian language than with the French; it abounds in Italian idioms, and not only do we find words exclusively Italian by their origin and their form, but grammatical terms and phrases which betray a Transalpine birth. The *Ystoire*, properly so called, is divided into eight books, each of which, comprising an unequal number of chapters, is preceded by a table of contents. The fifteen chapters of the first book treat of the Normans in general; the island *Nora*, their principal abode; their emigrations, occasioned by the overgrowth of the population; their pre-eminence in all the countries where they settled; finally, their invasions of Spain and of

England, and the fortuitous deliverance of the city of Salerne by a company of Norman knights on their return from the Holy Land. A large number of Norman lords took a part in these successive expeditions; much time had to be spent and a terrible sacrifice of human life made before any perceptible result was obtained; and it was only after the lapse of a century that the second son of the last of Tancred de Hauteville's children placed on his head the crown of Sicily. The chronicle ends at the death of Richard, Prince of Capua, which occurred on the Thursday in Passion Week of the year 1078. This prince and his brother, Robert, Duke of Calabria, are the two personages on whose high deeds of valour the Bishop of Nusco chiefly dwells, on account of "the good which these two lords did to our monastery."[1]

The chronicle of Robert Viscart, which follows *L'Ystoire de Li Normant*, describes more particularly the wars of the Normans in Italy; it forms two books, divided into forty-one chapters, the first of which mentions Tancred de Hauteville, whilst the last three, after having related the death of the Count Roger, give a few anecdotes on Roger II., King of Sicily, who died in 1154. An author, whose name is unknown, wrote a brief supplement to the work of Bishop Amatus, containing the enumeration of a few events posterior to the death

---

[1] "Le bien que firent à nostre monastier ces ij seignors."

of Roger II., and ending with the Sicilian Vespers and the crowning of Peter of Arragon, in 1281. This last poem, of a very unimportant character, was published by Muratori in the *Scriptores Rerum Italicarum*, together with the rest of the work; but it is not included in the volume of the *Société de l'Histoire de France*.

CHAPTER V.

THE CRUSADES—FOULQUES DE CHARTRES—GUIBERT DE NOGENT—"GESTA FRANCORUM"—WILLIAM OF TYRE AND HIS CONTINUATORS.

WE now come to the epoch of the Crusades; it may aptly be designated as the heroic age of Christianity. If we consider these expeditions fairly and dispassionately, and if we place ourselves mentally at the times when they happened, the reproach of extravagance so often addressed to them falls of itself; nor shall we be tempted to look upon them as having been merely the result of false zeal and of blind superstition. That was the theory adopted by the school of Voltaire and of the infidels of the last century—a school which still holds up its head, pretending to have the monopoly of truth, whereas the trenchant tone of its assertions is only equalled by its startling ignorance. It is easy now to assert that a small corner of Syria was, for all practical purposes, quite valueless, and that the expeditions known by the name of Crusades could not pay. But the religious spirit of the Middle Ages argued quite differently, and could not but do so. For the men of the twelfth and thirteenth centuries, Palestine, that small corner of Syria, was hallowed by all the associations of religion. There was born, and there died, for the salvation of mankind, the Founder of Christianity—the Son of God; there had been sown the first seeds of the Gospel, and there were the scenes hallowed by most sacred associations for those who believed in revealed truth. The child of Israel still turned his eyes towards the spot which was his fatherland; the Mahometan himself respected it, and its protection was one of the first articles of his faith. Could a Christian do less than a Jew, or than a follower of Islam? Could he cease to venerate those holy places which he had so long been accustomed to visit, and which were now shut against him by a tribe of barbarians? Was he not, on the contrary, bound, by the most sacred obligations, to punish in the severest manner those who closed against Christianity the road to the Holy Land?

It was from France that the great movement sprung, which lasted for more than a century and a half, and which precipitated the whole of western Christendom upon Palestine. "On avait pleuré en Italie," says Voltaire, "on s'arma en France." The French were nearly the sole actors in the first Crusade; they joined in the second with the Germans (1147); in the third (1190) with the English; in the fourth (1203) with the Venetians; the fifth (1217) and the sixth (1228) were unimportant; the seventh (1248) and the eighth (1270) were exclusively French. We cannot, therefore, wonder at Bongars, who published a valuable collection of the historians of the Crusades, entitling his work *Gesta Dei per Francos*. Even at the present day all Christians are designated, in the East, by the common name of *Franks*, to whatever nationality they belong.

Leaving aside Villehardouin and Joinville, whom we shall consider later on in detail, the principal chroniclers connected with the Crusades are Guillaume de Tyr, Bernard the Treasurer, Albert d'Aix, Raimond d'Agiles, Guibert de Nogent, Jacques de Vitry, Raoul de Caen, Foulques de Chartres, Baudri de Bourgueil, and Odo de Deuil. They have brought together a mass of information which, despite a large number of inaccuracies and misstatements, deserves to be thoroughly examined by all the students of history whose attention is directed towards the mediæval relations between the East and the West; and the excellent use made by M. Michaud of those chronicles in his *Histoire des Croisades* is the most conclusive proof of the attention to which they are entitled.

We have alluded just now to Foulques de Chartres. He is not the only author of that name who has treated of the expeditions of the Europeans in Palestine. Another Foulque, mentioned by the Benedictine compilers of the *Histoire Littéraire de la France*, announced in the following doggerel his intention of celebrating the heroes more immediately identified with the first Crusade:—

> " Inclyta gesta ducum perscribere magnanimorum
> Fert animus, patrum qui fortia facta suorum
> Non solum magnis successibus æquiparare,
> Sed majore fide certârunt exsuperare.
> Ardor inest, inquam, sententia fixaque menti
> Versibus et numeris transmittere posteritati,
> Qualiter instinctu Deitatis et auspice cultu
> Est agressa via memorando nobilis actu,
> Quo sacrosancti violantes jura sepulchri
> Digna reciperunt meriti commercia pravi." [1]

The author of this wretched Latin has devoted three books to a narrative of the first expedition. He begins with a description of the effect produced upon the mind of the Christians by the preaching of the Crusades; he then names the various leaders who took a part in the movement, relates their departure, and indicates the route which they severally followed in their march towards the Holy Land. The numerous adventures which the

---

[1] "I have a mind to write about the illustrious deeds of the magnanimous leaders, who not only strove to equal, by great successes, the brave actions of their fathers, but to surpass them by greater faith. I say, that an ardour possesses me, a fixed purpose has seized upon me, to transmit to posterity, in verses and numbers, a record of the events which led to the condign punishment of those who violated the Holy Sepulchre."

Crusaders met with supply abundance of materials for the second book, whilst the third is taken up by an account of the quarrel between Godfrey de Bouillon and the Emperor Alexis Comnenus. Foulque, the author of this poem, is neither a Villehardouin, nor a Joinville, much less a Tasso; but his poem is a valuable *mémoire pour servir*, and it would have been unfair to leave it unnoticed.

Odo or Eudes, born at Deuil in the valley of Montmorency, near Paris, is a chronicler of much higher merit than the poet we have just been noticing. Brought up at the abbey of Saint Denis, he became the friend of Suger, whom he succeeded in the government of the monastery. Previously to his election, he had accompanied Louis VII. to the Holy Land in the capacity of secretary and chaplain; and on his arrival at Antioch, he hastened to commit to writing an account of the events in which he had taken part. This narrative, subdivided into seven books, was sent to Suger, in the shape of a letter. The proclamation of the second Crusade, and the incidents which occurred till the departure of the king, supply the materials for the first book. We then follow the expeditions through Bulgaria to Constantinople (books ii. and iii.). The entry of the army into Roumania occupies the fourth book. The next book describes to us the misfortunes which befel the German Crusaders on their way from Nicomedia to Antioch, and their forced retreat to

Constantinople. The sixth division is taken up with the various adventures which occurred to the army of the French monarch; and in the last we are told why he embarked at Satalieh and returned to Antioch.

Odo of Deuil has no pretensions whatever to be a fine writer; but yet he is sometimes, as M. Michaud remarks, equal in conciseness to Sallust, and he becomes truly eloquent when he relates the misfortunes and the useless courage of the Crusaders. Like most of the annalists belonging to Western Europe, he thoroughly hates the Greeks, and alludes to their double dealing and their selfishness in the most energetic manner. His account of Constantinople is particularly interesting. He died in 1162.

Foulcher, or Foulques, of Chartres, born in 1059, died at Jerusalem in 1127. He took a part in the first Crusade as chaplain to Baldwin, the brother and successor of Godefroy de Bouillon. There is a kind of naïve conceit running through the otherwise valuable chronicle which he has left; *Ego Fulcherius Carnutensis* is a favourite phrase with him; he is very minute about the persons and things which he specially dislikes; the successes obtained by the Christians call forth his hearty thanksgivings, and when a battle is about to take place, he honestly wishes, like a mediæval Bob Acres, that he were safe at Orleans or at Chartres. The great feature in the chronicle of Foulcher is the abundance of details he supplies on Godefroy, and on the establishment of the early Christian settlements in the midst of the Mussulman population. Let us quote an extract which shall give some idea of what we mean: "He who was a Roman or a Frank has become a Galilean; the native of Reims or of Chartres has now become a citizen of Tyre, or of Antioch; we have already forgotten the place of our birth. This one possesses in a foreign land houses and slaves; that one has married a wife who was not born in the same country as himself—a Syrian, an Armenian, or even a Saracen, who has received the grace of Baptism. One cultivates vineyards, another tills the fields. All these colonists speak diverse languages, and already manage to understand one another; mutual trust and confidence brings side by side the races the most opposite by their origin, for it is said that the lion and the ox shall feed together. Every day our friends and our relatives come over to join us, abandoning the property they possessed in the West. Those who were poor in their native country have waxed rich here, by the grace of God; those who owned only a few crowns here possess a large number of besants; to those who had merely a farm, God has given a town, for He will not suffer those who have taken the Cross to pine away in misery and distress."

Our friend Foulcher, as we see, held out a tempting *programme* to the adventurous pilgrims, who, like Walter the Penniless, might feel disposed to exchange the certainty of beggary at home for the probability of a rapid fortune abroad. He tells us briefly the result of the expedition; we must look elsewhere for the preliminaries, the fervent addresses of Peter the Hermit, and the first enthusiasm which led French, English, and Germans to rush to arms, at the earnest summons of the preacher. Here Guibert, Abbot of Nogent, is our guide; and when we open his chronicle, we find ourselves on a totally different ground from that occupied by the annalist with whom we have just been tarrying. Guibert, in fact, criticizes most severely the narrative of Foulcher; he accuses him of credulity, of gross exaggeration, and finds fault with his style, which does not come up to his own notions of elegance, or even of grammatical correctness. It is remarkable that Guibert is far from being innocent of the offences for which he taunts the monk of Chartres; a writer who considers that the Crusades were clearly predicted by the prophets of the Old Testament, can scarcely be justified in bitterly denouncing the credulity of a *confrère*, and the affectation of his style is almost as intolerable as the ruggedness of Foulcher. However, Guibert, as we have just remarked, is an excellent authority on the early period of the first Crusade, and the noble individuality of Peter of Amiens stands forth in bold relief in the pages of his work. Guibert composed, besides, an autobiographical fragment (*De Vitâ suâ*), which is full of the most valuable information. Born at Clermont (Auvergne) in 1053, he died in 1124.

But there is another work which Guibert de Nogent himself, together with other compilers, made great use of; we mean the *Gesta Francorum et aliorum Hierosolomytanorum*, printed by Bongars at the beginning of his collection, and which gives the history of the first Crusade. It is the production of an anonymous writer about whom nothing certain is yet known. Was he a priest, or a layman? an Italian, or a Provençal? The answer must be doubtful. A passage might be quoted which seems to show that a stalwart knight, recording his own impressions, has for a season taken up the pen instead of the sword. On the other hand, the history of the Middle Ages, and, in particular, of the Crusades, abounds in instances of fighting clergymen; and the venerable Bishop of Le Puy, amongst many others, was equally ready at celebrating divine service and at slaying the Paynim dogs. We may further remark that several passages in the *Gesta Francorum* could not have been written by any but a clergyman. On the point of nationality it is equally impossible to decide; the expression "Franci tumebant superbia" would be quite as natural on the lips of a Provençal as on those of an Italian.

At any rate, the *Gesta Francorum* were handled

with the most extraordinary *sans façon* by the writers who undertook to give the history of the first Crusade. Peter Tudebode, a priest of Sivray (or Civray), in the diocese of Poitiers, was the earliest offender; we have already mentioned Guibert de Nogent; we must now say a few words about Baudri (Baldericus) de Bourgueil, the author of an account of the Crusade beginning with the Council of Clermont, and ending with the siege of Ascalon. The *Gesta Francorum* are comparatively laconic and matter of fact; Baudri is fond of expanding the statements they give, of adding rhetorical or poetical embellishments, and even of inserting facts intended to explain, or to extenuate, sundry details which were not much to the credit of the Crusaders. The monk of Bourgueil had announced his intention of giving a certain number of particulars which he had heard from credible witnesses, and which had been left unmentioned by the author of the *Gesta*. He, indeed, kept his promise, but it is sometimes difficult to distinguish in his additions truth from fiction; and, as a general remark, we may say that Baudri de Bourgueil's statements must be received with a considerable amount of caution. His work, however, seems to have enjoyed much popularity during the Middle Ages. The account of the first Crusade given by Ordericus Vitalis, in the ninth book of the *Historia Ecclesiastica*, is copied word for word from him; and an anonymous writer of the twelfth century, following in the same direction, compiled another narrative of the Crusade, taking Baudri as his chief authority, and introducing numerous additions, some original, some borrowed from the *Gesta*. Finally, a French poem, composed in the style of a *chanson de geste*, must be mentioned here, as expressly based upon the chronicle of our friend the monk of Bourgueil.

Baudri was elected to the post of abbot in 1079; he became Bishop of Dol in 1107, and died in 1130.

William, Archbishop of Tyre, has left on the history of the Crusades a work of far higher pretensions than any of those we have been examining. It is not the testimony alone of critics, such as Vossius, Natalis Alexander, and Renaudot, which must inspire us with confidence in the merit of his work, but the authority of recent *savants*, MM. Guizot, Lalanne, Michaud, and Poujoulat, amongst others. Aubert Lemire says of him, that his learning was remarkable, and put in a more agreeable shape than might have been expected from a man of his time; and a close study of his book serves only to confirm this favourable opinion. Respecting the life of William, we may just say that he was born in 1130, and died about the year 1193. It is doubtful whether he was a Frenchman by birth. Named Archdeacon of Tyre, he was subsequently promoted to the episcopal see established in that town by the Crusaders, and received the appointment of chancellor to his pupil, Baldwin, King of Jerusalem. The circumstances of his death are almost as obscure as the place of his birth; but it has generally been supposed that he was poisoned at Rome, where he had gone for the purpose of petitioning the Pope against the nomination of Heraclius, Archbishop of Cæsarea, to the patriarchate of the Holy City. "When Eracle," says a continuator, "knew that he had gone to Rome, he ordered one of his physicians to pursue him, and to poison him; he did so, and he (William) died."[1]

The chronicle of the Archbishop of Tyre comprises a description of the events which took place in Palestine from the year 1095, when the first Crusade was determined upon at the Council of Clermont till the year 1184, twelve months before the death of Baldwin IV., King of Jerusalem. In various passages of the work, the prelate refers both to the pains he had taken in collecting materials, and to the difficulty which an author has to encounter, if he aims at being strictly and uniformly impartial. The space of about ninety years covered by this chronicle was to have formed the materials of twenty-three books; the prelate did not live to finish the last one.

A number of continuators took up the thread of the narrative, and, as a matter of fact, the

---

[1] "Quand Eracle sut qu'alé à Rome, dist à un sien fisicien qu'il alast après, et qu'il l'empoisonast; et *cil si* [= *lui, ci ainsi*] fist, *si* [= *ainsi*] fut mort."

chronicle of William of Tyre, together with the supplements which were from time to time engrafted upon it, forms the most important *corpus historiarum* we have on the Crusades. M. de Mas-Latrie has recently discussed this question in an exhaustive way, and we cannot do better than borrow some of his remarks.

Let us notice, in the first place, how frequently the sources of mediæval European history offer us examples of original chronicles simultaneously continued after the author's death in various countries, and on lines totally different from those which the first compiler had thought fit to adopt. Thus, the biographies of the popes by Anastasius and by the Cardinal of Arragon, the chronicles of Sigebert de Gembloux, the annals of the abbeys of Waverley and of Mailross, and the chronicle of Fredegarius, were all followed up and completed in the manner we have just alluded to. We shall have presently to notice the additions made to the *Grandes Chroniques de Saint-Denis,* and the various arrangements to which was subjected the narrative of William of Nangis. The fact that the authors of these supplements and continuations, almost without exception, are anonymous, adds considerably to the difficulty of establishing anything like an accurate classification of their labours; and we may further observe that the habit they had of tacking upon the original narrative compositions of their own, accounts sufficiently for the contradictions we find in the appreciations of characters and events.

It is, says M. de Mas-Latrie,[1] by a system of that kind, a process of additions and accretions belonging to various epochs and to different countries, that the chronicles or histories of the Crusades, so popular in Europe during the Middle Ages, were formed. Manuscript copies, in great numbers, were disseminated about, and obtained extraordinary popularity under the titles of *Livres de la Terre Sainte, Chroniques d'Outremer ; Contes de la Terre d'Outremer, Romans de l'Histoire d'Outremer, Livre de Voyage de Terre Sainte, Histoires du Passage de Godefroy de Bouillon*, etc., etc.

The French translation of William of Tyre begins with the following phrase, exactly taken from the first chapter of the Latin text, where are described the conquests of the Emperor Heraclius, and his recovering the true cross from the Persians: —"Les anciennes estoires *dient*[2] que Eracles, qui *molt*[3] fu *bons Crestiens*,[4] governa l'empire de Rome," etc. This passage was quite enough for the old scribes and authors of catalogues, to induce them to designate the French translation of William of

---

[1] See M. de Mas-Latrie's *Essai de Classification des Continuateurs de Guillaume de Tyr*, in the edition of Bernard le Trésorier's chronicle, published by the *Société de l'Histoire de France*.

[2] *Dient* = *disent*.   [3] *Molt* (Lat. *multum*) = *beaucoup*.

[4] *Bons Crestiens*, in strict accordance with the Lat. nominative *bonus Christianus*.

Tyre as *Le Livre d'Eracles*, or *L'Histoire d'Eracles, Empereur de Rome*. Another title frequently found is *Livre du Conquêt* (*Liber acquisitionis* [*Terræ Sanctæ*]).

An attentive study of the work or works we are now considering leads us to conclude that the general compilation, touching the history of the wars carried on in the Holy Land, was made at four various epochs, corresponding to the following divisions :—

First epoch.—After the Crusade of the Emperor Frederic II. (1228-1229) and the arrival of John de Brienne at Constantinople (1231).

Second epoch.—Subsequently to the Egyptian Crusade of Saint Louis, and to his return to France.

Third epoch.—Between the second Crusade of Saint Louis and the loss of Saint Jean d'Acre.

Fourth epoch.—After the loss of Saint Jean d'Acre, the last seat of the kingdom of Jerusalem, taken from the Christians by Malec al Aschraf in 1291.

Amongst the sources which William had consulted in preparing his work, we may name the chronicle composed by Raymond d'Agiles, canon of the cathedral of Le Puy-en-Velay, who flourished during the last years of the eleventh century and the beginning of the twelfth, and who was present at the taking of Jerusalem by the Crusaders. Most of the facts he relates are borrowed from other contemporary works, and the additions he introduces refer chiefly to idle superstitions, which have no historical importance whatever. The Archbishop of Tyre could certainly derive better information from his own personal experience; and the opportunities he had for observation supplied him with details which no one else preserved so carefully.

It would take us too long to give an account of all the continuators of William of Tyre. We must be satisfied with a brief notice of the most important: Ernoul, Bernard the Treasurer, and two others whose names have not yet been successfully identified. Hernoul, or Ernoul, composed his chronicle when he was still a *varlet* or squire in the service of Balian d'Ibelin, one of the first barons of Syria, and lieutenant of the kingdom after King Guy de Lusignan had been made a prisoner at Kittin. Ernoul had witnessed, in the company of his master, the defeat at Tiberias, the capture of the king, and the surrender of the capital. The prologue to his work declares plainly that the author's purpose is not to describe the conquest of Jerusalem by the Crusaders. Other historians have already given the wonderful story, and he would not recapitulate the tale they have so well told. The loss of the holy city, recaptured by Saladin, is the theme on which he has to discourse; and, accordingly, after a short glance taken at the reigns of the early Latin princes who ruled in Palestine,

he begins the detailed part of his narrative with
1183, and it seems tolerably certain that he did not
go further than the year 1227. Ralph, abbot of
Coggeshal in Essex, and who had been one of the
heroes of the Crusade, composed, besides his
Chronicon Anglicanum, a *Chronicon Terræ Sanctæ*,
in which he described specially the siege of Jerusalem, where he was wounded in the face by an
arrow. With the view of apologizing for the
brevity of his narrative, he refers the reader to a
French history which gives more details, and which
was nothing else than Ernoul's chronicle: "If any
one wishes for further details, let him read the
book which the prior of the Holy Trinity in London
has caused to be translated from French into
Latin, in a style equally elegant and faithful."[1]

Next to Ernoul we must mention Bernard the
Treasurer, a monk who, as we know from incontestable evidence, wrote one of those popular
histories of the Crusades so widely circulated
during the Middle Ages, and forming an integral
part of the historical monuments known by the
common name of *Histoire d'Eracles* or *Histoire du
Conquêt*. Treasurer of the abbey of Corbie in
Picardy, Bernard deserves special mention as a
chronicler. He begins, like most of his *confrères*,

---

[1] "Si quis plenius scire desiderat, legat librum quem dominus prior Sanctæ Trinitatis de Londoniis ex gallicâ linguâ in Latinum tam eleganti quam veraci stilo transferri fecit."

with a rapid sketch of the history of the kingdom of Jerusalem, dwelling particularly on the share taken in the first Crusades by the Counts of Flanders, as would be natural to a writer belonging, by his social position, to that part of the country. A few brief sentences dispose of the reigns of Baldwin III. and Amaury I.; but, as he proceeds, he goes in detail over some of the facts he has previously mentioned, and his description of Jerusalem is specially interesting, because it shows on the part of the author the local knowledge of one who had actually visited the Holy Land. The historical prologue of Bernard, and the abridgment which follows, cannot be strictly considered as his work; it is with the year 1227 that he assumes the part of an original annalist, and he takes us to the year 1231. The subject on which the treasurer of Corbie dwells most is the Crusade undertaken by the Emperor Frederic II., after that monarch had been anathematized by Pope Gregory IX. He dwells repeatedly on the secret correspondence carried on by Frederic with the Sultan of Egypt—correspondence denied by historians belonging to the Ghibeline party, but which we find distinctly alluded to in the narratives of Eastern chroniclers. In the face of such evidence, it is difficult to understand how the opinion of Boiardo and other Italian authors could ever be entertained, who would make us believe that Bernard was treasurer of the Emperor of Germany.

Two other continuators of Archbishop William should not be left unnoticed, although they have not yet been identified, and must, for the present at least, remain anonymous. The one fills the gap between Ernoul and Bernard; the other takes up the pen where the treasurer of Corbie dropped it, and conducts us as far as the year 1240. The Latin empire of Constantinople does not fix his attention; but, dealing exclusively with the affairs of the kingdom of Jerusalem, he relates the capture of the holy city by the Arabs, shortly after the departure of Frederic II.; the expedition of Thibaut, Count of Champagne; and the temporary union of the Christians with the Syrian Arabs for the purpose of repelling the Kharizmians, who had contracted an alliance with the Sultan of Egypt. This anonymous chronicler does not conceal his hatred of the Emperor Frederic II., but he never suffers himself to be carried away beyond the limits of strict impartiality; and, notwithstanding M. Guizot's remarks, his description of the war between the Genoese and the Ghibelines of Pisa is tolerably accurate. On the whole, therefore, we may consider him as one of the annalists whose works enable us best to understand the sequence of events which occurred from 1230 to 1241.

In order to exhaust the subject of the Crusades, so far as chronicles properly so called are concerned, and still leaving out of consideration Villehardouin and Joinville, we shall mention here

Albert d'Aix, Jacques de Vitry, and Raoul de Caen. Of the first named, we can only say that he was a canon of the church of Aix in Provence, and that he published, under the title of *Chronicon Hierosolymitanum*, a narrative of the first Crusades, from 1095 to 1120. He lived during the twelfth century. Jacques de Vitry, Vicar of Argenteuil, near Paris, and who died at Rome April 30, 1240, preached a crusade against the Albigenses, and was afterwards made Bishop of Ptolemais (1217). He went to Syria, and from thence found his way to Egypt, where he was present at the siege of Damietta (1218); and, having returned to Rome in 1227, he was successively created cardinal (1228), Bishop of Frascati, legate to the Court of France, and Patriarch of Jerusalem. The work of Jacques de Vitry, which contains his reminiscences of the Holy Land, is entitled *Historia Orientalis*, and was published for the first time in 1597. Raoul de Caen is, strictly speaking, the biographer of Tancred de Hauteville, whom he followed to the first Crusade, and whose high deeds he described in a work published successively by Dom Martène, Muratori, and M. Guizot.

CHAPTER VI.

THE CRUSADES.—" LA CHANSON D'ANTIOCHE "—CHRONICLE OF THE DUKES OF NORMANDY—" LE ROMAN DE HAM "—GARNIER DE PONT SAINT-MAXENCE, AND HIS METRICAL LIFE OF THOMAS À BECKET.

THE Crusades could not but appeal strongly to the imagination of the *trouvères*, and it would have been wonderful indeed if the expeditions of Christian Europe, in the Holy Land and in Egypt, had not roused up the enthusiasm of the Langue d'Oïl poets, who were so busy relating and embellishing the life and exploits of Charlemagne, the Emperor of the West, the type and pattern of kingly prowess. The first Crusade took place at the very time when popular poetry was equally flourishing in the south and in the north of France, and it happened most opportunely to furnish the minstrels with a new and exciting theme for their metrical narratives. A *trouvère*, probably a native of Picardy, who had taken a part in the Crusade headed by

Godefroy de Bouillon, related the events connected with that campaign, and the legendary exploits of Charlemagne against the Saracens were revived, recast, and blended together with the reminiscences of the expeditions undertaken to rescue Palestine from the sway of the infidels.

The *Chanson d'Antioche* (such is the name of the poem we are alluding to) deserves, as much as the *Chanson de Roland* itself, a place in the historical compositions of the Middle Ages. Its author, Richard the Pilgrim, was a worthy companion of the heroes whom Godefroy de Bouillon led to the deliverance of Jerusalem and the conquest of Palestine; he is named twice in the course of the narrative, so that there can be no doubt as to his identity. The *chanson* itself soon obtained great celebrity, for we find it recorded more than once by the different minstrels, as late as a hundred years after, that they intended in their metrical works to follow both the rhythm and the general structure of the *Chanson d'Antioche*. One *troubadour* taunted his rival with not knowing Richard's poem; and, finally, the annalist, Lambert d'Ardres, complained bitterly that the exploits of a certain Count of Guines had been purposely forgotten by the *trouvère*. "Count Arnoul," says the chronicler, "performed under the walls of Antioch exploits which his great humility wished to keep concealed; but, in spite of his efforts, the knowledge of these high deeds was obtained by his fellow-Crusaders.

And yet we do not see his name mentioned in the *Chanson d'Antioche;* in fact, the *trouvère* who composed it, more anxious for a temporal profit than Arnoul was to obtain human praise, made a secret of the exploits and glory of the noble count, as a revenge for not having received from him a pair of scarlet hose (*chausses*) which he had asked. That is why the *Chanson d'Antioche* (in which certain personages are unduly praised, and others unfairly forgotten) makes no mention of Count Arnoul—a hero all the more worthy of glory, because he had not been afraid of exposing himself to see his claims frustrated, by refusing to entertain the sordid request of a contemptible *jongleur.*"

We know that the *Chanson d'Antioche* was revised and almost rewritten by Graindor of Douai, who lived in the thirteenth century; this *remaniement*, as our French neighbours would call it, need not astonish us. It was the time when the language of the Langue d'Oïl was subjected to a thorough transformation. Hitherto spoken, declaimed, and sung, it was now going through the ordeal of writing, and in consequence the most important changes were taking place in the prosody and the accentuation. A regular system of orthography was introduced, and the whole grammatical structure received improvements of every kind. It is no exaggeration to say that the *cantilènes* or poems of the twelfth century were, to a considerable extent, a dead letter for the readers of the thirteenth. Thus, the minstrel Adenèz, who lived about the year 1280, said, speaking of the old *trouvères:* "They sang, accompanying themselves on shields or blazoned bucklers; instead of bow, they used swords of steel; therefore they performed strains capable of tearing to pieces the ears of the Saracens, and the best way of obtaining paradise would have been to be patient enough to listen to them."[1]

However, we can say that the *Chanson d'Antioche*, the joint production of Richard the Pilgrim and of Graindor, is undoubtedly a composition of great historical, as well as literary, value. The introduction is worth translating :—

"Barons, hearken unto me, cease your quarrels, and I shall relate to you a fine *chanson*. He who wishes to hear about Jerusalem should draw near to me; in God's name, I entreat him to do so. I ask of him neither a palfrey, nor a charger, nor a

---

[1] "Ils vielerent tous d'une chanson
Dont les vieles *erent targe*[1] ou *blason*;[2]
Et *branc*[3] d'acier estoient li *arçon*;[4]
De leurs vieles *retraoient*[5] maint son
Grief a oïr à *la gent Pharaon*[6] . . .
Qui de tel maistre *retenroit*[7] la leçon
Il porroit bien avoir le haut pardon."

[1] *Erent* (Lat. *erant*) = *étaient;* targe (Eng. *target*) = *bouclier.*
[2] *Blason* = *écu.*
[3] *Branc* (Eng. *brand*) = *épée.*
[4] *Arçon* = *archet.*
[5] *Retraoient* (Lat. *retratebant*).
[6] *La gent (de) Pharaon.*
[7] *Retenroit* = *retiendroit.*

pelisse of miniver or grey, nor even a mere *denier*, unless he gives it to me for the sake of God, who will reward him. I wish to speak to you about the holy city, and to tell you how the gentle barons, whom God wished to bless, went beyond the seas for the purpose of avenging the injury done to it. The first army suffered great disasters; all those who composed it perished, or were made prisoners without being able to find any refuge. Peter alone escaped and returned. Then many princes and noble warriors had assembled together; there was Hugh the Great and all his knights, Tancred and the wise Bohemond, Duke Godfrey so loved of God, the Duke of Normandy and his Normans, the Picards, Robert of Flanders, and his brave Flemings. When they had assembled under the walls of Montpellier, history tells us that they numbered full one hundred thousand. They captured by force Nicæa and its palaces, Robais, and Antioch with its numerous churches; then they broke open the walls of Jerusalem. But, in the first place, they had to fast and to watch, to suffer from rain and storm, snow and hail. Here then begins the song wherein there is so much to learn."

The poem of Richard the Pilgrim was finished before the arrival of the Crusaders at Jerusalem. It is thought that he was one of the retainers of the Count of Flanders, and that he died shortly after the taking of Arches, or Archas, the last event which he recorded; he did not live, at all events, to see the capture of Jerusalem. The best guarantee of the historical importance of the *chanson* lies in the fact that the author was an eye-witness of the events he relates. Every page of his narrative bears evidence of this, even in the most indifferent and casual circumstances. Talking, for instance, of three knights who refused to do their duty, he says, " I know well who they are, but I shall not name them." Thoroughly conscientious, Richard the Pilgrim describes faithfully all the episodes of the Crusade, and analyzes with much impartiality the characters of the various leaders. Thus, Bohemond is represented more than once as trembling, and needing to be reminded of his duty. The Duke of Normandy appears exactly as the local historian describes him to have been: brave, but light-hearted, impetuous, easily put out of temper, and allowing himself too often to be prejudiced. A native of Northern France, our *trouvère*, however, dwells especially upon the heroism of his *compatriotes*. The warriors of Flanders, Artois, and Picardy are those in whom he feels chiefly interested. Thus, he relates in detail the farewell meeting between the Countess of Flanders and her husband, the exploits of Baldwin Cauderon, of Gontier d'Aire, of Enguerrand de Saint-Pol, and of Raimbaud Creton, in whose honour the present *chanson* was composed. Independent authority shows us that Creton really deserved the special distinction bestowed upon him by Richard the Pilgrim. He was the fourth to scale the walls of Antioch, and Ordericus Vitalis informs us that he appeared first on those of Jerusalem; hence his motto—"*Vaillant sus la creste.*" On his return from the Holy Land, he followed Louis the Fat in his expedition against Bouchard IV. of Montmorency, and was killed at the siege of that town in 1101.

The *Chanson d'Antioche,* we have already remarked, is equally striking as a work of art; it has nothing of the dryness of a mere rhymed gazette, and the author, whilst adhering strictly to historic truth, succeeds admirably in working out episodes where some allowance must be made for imagination. Nothing, for instance, is more simply and naturally expressed than the joy of Dacian, the rich Saracen, appointed to defend one of the gates of Antioch, when he presses in his arms his son, who had been made prisoner during a sally, and whom the Christians send back to him covered with a magnificent dress, and with a rich armour:

". . . in the French style,
And of the smallest armour that could be found.
The father comes to meet him; he has taken off his armour;
He kisses and embraces him; he has longed for him so much!
God has thus allowed it, the King of Paradise . . .
By that child were conquered the town and the country."[1]

---

[1] ". . . à la guise Françoise
Et des plus petites armes qu'on ait pu trouver."

Struck with gratitude, the Paynim becomes a convert to Christianity, gives up his palace to the Crusaders, and introduces them into the city of Antioch.

The few lines we have just been quoting are from a modern French transcript of the *Chanson d'Antioche*, for which we are indebted to the Marchioness de Sainte-Aulaire.[1] Of metrical narratives composed on the subject of the Crusades, very few have been handed down to us, and these have reached us only under very modified forms. Thus, we possess absolutely no details about the poem of Gregory of Bechada, except what we learn from the evidence of the Prior of Vigeois. The same remark applies, as we have seen, to the *Chanson d'Antioche*, for Graindor's revision is, of course, a work entirely distinct from the original *geste* composed by Richard the Pilgrim; but, to conclude this notice, we cannot do better than quote the authority of a distinguished French critic, M. Géruzez, who describes the *chanson* as surpassing in accuracy even the chronicle of William, the Archbishop of Tyre.[2]

Le père vient à sa rencontre, il l'a désarmé,
Il le baise et l'étreint ; il l'a tant désiré !
. . . . . .
Dieu l'a ainsi permis, le roi du paradis . . .
Par cet enfant fut la ville et le pays conqués. . . ."

[1] Paris, Techener. 12°. 1848.
[2] *Histoire de la Littérature Française*, vol. i. p. 61.

We have already described a chronicle treating of the Dukes of Normandy; the work we shall now notice is later in point of date. It was published in 1840, by M. Francisque Michel, for the *Société de l'Histoire de France*, and must not be forgotten in our review of mediæval documents. It is divided into two parts of unequal value, and, according to all probability, is the work of two different authors. The first section, extending from the arrival of the Northmen into France, down to the reign of Richard Cœur de Lion, is nothing else but a *résumé* of the *Historia Normannorum*, composed by Guillaume de Jumièges, together with a short supplement. The second part continues the narrative as far as the year 1220, shortly after the coronation of Henry III., King of England; the last event recorded being the raising of the body of Thomas à Becket, *le beneoit martyr*. This portion of the work is full of minute and precise details which are to be found nowhere else, and M. Francisque Michel is led to suppose that the author, having come to England with a number of Flemish adventurers who were anxious to make their fortune, was an eye-witness of a great many of the events which he relates. There is no precise indication of the author's name, or of his nationality; on this latter point, however, we have plenty of indirect information, which can enable us to come to an almost certain conclusion. Let us note that when he alludes either to the persons whom he loves, or, on the contrary, to those who are the object of his hatred, he exclusively mentions knights belonging to the provinces of Artois or of Boulonnais. Thus, giving us an enumeration of the barons who consented to follow Louis in his expedition to England, he assigns the foremost place to the lords of Artois, naming the Frenchmen only next in order. Again, speaking of the siege of Windsor by the Count de Nevers and the Count de Dreux, he adds, "A knight of Artois, by name William de Cerisi, was killed there; he was little regretted by many people, for he was much hated."[1] Further on, describing the siege of Dover, he says, "At the siege Guichars de Beaujeu died; he was taken to be buried in his estates. A knight of Boulonnais also died, who was much regretted; his name was John de la Rivière. He was also taken to be buried at Boulonnais."[2] We think that these three instances, which might easily have been multiplied, are quite conclusive. As M. Michel remarks, no

---

[1] "Uns Chevaliers d'Artois, ki estoit apielés Guillaume de Cerisi, i fu ocis, ki *assés poi*[1] fu plains de maintes gens; car molt estoit haïs."

[2] "Guichars de Beaujeu moru a *cel*[2] siege, si fu portés *enfouir*[3] en sa tierre; mais *ançois*[4] moru uns Chevaliers de Boulenois qui moult fu plains, Jehans de la Rivière *ot à non;*[5] et il fu *autresi*[6] aportés enfouir en Boulenois."

---

[1] *Assés pol* = *assez peu*.
[3] *Enfouir* (Lat. *fodire*) = *enterrer*.
[5] *Ot à non* = *eut à (pour) nom*.

[2] *Cel* = *ce*.
[4] *Ançois* = *aussi*.
[6] *Autresi* = *aussi*.

chronicler would have troubled himself about such insignificant details, in the midst of the important events which marked the reign of King John, if he had not been urged on by the pride of nationality.

The circumstance which recommends to our attention the chronicle we are now considering, is that it gives us all the particulars of the expedition made against England by the son of Philip Augustus—an enterprise about which we had, till recently, but very little original information. English historians, very naturally, did not feel anxious to hand down to posterity an account of the successes of the French on this side of the Channel; the French, on the other hand, were equally silent, because the hopes which they entertained of a second conquest of England speedily disappeared, never to revive again. The anonymous author of our chronicle, being neither French nor English, had not the same difficulty, and this piece of good fortune has produced a narrative which fills up a gap in the history of France during the twelfth century.

Louis, says the old annalist, Matthew Paris, "cum opprobrio sempiterno ad Gallias transfretavit;" after the peace had been concluded, he found himself so utterly destitute of resources that he was obliged to borrow from the London citizens a sum of five thousand pounds, and with this help he returned to France.

The chronicle published by M. Francisque Michel contains numerous details on the barons of Northern France, and this fact has induced the learned editor to print, by way of appendix, a metrical narrative entitled *Le Roman de Ham*, which was composed in 1278. The author is a *trouvère* of the name of Sarrazin. Guillaume de Nangis informs us that Saint Louis, having heard from the pope, in 1268, the news of the disasters experienced in the Holy Land by the Crusaders, had issued a decree forbidding the holding of tournaments for the space of two years, and directing that the only pastimes allowed should be practising with the bow and cross-bow. In the preface to his poem, Sarrazin remarks bitterly on the fatal consequences which such a prohibition is likely to bring about. In the first place, there will be an end of the profession of the *jongleurs*, who used to go from place to place, earning their livelihood by entertaining with tales and romantic stories the knights who had been wounded in the tournaments. Then, what a loss for the saddlers, armourers, harness-makers, smiths, farriers, and other tradesmen and artificers, whose occupations depended almost entirely upon the existence and popularity of martial exercises! Finally, a serious decay of morals must speedily follow; and Dame Courtesy is introduced, looking back with fond regret upon the days of King Arthur, and of the Knights of the Round Table;—as the practical teaching of chivalrous virtues is now forbidden, let the youths learn from the romances of Chrestien de Troyes lessons of urbanity.

    The subject of Sarrazin's poem is the holding of a tournament at the castle of Ham, in Picardy. The lords of Longueval and of Barentin are commissioned to proclaim it throughout all the provinces of France and England. A number of English knights and ladies, supposed to represent King Arthur, Queen Guinevere, and other stars of the Arthurian court, and amounting to upwards of seven hundred persons, appear at this tournament, where for the space of three days deeds of valour are performed by warriors who have assumed names well known in the annals of the Round Table. The enumeration given by the *trouvère* includes many celebrated French and Anglo-Norman barons, such as the lords of Harcourt, Montaigu, Neville, Ver, Bailleul, Blosseville, Tesson, Hangest, Carbonel, Ferrières, Esneval, Trie, etc. All these names are also to be found in the anonymous chronicle we have just been describing, and we notice that Enguerrand de Bailleul is made the subject of special praise. The poem is written in octosyllabic lines, and although the constant recurrence of fictitious characters produces a singular effect, yet, to a considerable extent, we have in the *Roman de Ham* an historical document which deserved to be published, if only as a kind of biographical summary or catalogue of the noble families of England and France towards the end of the thirteenth century. We may add that the edict of Saint Louis caused a great deal of sensation when it was issued, as being contrary to all the usages and traditions of chivalry. It is alluded to in many contemporary writings, and forms the subject of a story in the Italian book entitled *Libro di Novelle è di bel Parlar Gentil.*

Amongst the historical poems which the Middle Ages have bequeathed to us, we must not forget the one composed on the life and death of Thomas à Becket, by Garnier de Pont Saint-Maxence. The subject is essentially English, but the author was a Frenchman, and therefore deserves a place in our sketch; it is interesting, besides, to ascertain how the great Archbishop of Canterbury was appreciated on the other side of the Channel. We all know that, a short time after the death of Thomas à Becket, four priests, attached to his person and honoured with his friendship, wrote memoirs of his life, viz., John of Salisbury, Herbert of Bosham, William of Canterbury, and Alan, Abbot of Tewkesbury. The details given by these four authors were afterwards compiled together, under the direction of Pope Gregory XI., so as to form one single work, entitled *Quadrilogus* or *Historia Quadripartita;* the compiler of this new production taking care, at the same time, always to name for each fact the one of the original biographers on whose authority it was given.

The poem of Garnier de Pont Saint-Maxence is extremely valuable, because it is an independent work. "If you wish," says he, "to read the life of the holy martyrs, you can learn it from me in its completeness, without either omission or error. I have spent at least four years in making and perfecting it, retrenching, adding, without taking any account of my trouble. In the first place, I had written it for my own pleasure, and more than once was guilty of untruth (*et suvent ai menti*). Since then, I went to Canterbury, for the purpose of getting the truth from the friends of Saint Thomas, and from those who had served him ever since he was a child. I had already laboured much in correcting and adding, but certain scribes stole from me this first romaunt before I had had time to finish it, and to soften down what there was in it too hard or too rough. I had not yet suppressed what was unnecessary, nor filled up what was deficient; many places are either false or incomplete; and yet no more exact account is to be found as yet, and many wealthy men have purchased it from me. May those who have stolen it from me be blamed for such a deed! As for the present romaunt, I have entirely corrected and completed it. In all the other narratives composed on the martyr, by either clerks or laymen, monks or ladies, I find errors; they are neither true nor complete. Truth and integrity you may expect here, for I would not depart from the truth for any damage or death I might endure (*n'isterai*[1] *de vérité pur perdre u pur murir*)."

The poem in question is written in Alexandrine verses; the author thus gives us his name and the place of his birth:—

"Since now, and so late a time (in the history of the world), a new martyr is given to you, Garnier the *clerc*, a native of Pont Saint-Maxence, thinks it right to tell you the date of this event; it took place full eleven hundred and seven years after the Incarnation."

It is impossible to read the poem of Garnier without being convinced that it deserves serious attention as a trustworthy historical document. He is thoroughly acquainted with English customs, and the care he displays in describing and accounting for them, shows an amount of observation perfectly wonderful for a *trouvère* of the twelfth century. Nor can we doubt that he derived much information from the relatives and friends of the archbishop, so minute is he in his description of Thomas à Becket's life, his habits, the appearance and circumstances of his house, etc. He goes so far as to clothe in rhyme the correspondence of the prelate, and even the charters issued by Henry II. in the course of the debates which form the subject of the poem. Now, as these official documents are still extant in their original shape, it is quite easy to compare them with Garnier's version, and

---

[1] *Isterai* = *sortirai*; from the old French verb *issir* (Lat. *exire*).

thus to verify his claims to the position of a conscientious and well-informed historian.

As far as the general plan is concerned, and the course of events, there is considerable agreement between the *Historia Quadripartita* and the metrical biography; it is in matters of detail that the differences appear so strongly as to shield Garnier from the accusations of having plagiarized the Latin work. Herbert of Bosham, and the three other monks, his *collaborateurs*, describe Thomas à Becket as a patient, meek, and humble martyr; our friend of Pont Saint-Maxence gives us the full-length portrait of a haughty prelate, impatient of contradiction, irritable, and restrained only by the sense of his episcopal dignity from giving way to fits of passion. Several of the circumstances related in the poem do not appear in the *Historia Quadripartita*; thus, the manner in which Thomas à Becket received the *pallium* from Pope Alexander III. One of the most curious passages is the one where Garnier discusses the pretensions of Henry II. with reference to the political status of the Church; he examines the whole question from the point of view of a canonist, and his opinion represents that of the clergy during the twelfth century. "I appeal," says he, "to the king and to the *clercs*, which are the laws best calculated to govern Christians— those which have been established by heathens and barbarians, or those drawn up by holy men in the shape of a constitution?" A little further on he discusses, article by article, the charter of Henry II., which the bishops had accepted in the Westminster assembly, and which reduced ecclesiastical jurisdiction to so humble a degree when compared with that of the Crown. "The prelates," he remarks, "are the servants of God, and princes, therefore, ought to cherish them; they are above kings, who should bend under them (*et si seint chiefs des rois, li rois leur doit fléchir*)."

Garnier's chronology is not uniformly faultless, and he does not always give us the events in their real sequence; but the great episodes of Thomas à Becket's biography are all recorded—the meeting of the prelates at Northampton, the archbishop's condemnation, his flight into France, his interview at Sens with Pope Alexander III., his exile at Pontigny, the visits paid to him by the French king, Louis VII., etc. The poem is an interesting drama, written with a considerable amount of vigour, and by no means destitute of literary merit.[1]

---

[1] See an interesting article by M. le Roux de Lincy, in the *Bibliothèque de l'École des Chartes*, vol. iv.

CHAPTER VII.

REIGN OF PHILIP AUGUSTUS.—CRUSADE AGAINST THE ALBIGENSES. — RIGORD. — GULIELMUS BRITO.

THE majestic figure of Charlemagne still appeared as the representative of the monastic principle in all its grandeur, and the old *trouvères* seemed anxious to associate it with heroism of every kind, daring, and generosity. Their disposition to do so was, perhaps, increased when they looked about them, and considered into what hands the sceptre of France had fallen during the tenth and eleventh centuries. At last Philip II. came to the throne, and although he cannot be regarded as equalling in genius or in administrative powers the founder of the Carlovingian dynasty, yet it would be unfair to refuse him the qualities of a great king. He strengthened the royal authority, which the turbulent vassals were still too much disposed to set at nought, and, whilst braving the thunderbolts of the Holy See, he managed to secure the goodwill of the French clergy. The cares of home administration seemed to engross his attention; he divided his dominions into seventy-three *prévôtés*, each placed under the rule of a bailiff; then the establishment of *la quarantaine-le-roy* attacked feudalism in one of its most important privileges, the right of private warfare. This name was given to the interval of forty days occurring between every murder or insult and the revenge which the aggrieved party had a right to exercise. During this space of time, anger might subside; it was a kind of truce, which the king took advantage of to interfere, and enforce the claims of justice. The architectural works commenced under the reign of Philip; the protection and encouragement he granted to the University of Paris; finally, his conquest of Maine, Anjou, Normandy, Touraine, and Poitou, together with the acquisition of Auvergne, Artois, and Picardy, justified the title of *Augustus*, which was universally bestowed upon him. We find it mentioned for the first time in the chronicle of Rigord (Rigordus, Rigoltus, Rigotus), who is one of the chief authorities respecting the reign of Philip. A native of Languedoc, Rigord, about whose birth we have no certain data, save that he belonged to the twelfth century, had intended, in the first place, to follow the medical profession; want of success, however, determined him to alter his plans, and, leaving his country, he took up his abode in the abbey of Saint Denis, which the administration of Suger had rendered so justly celebrated. We are informed that about the year 1190, and probably at the instigation of Hugh, abbot of the community, Rigord undertook to write the history of Philip Augustus. He spent ten years in preparing his work, but was so dissatisfied with what he had accomplished, that he would have destroyed the portion he had already committed to writing, had not his superior dissuaded him from doing so. Better advised, Rigord dedicated his life of the king to Louis VIII., his successor, who was then a youth of thirteen. Philip Augustus appreciated so highly the composition of the monk of Saint Denis, that he ordered copies to be placed among the public records, and he named Rigord his historiographer. The history begins at the coronation of the king in 1179; after having related the events connected with the first five years of the reign, Rigord stops suddenly, and launches forth into a discussion about the origin of the French nation, which he traces up to the fabulous Francus; he next gives the succession of all the kings, and then, resuming the thread of his narrative, goes down as far as the year 1207. There death alone appears to have stopped him; and, according to the *Nécrologe* of the abbey of Saint Denis, he died, at a very advanced age, on the 27th of November.

The other historian of the reign of Philip Augustus is a man whose literary talents leave those of Rigord quite in the shade, and who, like the old monk Abbo, attempted to hand down to posterity, through the medium of poetry, the events it had been his lot to witness. Guillaume le Breton, to call him by his French name, was in every respect a far more distinguished personage than his predecessor. A Breton by birth (? 1165), he took orders at an early age, and became chaplain to Philip Augustus, who entrusted him with several political missions of great importance; sending him, for instance, to Rome for the purpose of obtaining his divorce from the Princess Ingelburgha of Denmark. Gulielmus Brito enjoyed considerable influence over the mind of the king; he took a leading part in the councils of the crown, and accompanied his master in most of his military expeditions. We do not know the date of Brito's decease; but in all probability he survived Louis VIII., whose death occurred in 1226. The works of this author are two in number, the first being a mere prose continuation of Rigord down to the year 1219, and the other, the *Philippid*, has already been alluded to. M. Walckenaër remarks that Guillaume le Breton's chronicle contains a number of interesting particulars on the author's native country, and he may be considered as the annalist of Brittany for the epoch embraced in his narrative. For a detailed account of the events which occurred between 1209 and 1219, Guillaume is invaluable—he had never left the king's side during the campaigns of Flanders; and his book is equally minute and accurate. The poem, on the other hand, may be regarded as throwing considerable light, not so much upon historical events, as on geographical details, manners and customs. The style here, we need scarcely say, is very far from perfect; whole lines copied from Virgil, Ovid, and Statius merely help to make the surrounding Latin look more wretched; and, if the description of the battle of Bouvines can be quoted as an exception, its comparative merit is due probably to the author's patriotism alone.

Philip Augustus refused to take a share in the Crusade against the Albigenses, although he had allowed his son Louis to join for that purpose the standard of Amaury de Montfort. This momentous event, which led to the destruction of Languedoc thought and culture, and which resulted in the triumph of Teutonic over Latin civilization, has been recorded in several chronicles, which we must proceed to enumerate. Alluding to the Crusade itself, Sir James Stephen remarks—

"The imputations of irreligion, heresy, and shameless debaucheries, which have been cast with so much bitterness on the Albigenses by their persecutors, aad which have been so zealously denied by their apologists, are probably not ill founded, if the word *Albigenses* be employed as synonymous with the words *Provençaux* or *Languedocians*. For these were apparently a race among whom the hallowed charities of domestic life, and the reverence due to divine ordinances, and the homage due to divine truth, were often impaired, and not seldom extinguished, by ribald jests, by infidel scoffings, and by heart-hardening impurities. Like other voluptuaries, the Provençaux (as their remaining literature attests) were accustomed to find matter for merriment in vices which would have moved wise men to tears."[1]

There seems no doubt that a broad distinction must be made between the *Albigeois* and the *Vaudois*, whose dissent from the doctrines of the Church of Rome was their only fault, and against whom even the charge of heresy must be received with considerable caution; but, at the same time, we should not forget that the writers of the thirteenth century do not acknowledge the difference which fair dealing obliges us to admit, and the author of a poem, to which we shall presently refer more in detail, classes the Vaudois amongst outlaws and highwaymen. "Knowest thou," says Bishop Folquet, addressing the pope, "that the Count de Montfort has remained in the district of Carcassis for the purpose of destroying the wicked and establishing the good, for the purpose of driving out the heretics, the *routiers*, and the Vaudois, and peopling the country with Catholics, Normans, and French?"[2]

---

[1] *Lectures on the History of France.*
[2] *Croisade contre les Alb.*, lines 3500–3503.

At any rate, the history of the Crusade against the Albigenses has been made the subject of several works, which may be found in the nineteenth volume of the *Recueil des Historiens*, and the principal of which, translated into French, form part of the collection of documents published by M. Guizot (vols. xiv. and xv.). Let us first mention the memoirs of Pierre de Vaulx-Cernay, who died about the year 1218, and who took an important share in the terrible deeds he relates. It is curious to note the expressions of his zeal for the Church of Rome; to watch him as he travels from one end of France to the other, recruiting for the Crusade, preaching, confessing, exhorting his erring brethren, and assisting, as he acknowledges himself, "with unutterable joy," at massacres and *auto-da-fé*. The uncle of Pierre de Vaulx-Cernay, Guy, abbot of the same monastery, became Bishop of Carcassonne after the domains of the Count of Toulouse had been conquered by Simon de Montfort. Sharing the fanaticism of his nephew, he threw all his energy into the Crusade, and appears as one of the leading characters in the stirring drama unfolded by the monk. The history we are now alluding to, being the work of a partisan, is not very reliable. Peter distorts or omits, not only the circumstances favourable to the Count of Toulouse and to his followers, but all the facts which tell against the Crusaders. You rise from the perusal of his book knowing absolutely nothing about the petty rivalries of the orthodox barons, their greed, their ambition, the reproaches frequently addressed to them by the pope. In the opinion of the annalist, Simon de Montfort is an immaculate hero, to whose glory he does not hesitate to sacrifice indifferently friends and foes. On the other hand, as M. Guizot remarks, there are few historical productions so thoroughly interesting as the work of Pierre de Vaulx-Cernay—few which make us so well acquainted with the character of the times, the spirit which animated the Crusaders, and the whole policy of the expedition. The work begins with the supposed origin of the Albigensis heresy, and ends with the death of Simon de Montfort.

The next chronicle to which we shall call the attention of our readers is a metrical one, published for the first time by M. Francisque Michel in the *Collection de Documents Inédits*, begun during the reign of Louis Philippe, and a new edition of which, prepared by M. Paul Meyer, is now in course of publication under the auspices of the *Société de l'Histoire de France*. This poem is the work of two distinct authors—Guillaume de Tudela, and a troubadour, who seems to have been a native of Toulouse, or of the immediate neighbourhood. The fact of its being *a poem* might lead some critics to suppose that it is destitute of historical importance, and that its only merit is that of a literary composition, in which a few events and characters are introduced as the pretext for giving a kind of material in which the author's fancy could freely display its powers. Now, it is quite true that Guillaume de Tudela talks of his work as of a *chanson*, but exactly in the same manner as Robert Wace called his poems *romances*. There is, of course, some share to be given to fancy, but the metrical composition we are examining is, to all intents and purposes, a history. It contains the narrative of events which the author has either witnessed himself, or heard from the lips of credible and trustworthy persons. We may notice here that whilst writing his account of the Crusade, Guillaume de Tudela, anxious, no doubt, to earn reputation as a *littérateur*, endeavoured to take for his pattern some of the most popular of the *chansons de geste* which were then current. Thus, in giving an interesting description of the siege of Beaucaire by the young Count of Toulouse, he introduces to us the French knights who were defending the citadel for the Count de Montfort, reduced to the greatest distress, and deliberating on the best course which they should adopt :—

"Raynier de Chanderon is the last to speak. 'My lord,' says he, 'remember Guillaume au Cort-nez. What fatigues he endured at the siege of Orange! Let us all be knights, both for life and for death, and let us disgrace neither France nor Montfort.'"[1]

---

[1] Lines 4106 and foll.

This allusion evidently proves that the author had seen one of the old *chansons de geste* relating the wars of Guillaume au Cort-nez with the Saracens, and that the *chanson* was well known in Languedoc.

In another passage, describing the arrival of the Crusaders under the walls of Carcassonne, we find the following allusions to a supposed incident which took place in the siege of that town by Charlemagne:—

"Charles, the emperor, the powerful crowned king, kept the town, as we are told, besieged for the space of more than seven years, without being able to take it either in summer or in winter. But when he departed, the towers bent forward to do homage to him, so that he captured it on his return, if the *geste* can be trusted; and it would have been impossible for him to take it otherwise." [1]

Until quite recently, the poem we are now describing was regarded as being one work, composed throughout by one and the same author. Such was the theory put forth by MM. Fauriel and Francisque Michel—a theory so absurd that it will not bear investigation; for, if we accept it, we find ourselves face to face with an historian writing the commencement of his chronicle from one point of view, and finishing it under the influence of diametrically opposite principles. Up to the account of the battle of Moret, where the

---

[1] Lines 562 and foll.

King of Arragon was killed (1213), the political and religious sympathies of the author are entirely on the side of the Crusaders; Simon de Montfort is his hero as he was that of the monk of Vaulx-Cernay, and the heretics deserve nothing but destruction. After this event, the whole character of the work is changed; the Albigenses become the object of the poet's good wishes, and the orthodox party are treated by him with a severity which their deeds of cruelty only too thoroughly justified. At the same time, he professes to be a fervent Catholic, and his condemnation of the manner in which the authority of the Church was maintained does not, in the slightest degree, shake his attachment to the Church itself. M. Paul Meyer's solution of the problem clears away every difficulty, and we are no longer puzzled by the apparent want of consistency, when we find that the romance is, in reality, the artificial association of two distinct works, representing two opposite views of religious policy. M. Francisque Michel takes care to note the principal passages, where much has evidently been allowed to imagination; the most remarkable is the episode of the famous Council of Lateran and of the resolutions which were taken there. "It is," said the learned editor, "a poetic creation where history is handled with very little scruple." At the same time, even there we find historical statements which have been abundantly confirmed by other evidence; and the conduct of Pope

Innocent III. towards Simon de Montfort, amongst other things, is accurately stated and ascribed to its true causes. The poem of the Crusade consists of nearly 9580 Alexandrine lines, arranged in 1214 stanzas of unequal length; it gives us the events of the war from the year 1208 to the taking of Toulouse in 1219.

Another chronicle on the same epoch, reprinted in M. Guizot's collection, deserves special mention, because it was evidently written as a paraphrase of the metrical account we have just been examining, and the one is a mere reproduction of the other. The facts are presented in the same manner, explained by the same motives, and the only difference between the prose and the metrical narratives consists in peculiarities of style and of literary composition. From various circumstances and allusions given in the course of the work, the Benedictine Dom Vaissète, who published it for the first time in his *Histoire du Languedoc*, was led to conclude that it belongs to the middle of the fourteenth century, or even, perhaps, to a more recent date.

Guillaume de Puy-Laurens, who flourished about the end of the thirteenth century, and was chaplain to Count Raimond VII., must not be forgotten amongst the historians of the war against the Albigenses. Beginning quite *ab ovo*, and discussing fully the origins of the heresy, he takes us down to the year 1272; and his account is the more valuable because he has related a number of facts omitted by other writers. We must give him credit, also, for an endeavour to be impartial, and for the comparative freedom with which he appreciates the events and personages he has to review. The great drawback to his work is the chronology; there Guillaume de Puy-Laurens signally fails, especially when, wandering away from the main subject he has in hand, he attempts to survey the general course of European history.

The last chronicle which we shall mention here, in connection with the Crusade against the Albigenses, is a very brief one, generally known by the name of *Chronicle of Simon, Count de Montfort.* It extends from 1202 to 1311, and is disfigured by blunders of every kind, which detract considerably from its merit. It will be found in the fifteenth volume of M. Guizot's collection.

CHAPTER VIII.

SAINT LOUIS—GUILLAUME DE NANGIS AND HIS CONTINUATORS—JEAN DE VENETTE.

WE have thus arrived at the thirteenth century, the most remarkable epoch in the whole Middle Ages. Two great prelates, Innocent III. and Innocent IV., occupied the papal chair. A saint ruled over France, and the empire was under the sway of Frederic II.—a monarch who, at any time, would have attracted the notice of the whole world. The quarrel of the investitures between Rome and Germany had come to an end, and Italy was once more throwing off the yoke of its Teutonic oppressors. England established the foundation of its liberties. The results of the Crusades were beginning to manifest themselves in a remarkable intellectual, industrial, and commercial movement. The love of study had spread far and wide, monuments of national literature were appearing, and in the various walks of philosophy, science, divinity, and *belles lettres*, the progress accomplished was of the most extraordinary character. Let us see how historical composition was affected by this general revival, and ascertain what impression the development of mediæval civilization had produced upon the writers whose business it was to record passing events, and to delineate the portraits of leading personages in Church and State. We have already mentioned Rigord and Guillaume le Breton. For the biography of Saint Louis, we can profitably consult the confessor of Queen Margaret, his consort, besides Geoffroy de Beaulieu (? 1274), who was, during the space of more than twenty years, his own spiritual adviser; Guillaume de Chartres, his chaplain and his fellow-captive in Palestine (? 1225-1280); Albéric des Trois Fontaines, and Baudouin d'Avesnes. Most of the historical documents or compilations written by these annalists have been printed in the collections of Duchesne, Dom Bouquet, and Leibnitz.

Guillaume de Nangis and his continuators are entitled to a separate mention, on account of the exceptional merit of the chronicle with which their names are associated—a chronicle edited, a few years ago, for the *Société de Histoire de France* by M. Géraud. Of Guillaume himself very little is known, for not one of the writers belonging to the thirteenth and fourteenth centuries has mentioned him, and he is provokingly reticent about his own biography. Was he born at Nangis, a small town in the department of Seine-et-Marne? Even that is far from being ascertained, and the words *de Nangiaco*, which accompany his name in the original manuscripts, afford the only fact upon which we can rest this supposition. He was a Benedictine monk of the abbey of Saint Denis, and died shortly after the year 1230. The history of Guillaume's works is not, to quote Lacurne de Sainte-Palaye, as barren as that of his life. He has left behind him a biography of Saint Louis, and one of Philip the Bold, in Latin; a Latin chronicle extending from the creation of the world to the year 1300; and a small account of the kings of France, written in French. He is, moreover, supposed by some critics to have translated into French his biography of Saint Louis and his general chronicle. Guillaume de Nangis does not pretend to any originality in the first of these works; his guides, he says, are Geoffroy de Beaulieu and Gilon de Reims. The memoir of the confessor of Saint Louis still exists; it is what we should call strictly a work of edification, and therefore we are led to conclude that the narrative of the wars in which the king took a part, and the account of his administration, were borrowed by Guillaume de Nangis from Gilon de Reims, whose own composition is lost. Now, if our author has followed this writer as he has done in the case of Geoffroy, we need not regret very much that Gilon's *ipsissima verba* are not to be found at present in any library, either public or private. The history of Philip III.

deserves still more confidence, and is still more reliable. Here Guillaume de Nangis required no guide; he described what was taking place under his own eyes, events in which he sometimes had a share.

The chronicle, as far as the year 1300, is a mere compilation from the works of Eusebius, Saint Jerome, and Sigebert de Gembloux; subsequently to that date, it assumes the appearance of an original work, and is nearly the only authority for the first sixteen years of Philip the Fair, the portion of the chronicles of Saint Denis corresponding to that epoch being nothing else but a translation of Guillaume's own composition. Guillaume de Nangis, like Guillaume de Tyr, had his train of continuators, all monks of Saint Denis, *commonachi nostri*, and of whom we need not say much till we come to a certain Jean de Venette, who took up the thread of the narrative at the year 1340, and brought it down as late as 1368. Master Jean de Venette *dit Fillons*, born about 1307 or 1308, and a Carmelite friar, was a man of somewhat irregular habits, if we may judge from the following curious extract, which readers interested in antiquarian lore may find in his poem on the three Marys. Talking of the miracle at Cana, he exclaims feelingly—

"Would to Heaven, for my solace,
That I had three or four bottles (shares=*lots*) of it,

Yea, a jar quite full !
I would drink hard." [1]

This is tolerably good French, if somewhat of a bacchanalian character. Venette's Latin, on the other hand, is uncouth in the extreme, and he frankly acknowledges it himself: "Ad ea ... recitanda me verbis rudibus applicabo ruditer, cum sim rudis." But, as the latest editor of our chronicle well remarks: "How superior to his predecessors he is by his manner of understanding and writing history! Previous to him, history is a mere record of facts stated in all their simplicity, with no other connection except chronological sequence. No criticism, no comments; the reader is left to unravel cause and effect, to appreciate men, things, institutions: the historian seems to make a merit of concealing himself, and courts oblivion. Jean de Venette follows an entirely different method; his bold and independent pen not only puts down the facts he has witnessed, or those which have been related to him, but also the impression he has received from them. He discusses, censures, approves with equal freedom the acts of the crown, the excesses of the feudal lords,

---

[1] "Pleust à Dieu, pour moy esbatre,
Qu'en tenisse trois los ou quatre,
Voire[1] une isdrie[2] toute plaine !
Si en buvroie a grant alaine.[3]

[1] *Voire* (Lat. *verè*) = *vraiment*.
[2] *Isdrie* (Gr. 'ύδριον) = *cruche*.
[3] *Alaine* = *halline*.

the resistance of the people. Engaged by his sympathies, and perhaps by a direct share, in the internal struggles which, during his lifetime, deluged France with blood, he stamps his narrative of events with all the independence of his ideas and the warmth of his convictions. Passion stands for him in the stead of style and of literary talent, and for the first time, under the barbarous Latin of the Middle Ages, history becomes animated, and assumes a dramatic form to which it had not been accustomed."

It is curious to compare Jean de Venette with Guillaume de Nangis. The older chronicler is the pattern of a staunch conservative. The idea which runs through his book is that of complete submission to the powers that be; the greatest misdeeds committed by the kings of France are recorded without any reflection or expression of blame, as if it was quite impossible for a monarch to do anything wrong. Jean de Venette, on the contrary, never misses the opportunity of inveighing against the nobles, and, next to the English, he hates them with an earnestness which is sometimes quite amusing. Belonging probably by his birth, and certainly by his convictions, to what our neighbours would call *le petit peuple*, he accepts as a challenge the famous sobriquet of *Jacques Bonhomme*, applied by the feudal barons to the country population. Jacques Bonhomme is the object of all his care; the miseries of the people engross his attention; the triumphs and virtues of the people monopolize his praises. Relating a well-known episode in the wars against the English, he first alludes to the treaty of peace concluded in 1359 between the Regent of France and the King of Navarre, and then goes on:—

"Dissatisfied with this place, the English endeavoured to do still greater harm to France; but their designs did not always meet with the success which they expected, for, by the permission of the Lord, they were defeated in several private combats. I wish to relate one of these such as I heard it from the mouth of trustworthy witnesses, and I do so the more willingly, because the event took place near the village where I was born, and was stoutly despatched by Jacques Bonhomme. *Et fuit negotium per rusticos, seu Jacque Bonhomme strenue expeditum.*"

We cannot wonder at finding Jean de Venette accused of being a democrat in the modern sense of the words; but a close attention to his chronicle will lead an impartial critic to modify this opinion very materially. Let us again quote from M. Géraud's excellent preface:—

"Jean de Venette never dreamt that the people, the object of his predilection, should obtain any privilege; taxes, services, impositions, were so many sacred obligations to which they must submit without a murmur. But, on the other hand, the faithful and conscientious discharge of all these burdens should, as a matter of justice, guarantee to the people the right of working with security, and of enjoying the fruit of their labours; and if the nobles, whom Jean de Venette regarded as the born defenders of the country, deserved to be called to account, it was because they had not protected the land against foreign invasion, and because they had plundered the lower classes instead of assisting them. If the regent, notwithstanding the supreme authority with which he was invested, merited the severest blame, it was because he had done nothing to repress the insolence and exactions of the barons."

The chronicle of Jean de Venette was evidently written subsequently to the year 1358, when the treacherous conduct of the King of Navarre and of Etienne Marcel had become notorious. He does not attempt to palliate this crime; in fact, he ascribes to Charles le Mauvais the burning of Saint Lazare, of Saint Laurent, and of the stores preserved in the neighbourhood of Paris. What, then, was the secret hope which governed the mind of that faithless prince and of his adherents? Nothing else, our author answers, but the ambition of obtaining the crown of France: *ad hoc totis viribus anhelabat.* If Etienne Marcel favoured the views of Charles le Mauvais, by attempting to open to him the gates of the capital, it was because the Parisians dreaded the wrath of the regent, whom the catastrophe of Robert de Clermont and of the Marshal of Champagne, both murdered under the eyes of Charles V., had justly infuriated. The account of the death of Etienne Marcel is one of the most striking episodes in Jean de Venette's narrative, and the sentiments of the Parisians are expressed with singular *naïveté*. We have been led to dwell at some length on these circumstances, for the purpose of showing that Jean de Venette was not, as Lacurne de Sainte-Palaye and other critics have supposed, an admirer of the King of Navarre. If ever he was so, remarks M. Géraud, he had completely altered his original opinion, and no adherent of Charles le Mauvais could have spoken with such evident delight of the defeat of the Captal de Buch, and of the Navarrese, at Cocherel in 1364.

CHAPTER IX.

VILLEHARDOUIN—JOINVILLE—ROBERT DE CLARI.

IN order not to separate Guillaume de Nangis from his continuators, we have been obliged to neglect two historians, whom we shall now examine somewhat in detail, because they combine literary merit of the highest kind with all the qualities of excellent and trustworthy memoir-writers. We mean Villehardouin and Joinville, whose works have recently been edited by M. N. de Wailly in the most scholarly manner. We may affirm, without fear of contradiction, that they stand by themselves as brilliant specimens of mediæval French literature. Villehardouin gives a lively and interesting, and, on the whole, a faithful, account of the fourth Crusade. The foundation of a French empire at Constantinople, the taking of that city, and the transportation of the whole system of feudal institutions to the shores of the Black Sea, amongst the descendants of the ancient Hellenes, were facts startling enough, and well calculated to draw forth the powers of an observer. Villehardouin had the advantage of taking a part in the expedition as a soldier and a diplomatist. He relates the things which he saw, and the sobriety and simplicity of his narrative are among its greatest merits. As M. de Wailly well observes, Villehardouin is the father of French vernacular history. It is true that at the same epoch, or even a few years previous, other writers had attempted to describe contemporary events in the language of their country. Thus, we have seen that a Crusader of the name of Brehada composed in the Romance language a history of the first Crusade; but his work has not reached us. Then, again, the first translations of Aimoin and Eginhard seem to belong to the beginning of the reign of Philip Augustus; but they are only translations, whilst the *Conqueste de Constantinoble* is the first original French work of a thoroughly historical character. We shall not dwell long on Villehardouin's biography. Born about the year 1167, in a château situated between Bar and Arcis-sur-Aube, belonging to one of the most ancient families of Champagne, and to one of those who enjoyed most influence at the court of the lord of that province, he had for some time discharged the duties of marshal, when, in 1199, Count Thibault, happening to be at a tournament with all the nobility of the neighbourhood, announced that he was about to undertake the voyage to Jerusalem, and to do his service as a Crusader. A considerable number of barons, Geoffroy de Villehardouin amongst the rest, took the cross on the occasion. They assembled first at Soissons, then at Champagne, for the purpose of determining the epoch of their starting and the road they would take. Villehardouin, as we have already said, was a personage of much political importance; with the chivalrous courage of which he gave repeated proofs, he combined the eloquence of a debater and the experience of a statesman. As he had a prominent share in all the negotiations, as well as in the military exploits of the Crusade, it is almost a subject of wonder that he should have found time to describe the romantic expedition which his memoirs make so well known. At any rate, it is not too much to say that his work is a masterpiece of candour and of veracity. He begins by enumerating the various lords and barons who joined in the war. The chiefs were the Count de Brie; Louis, Count de Blois and de Chartres; Baudouin, Count de Flanders; and his brother. Amongst the Crusaders belonging to Champagne, we notice Geoffroy de Joinville, the uncle of the celebrated friend and biographer of Saint Louis. The years 1199 and 1200 were spent in all the necessary preparations. The commander decided at last upon despatching six messengers or deputies, the best that could be found; and these forerunners, if we may use the expression, Geoffroy de Villehardouin being amongst them as a matter of course, started for Venice, where they arrived in

February, 1201. It is not our intention to describe here the events of the fourth Crusade; we shall merely say that, after the taking of Constantinople in 1204, the Marshal of Champagne, as a reward for his services, received from the Marquis of Montferrat the grant of a fief situated in Thessaly, where he died about the year 1213. The *Conqueste de Constantinoble* comprises the history of the events from 1198 to 1207.

It is a matter of regret that we should not possess the original text of the Maréchal de Champagne; but an attentive study of the six manuscript copies which are still extant has enabled M. de Wailly to give us an edition far surpassing those of Ducange (1657), Dom Brial (1822), M. Paulin Paris (1838), and M. Buchon (1840). The best of the six copies alluded to is one which was done during the reign of Philippe de Valois, by an Italian. It was preserved for a long time in one of the Venice libraries. The transformations undergone by the French language from the eleventh century to the fourteenth have often been a source of great confusion to scribes; and we know, besides, that persons working on texts belonging to the early Middle Ages purposely altered the original which they had to copy, in accordance with the grammatical fashion of their own times. We shall have to note this circumstance when we treat of Joinville; the *Chronique de Constantinoble* gives us an opportunity of mentioning it now. Fortunately, in the case of this work, the Italian *amanuensis* knew nothing about the difference existing between the French of the fourteenth century and that of the thirteenth. He was, moreover, totally incapable of understanding the character of the variations introduced into the etymology and the syntax. His copy, therefore, may be accepted as a faithful transcript of the original, and the blunders he has committed are not deliberate alterations, but the result of carelessness; he never had the intention of modernizing the narrative he was directed to reproduce.

Next to the Venice manuscript, as it is called, comes *Longo Intervallo*, another one, in all probability due to a native of Ile-de-France about the beginning of the fourteenth century. Here considerable liberties have been taken with the text. Long phrases are abridged, entire sentences condensed, synonyms introduced, and orthographical modifications applied for the purpose of giving to Villehardouin's idiom the colour of the locality to which the copyist belonged. M. de Wailly notices, however, that the manuscript in question is still of great importance, and that it helps, in many instances, to rectify the blunders of the Italian *codex*. A series of three transcripts, of evidently like origin, because they exhibit the same alterations, suppressions, and mistakes, then deserves to be mentioned here. The dialect used in the three is that of Picardy or of Flanders, and we have, therefore, a text totally different from the Champenois original of Villehardouin, such as we find it in the Italian manuscript. These three copies belong to the thirteenth, fourteenth, and fifteenth centuries respectively.

After having thus briefly given our readers an idea of the *letter*, if we may so say, of the *Chronique de Constantinoble*, we shall now offer a few remarks on the work itself. The critical appreciations made of it by M. Villemain, M. Géruzez, M. Demogeot, and other eminent writers, have all given a true estimate of its merits, and we can only re-echo the verdict thus passed.

Compelled to speak often of himself, Villehardouin always does so with the greatest modesty possible, and his narrative is singularly untainted by that affectation which detracts so much from the merit of the great majority of memoir-writers. Critics have often found fault with our author on the score of obscurity and of want of elegance. Now, it would not be difficult to show that the supposed obscurity with which he is charged arises from the ignorance or carelessness of copyists, who undertook to transcribe the chronicle; for we presume that, when Villehardouin is accused of being obscure, this epithet merely implies that his indications of persons and of localities are not always given with sufficient distinctness.

As for the want of elegance, we can hardly understand the weight of such a reproach, for

the slightest study of Villehardouin's prose will
convince the reader that no mediæval French
author can be named, more noteworthy for clearness of style, neatness of composition, and admirable delineation of character. M. de Wailly
very aptly remarks that, in the thirteenth and fourteenth centuries, France numbered nearly as many
dialects as there were provinces. The most elegant
of these dialects—those which have had the greatest
share in moulding the French of the present day—
were those of Anjou, Ile-de-France, and especially
Champagne. The Norman parlance was deemed
the most disagreeable; those of Artois and of
Picardy, with their harshness and abruptness, were
equally neglected, as unfit for the usages of polite
and courtly society. The critic who must be held
chiefly responsible for the accusation we have just
alluded to is Etienne Pasquier; he names Villehardouin as an indifferent writer, and talks con-
temptuously of him, as having adopted the *ramage
de son pays*. Now that *ramage*, to quote once more
M. Natalis de Wailly, was the most elegant language of the time. Thanks to Marie de France,
widow of Henry I., and daughter of Eleanora of
Guienne, the court of Champagne had become,
even to a greater extent than the court of the
sovereign, the favourite abode of all the most
distinguished poets and prose writers. Gautier de
Coinsy, the Châtelain of Coucy, Auboins de Sé-
zanne, Chrestian de Troyes, are all well known

amongst the leading French mediæval poets; they were all natives of Champagne. If we compare their works with those of Blondel de Nesle, for instance, or with the metrical romances of Robert Wace, we shall see at once the decided superiority of the Champenois *littérateurs*. One short extract from Villehardouin's *Conqueste* will serve to give an idea of his style:—

"When they had arrived at the palace, they alighted at the gate, and went in, and saw the emperor Isaac the father, and the emperor Alexis his son, sitting side by side in two chairs; next to them was sitting the empress, who was wife of the father. and stepmother of the son, and sister to the King of Hungary, a handsome and kind lady. And with them were many people of distinction, and it certainly seemed the court of a powerful prince. By the consent of the other messengers, Quèsnes de Béthune, who was very wise and eloquent, spoke, and he thus said: 'Sir, we have come to you in the name of the barons of the host, and of the Doge of Venice. And know that they reproach you for the great service they have rendered you, as your own people are aware, and as is quite apparent. You have sworn, you and your father, to keep the agreement you had promised, and they have your written deed to the effect. You have not kept it as you ought. More than once have they summoned you to do so, and we now summon you again, in the presence of all your barons.

If you comply, it will go well with them; if you do not, they hold you neither as their lord, nor as their friend; but they will endeavour to obtain their right in every possible way. And they send you word that they would harm neither you nor any one else, without first challenging you, for they have never been guilty of treachery, and in their country treason is not known. You have heard what we have said; decide, then, what you please.' The Greeks took this challenge as a wonderful thing and a great insult; and they said that never had there been a man in the world so bold as to defy the Emperor of Constantinople in his own room."[1]

---

[1] "DISCOURS DE QUÈSNES DE BÉTHUNE À L'EMPEREUR DE CONSTANTINOBLE.[1]

"Quant ils furent venus jusques au palais, il descendirent à la porte et entrèrent *ens*,[2] et trovèrent *l'Empereour*[3] *Kyrsac*[4] le père, et l'Empereour Alexis son fil, séant *ambedui*[5] *les-à-les*[6] en dui *chaieres*,[7] et de lès els séoit *l'empereris*,[8] qui feme estoit au père et

---

[1] The want of faith on the part of the Greek emperor Isaac, so energetically denounced by Quèsnes de Béthune in his speech, led to the storming of Constantinople, and to the partition of the empire between the conquerors, viz. Baldwin IX., Count of Flanders; Boniface II., Marquis of Montferrat; and the Republic of Venice.

[2] *Dans*, Lat. *intus*.

[3] Accus. sing. of the substant. *emperères*. In the French grammar of the twelfth and thirteenth centuries, all substantives ending in *ères* take the termination *eour* in the oblique cases.

[4] *Isaac*.

[5] *Both*, Lat. *ambo, duo;* in the obl. cases, *ambedeus*.

[6] *Side by side; les*, or *lès*, from the Lat. *latus*. The word still occurs in various compounds; thus, *Plessis-lez-Tours, Saint-Pierre-lez-Calais*.

[7] For *chaises*.

[8] *Impératrice*. The old feminine *emperière* occurs likewise.

The Latin empire founded in the East by the
heroes of the fourth Crusade was not of long

---

marastre au fil, et estoit *suer*¹ le Roi de Hongrie, bele dame et
bone. Et avoec els avoit grant *planté*² de bone gens, et mout
sembloit cour à riche prince. Par l'assentement des autres messages
monstra la parole Quèsnes de Béthune, qui plus estoit sages et bien
*emparlés*³ que nus des autres, et dist en tele manière : 'Sires, nous
somes à vous venu *de part*⁴ les barons de *l'ost*⁵ et de part le *Duc
de Venise ;*⁶ et sachiés que il reprouvent le service que il ont à vous
fait, tel come tot la gens sevent, et come il est aparissant ; vos et
vostre pères lor avés juré leur *convenances*⁷ à tenir ; il en ont vos
chartres. Vous ne leur avez *mie*⁸ is bien tenu come vous déussiez.
Meintes fois vous en ont *semons*⁹ et encore vous en semonnons-nous,
voiant tous vos barons, se vous le faites, moult leur sera bel, et *se ce
non*¹⁰ il ne vous tiennent ne pour seigneur ne pour ami. Ensi por-
chaceront que il auront leur raison, en toutes les manières que il
porront : et bien vous mandent ce ; que, sans *deffiance*¹¹ ils ne
feroient mal ne à vous, ne à autrui, car il ne firent *oncques*¹² trahison,
et en leur terres n'est-il mie acoustumé que il le facent. Vous avés
bien oï ce que nous vous avons dit ; si¹³ vous consellies ensi que il
vous plaira.' Mout tindrent le *Grieu*¹⁴ à grant merveille et à grant
outrage ceste deffiance, et distrent que *onques mès*¹⁵ nul home el
monde ne fu tant hardis qu'il osast deffier l'Empereour de Constantinoble en sa chambre méismes."

---

¹ For *sœur du roi*.
² Eng. *plenty*, from the Lat. *plenitas*. Hence the adject. *plan-
tureux*, which is still used, and which should be spelt *plentureux*.
³ *Eloquent*.
⁴ Another example of the genitive employed without a connecting
preposition ; see above, note 1.
⁵ *Hostis*.   ⁶ The Doge, Henry Dandolo.
⁷ *Convenances*, covenant.
⁸ *Pas*, from the Lat. *mica* ; ne . . . *mie* ; lit. *not a crumb*.
⁹ The verb is *semondre*, to summon ; Lat. *submonere, summonere*,
from which is also derived the verb *sommer*. The substant. *semonce*
is frequently employed in the sense of *a scolding, a reprimand*.
¹⁰ *Se ce non*, if not.   ¹¹ *A challenge*.
¹² *Ever*, Lat. *unquam*.
¹³ *Si (ainsi) vous consellies = consellier vous*.
¹⁴ *Grecs*.   ¹⁵ *Onques mès = jamais*.

duration; Villehardouin's record of it, to quote a recent critic, has outlived it, and it is no exaggeration to say that it will subsist as long as the French language. A captain, a statesmen, and an historian, he reminds us sometimes of Thucydides, more frequently of Herodotus. His actions, as well as his language, belong to epic times. When we peruse his entertaining work, we fancy we can see before us the *jongleur* Taillefer, celebrated by Robert Wace, riding in front of the Norman lines at the battle of Hastings, singing the exploits of Charlemagne and of Roland, then pushing his charger through the ranks of the Saxons, and striking the first blow upon one of the standard-bearers of King Harold. M. de Ségur's *Histoire de la Grande Armée* has often been called the epic of Napoleon; might we not, in like manner, designate *La Conqueste de Constantinoble* as the epic of the Crusades?

Another question, and a more important one, must be briefly alluded to here; it affects not the style, but the truthfulness of Villehardouin's assertions—of some of them, at least. The discussion carried on by M. Natalis de Wailly and Count Riant[1] seems to prove that, although the Marshal of Champagne's narrative must be regarded as of the highest authority respecting the military progress of the Crusade, it is by no means of equal value as a political appreciation; and when we find some of the statements contradicted

---

[1] See the *Revue des Questions Historiques*, vols. xvii., xviii.

by those of Pope Innocent III. in his official despatches, we should naturally give the preference to letters written whilst the events were taking place, over a chronicle composed some time after the end of the Crusade, and in the preparation of which the author was not always faithfully assisted by his memory.

Villehardouin's continuator, Henri de Valenciennes, must not be forgotten; his short chronicle is so far curious, that it is thrown into a kind of romantic shape, and has about it a poetical appearance which cannot be mistaken, although, like the *Conqueste de Constantinoble*, it is in prose. M. Paulin Paris is of opinion that Henri wrote it first as a metrical composition, and that it formed part of a *chanson de geste*, like the well-known romances of Godefroy de Bouillon, Baudoin de Sebourc, and the poem on the Crusade against the Albigenses. The length to which the speeches extend, the minute descriptions of single combats, are further proofs of the assertion put forth by M. Paulin Paris; we may also notice that the chronological order is not uniformly adhered to, and that some of the events described are of a very improbable character. Notwithstanding all these drawbacks, Henri de Valenciennes deserves to be studied by readers who are anxious to know the history of the fourth Crusade, because his narrative embraces years on which Western annalists say absolutely nothing, and Eastern ones very little.

Robert de Clari is another hero of the expedition to Constantinople; "quoiqu'il ne l'ait point aussi bellement contée que l'eussent fait maints bons auteurs, il en a toutefois conté la droite vérité." His narrative, covering the same ground as that of Villehardouin, differs from it in many important respects. Both begin their memoirs by a long list of the Crusaders, in which the same names occur; but Robert de Clari arranges his characters under two classes, the rich and the poor, and he devotes an equal amount of attention to the one and to the other. A friend of the leaders of the expedition, the Maréchal de Champagne bids us accompany him to their council board, and lets us into the secrets of their policy; Robert de Clari, whose companions are the *petites gens*, the soldiers and humble members of the Crusade, tells us what is spoken aloud, and describes the events which have taken place in the broad daylight. Another important difference between Villehardouin and Robert de Clari is to be found in the descriptions. The sketches of the former are mere sketches, boldly dashed off, so as not to interrupt the progress of the narrative. The latter, on the contrary, goes into details; he enumerates the various kinds of ships of which the fleet consisted, gives a list of the instruments of music which helped to stir up the courage of the Crusaders, and is very minute in his account of the tents, pavilions, standards, etc. Robert de Clari was, no doubt, one of the first to visit the monuments of Constantinople, and the numerous particulars he gives us are not the least remarkable portion of his work. A few lines suffice to Villehardouin for the purpose of expressing the astonishment of the Crusaders at the sight of the city "which was sovereign amongst all others;" Robert de Clari takes us from street to street, considers leisurely, and makes us share the interest with which he surveys the wonders of a civilization so totally different from that to which he was accustomed. In short, the chronicle we are now appreciating, despite several rather notable inaccuracies, deserves a conspicuous place in the list of the memoir-writers of the thirteenth century, side by side with Geoffroy de Villehardouin.

We now turn to Joinville, the adviser and friend of Saint Louis, the man whom we should be disposed to consider as the best model of a feudal baron, just as his master was the most accomplished type of the king. There is scarcely any doubt that if all the members of the mediæval nobility had been cut out on the pattern of Joinville, and if the sceptre had been always placed in the hands of monarchs such as Saint Louis, the feudal system would not have been open to the objection so loudly and so justly directed against it. The biography of Saint Louis, which has immortalized the Sénéchal de Champagne, and which will endure as long as the French language, was composed long after the author's return from the Crusade, when he was stricken down by age, and without the slightest pretension on his part to obtain literary fame, or to pass himself off as a scholar.

"To his good lord, Louis, son of the King of France, by the grace of God King of Navarre, Count Palatine of Champagne and Brie, John, Sire de Joinville, his sénéchal of Champagne, greeting, love, honour, right willing service.

"DEAR SIRE,

"I make known to you that madam the queen, your mother, who loved me much (to whom God be merciful!), entreated me as earnestly as she could, that I would cause a book to be written of the holy words and good deeds of our sainted King Louis. I made her that promise, and by God's help the book is finished, in two parts.

"The first part relates how Saint Louis ruled himself throughout his whole life, according to God and the Church, and for the good of his realm.

"The second part of the book speaks of his great deeds of arms."

Jeanne de Navarre had, no doubt, often heard Joinville relate the *souvenirs* he had treasured up on Saint Louis; she had been entranced by the narrative of the battle of Massorah, and of the sacking of Sidon; the character of the king, his piety and love of justice, could not also but excite her admiration, and she naturally felt anxious that all Frenchmen should know something about the life of a monarch who had done so much, both for the glory of God, and for the happiness of his country. Hence the memoirs we are now attempting to describe. The plan adopted by the author is not the best possible, if we examine it from the literary point of view; but, as we have already said, his intention was not so much to produce an artistic or rhetorical composition, as to leave behind him a work of edification. Hence also the repetitions, which are of frequent occurrence, and which Joinville might easily have dispensed with, if he had aimed at anything like dramatic effect.

It is unnecessary to dwell here upon the merely *material* part of Joinville's work—that is to say, upon the authority we have for the text as it now stands in M. de Wailly's splendid *Édition Définitive;* a few remarks will suffice. The original manuscript of the *Vie de Saint Louis* does not exist; three copies alone have been handed down to us, the most ancient and best being now preserved in Paris amongst the treasures of the *Bibliothèque Nationale*, after having belonged to the library of the Dukes of Burgundy and Brussels. It was done about the end of the fourteenth century, by a scribe who modernized the text, and substituted the style of the reign of Charles V. instead of the picturesque and terse idiom of Joinville's epoch. The second copy, discovered at Lucca by Lacurne de Sainte-Palaye, in 1741, is of a still more recent date, for it cannot be assigned to a higher period than the fifteenth century. It belongs, like the one just named, to the Paris *Bibliothèque*, and is valuable as reproducing a certain number of archaic expressions contained evidently in the manuscript which the copyist was using. The third *codex*, forming part of a private collection, also gives us a Joinville dressed up in the French of the Reformation era. From these remarks, it will appear that all the editions of the worthy seneschal published between 1761 and 1867, although they certainly give us the *thoughts* and the substance of the original work, do not reproduce the text; and it was reserved for M. de Wailly to place before us, so far as can reasonably be expected, the *ipsissima verba* disfigured and altered by the conceit of scribes, whose refined taste could not endure the roughness of the primitive draft. In doing this, the learned critic had to guide him *twenty-six charters* and other official documents, drawn up by Joinville's own clerks, and extending from the year 1238 to the death of the chronicler. These pieces, together with a letter addressed to the king by Joinville himself, and with the *Credo* which he composed, according to the pious habit of those days, supplied the necessary materials for a restitution of the original reading; and in the absence of the author's own manuscript, we must acknowledge that we now possess its next best substitute. We are told distinctly, both at the commencement and at the and of the work, that Joinville *a dicté et fait écrire ce livre ;* and it is not, therefore, too bold to suppose that the scribes who wrote it under his dictation were also those who drew up the twenty-six charters just alluded to.

It has been remarked that Villehardouin is often touching, but that he never smiles. Equal in beauty to the *Conqueste de Constantinoble*, but superior in point of attractiveness, the life of Saint Louis is also the narrative of the Crusade; but it is something more, and the history of the war may be considered as the framework destined to set off and bring out in strong relief the character of the king. A few quotations will serve to illustrate the nature and style of Joinville's memoirs; and, first, let us watch the Crusaders, as they take their departure for the Holy Land.[1] We add the original text as an interesting specimen of the seneschal's French :—

"The day we embarked, the door of the vessel was opened, and the horses were led inside that we were to take with us; then they fastened the door, and closed it up tightly, as when one sinks a cask, because when the ship is at sea the whole of the door is under water. When the horses were in, our sailing master called out to his mariners, who were at the prow, 'Are you all ready?' And they

---

[1] The English extracts are taken from the translation published by Mr. James Hutton. London, 1868.

replied, 'Sir, let the clerks and priests come forward!' As soon as they had come nigh, we shouted to them, 'Chant, in God's name!' And they, with one voice, chanted, '*Veni, Creator Spiritus.*' Then the master cried to his men, 'Set sail, in God's name!' And they did so. And in a little time the wind struck the sails, and carried us out of sight of land, so that we saw nothing but sea and sky; and every day the wind bore us farther away from the land where we were born. And thereby I show you how foolhardy he must be who would venture to put himself in such peril with other people's property in his possession, or while in deadly sin; for when you fall asleep at night, you know not but that ere the morning you may be at the bottom of the sea."[1]

---

[1] " A celle journée que nous entrames en nos *neis*[1] fist l'on (on fit) ouvrir la porte de la nef, et mist l'on tous nos chevaux ens (dedans) que nous deviens mener outre-mer; et puis reclost l'on la porte et l'enboucha l'on bien, aussi comme l'on naye (noie) un tonnel, pourceque quand la neis [est] en la grant mer, toute la porte est en l'yaue.

"Quant li cheval furent ens, nostre maistres notonniers escria à ses notonniers qui estoient ou bec (proue) de la nef et lour dist : 'Est arée (prête) votre besoigne?' Et il respondirent : 'Oïl, sire. Vieignent avant li clerc et li provere (prêtres).' Maintenant que il furent venu, il lour escria : 'Chantez *de par Dieu!*'[2] Et il s'escrierent tuit à une voix, 'Veni, Creator Spiritus.' Et il escria à ses notonniers, 'Faites voile de par Dieu!' Et il si (ainsi) firent.

"Et en brief tens, le vent *se féri ou*[3] voile et nous ot tolu (enlevé) la vue de la terre, que nous ne veismes que ciel et yaue : et

---

[1] *Neis*, Lat. *naves*.   [2] *De par Dieu* = de la part de Dieu.
[3] *Se féri ou* . . . = *frappa dans la* . . . Lat. *ferire*.

The relations between Saint Louis and Joinville had always been cordial without being intimate ; the crossing from Egypt to Palestine brought the monarch and the seneschal into habitual intercourse with each other, and a memorable circumstance sealed their friendship. Contrary to the advice of the legate and of the principal leaders of the expedition, Joinville had, one day, in a full council, urged the king not to return to France, but to remain in the Holy Land. On leaving the assembly, he had been assailed with taunts and jokes, and, the same day, during the dinner, the king, contrary to his custom, had not addressed him a single word.

"While the king was listening to the thanksgiving, I went to a barred window that was in a recess near the head of the king's bed, and I passed my arms through the bars. . . . Whilst I was standing there, the king came and leaned upon my shoulders, and put his two hands upon my head. I thought it was Monseigneur Philip de Nemours, who had annoyed me incessantly all that day because of the counsel I had given the king,

chascun jour nous esloigna li venz des païs où nous aviens estei neis. Et ces choses vous moustré-je que cil (celui-là) est bien fols hardis, qui se ose mettre en tel péril a tout *autrui chatel*[1] (avec le bien d'autrui) ou en péchié mortel ; car l'on se dort le soir, là où l'on ne scait se l'on se trouvera ou font de la mer."

---

[1] *Autrui chatel* (Eng. *chattel*) = *les biens d'autrui* (Lat. *alterius*). Note the genitive pronoun *autrui* used without the preposition *de*, much more logically than the modern form *d'autrui*.

and I said, 'Leave me in peace, Monseigneur Philip!' By accident, as I turned my head round, the king's hand slipped down over my face, and I saw it was the king by a emerald he wore on his finger. And he said to me, 'Keep still, for I want to ask you how so young a man as you had the hardihood to venture to counsel me to stay here, contrary to all the great and wise men of France who advised me to depart?'

"'Sire,' said I, 'if I had evil in my head, still I would advise you not to depart at any cost.'

"'Do you say,' he asked, 'that I should act wrongly, if I went away?'

"'Yes, sire,' I answered, 'so help me God!'

"'Then,' said he, 'if I remain, will you remain?'

"'Yes, sire, if I can; either at my own charge, or at that of some one else.'

"'Be at ease, then,' he answered; 'for I am greatly obliged to you for the counsel you gave; but do not say so to any one all the week.'"

From that time forward, Saint Louis took Joinville in his own pay, and found in him not only a faithful knight and a sincere adviser, but a friend, who shared his toils, was the companion of his walks, and the comforter he could rely upon in all his troubles. The worthy seneschal often amused the king by sallies of wit, and the harmless jokes in which he indulged relieved the monotony of the evenings spent under canvas in the plains of Egypt and of Palestine. On one occasion, before leaving the Holy Land, Joinville, who had been on a pilgrimage to Our Lady of Tortosa, brought back with him some relics given to him by the Prince of Tripoli, and a hundred pieces of camlet of variours colours, which the king had ordered him to buy. This was an excellent opportunity for Joinville to make a present to Queen Margaret. She was hoping to receive the relics—he had thought only of the pieces of camlet, and he sent them to her by one of his knights.

"The knight who took them carried them wrapped in a white cloth. When the queen saw him enter the room where she was, she knelt down before him, and the knight, in his turn, knelt down before her; and the queen said to him, 'Rise, sir knight; you, the bearer of relics, ought not to kneel down.' But the knight replied, 'Madam, these are not relics, but pieces of camlet which my lord sends to you.' When the queen heard that, she and her maidens began to laugh, and the queen said to my knight, 'Tell your lord that I wish bad luck to him, for making me kneel before his camlet.'"

Time will not allow us to dwell any longer in the company of the excellent Sénéchal de Champagne, however much we might wish to do so, or to enjoy the wonderful beauty of that style, which is equally admirable when the author describes touching episodes, or when he attempts a piece of quiet, good-humoured satire, or a naïve outburst of badinage. A modern writer[1] has well pointed out the difference which separates Villehardouin from Joinville: the former is the brilliant exponent of feudal independence; the latter, by the biographical mould into which he has cast his narrative, already expresses the growing importance of the monarchical principle.

---

[1] M. Demogeot, *Histoire de la Littérature Française.*

CHAPTER X.

SECOND CRUSADE OF SAINT LOUIS—GUILLAUME ANELIER — GRINGORE'S "VIE MONSEIGNEUR SAINT LOYS" — PHILIPPE MOUSKES — "RÉCITS DU MÉNESTREL DE REIMS."

THE second Crusade of Saint Louis has not been described by Joinville, who declined to take part in it; fortunately we have, as a source of information on that campaign, the metrical chronicle of Guillaume Anelier, which was published for the first time in 1856, by M. Francisque Michel, in the *Collection des Documents sur l'Histoire de France*.

We must repeat about the old troubadour what we have so often been already obliged to say, and what we shall, no doubt, have to confess more than once, viz. biographical details are absolutely wanting. The title of the manuscript used by M. Michel bears the following indication: *Guillelmus Anelier de Tolosa me fecit;* and we know that he lived during the latter part of the thirteenth century, but that is all we do know with any amount of certainty. One important circumstance deserves to be noted; he was an eye-witness of most of the events which he relates, and thus his work has an historical value which cannot be contested. Alluding to the sailing of Louis IX. from Aigues-Mortes, he observes—

"The Crusade was a great one, and they went to prepare themselves
At the port of Aigues-Mortes. What I have seen, I can relate." [1]

Further on, describing the civil war which broke out at Pampeluna, he makes use of the same expression; when he relates the siege of a farm, he talks of *us*, showing that he had taken part in the action; in the middle of a narrative he breaks out with the phrase "*e œ adonx yeu vi lo*" (and then I saw it).

The poem we are now examining professes to relate the war of Navarre in 1276 and 1277; but Guillaume Anelier, after a prologue of twelve lines, begins with the battle of Las Navas de Tolosa, which the King of Navarre, Sancho VIII., surnamed *the Strong*, together with the Kings of Arragon, Leon, and Portugal, won, on the 16th of July, 1212, over Mohammed el-Nassireddin-Allah, Sultan of the Almohades, who never recovered from the blow they there received. It is well known that Thibault, Count of Champagne and of Brie, nephew of Don Sancho, ascended the throne of Navarre in 1234, and founded a new dynasty. He died in 1253, and was succeeded by his son,

---

[1] "La Crozada fom granda e ancron s'aprestar
Lai al port d'Aigas-Mortas. Ço qu'eu vi puis contar."

Thibault II., a prince whose piety Anelier celebrates as something quite remarkable. It is, probably, with the view of illustrating this quality of the monarch that our troubadour passes on *ex abrupto* to the narrative of the Crusade which happened only a long time after, in 1270. Perhaps, also, he was eager to come to facts of which he had been a witness, and which he could, therefore, describe more accurately. Even if he had not expressly stated that he was present with the invading army under the walls of Tunis, we might have expected so, from the minuteness with which he relates the events of the campaign, and the details he gives. The Toulousan poet, having become a Navarrese by the result of political circumstances, is loud in praise of his new *compatriotes*, and he contrives to make the Saracens themselves pronounce the panegyric of King Thibault's followers:—

"And the Navarrese, who saw their lord hard beset, exclaimed, 'Barons, let us go and protect our lord, and let us all die with him rather than allow him to be forced.' Then you might see crossbows stretched and let loose, spears strike and darts hurled, and the Navarrese jumping about here and there in their shirts. And the Saracens, when they saw them thus rushing about, said, 'These are not men, by Mahomet; but it seems that they are living devils, since we see them thus jumping for they are not afraid of death, nor do they fear to be wounded, and certainly it is no good fighting with such men'" (lines 400-414).

Saint Louis, the leader and soul of the Crusade, died in 1272; Thibault II. soon followed him to the grave, leaving the throne to his brother Henry. The civil war which was the result of this arrangement, and the consequent interference of the King of France, Philip III., form the subject of the remainder of the poem, which, unfortunately, is very much mutilated towards the end. It consists of 5118 lines arranged into assonant stanzas of unequal length. M. Francisque Michel shows very conclusively, in his preface, the historical importance of Anelier's work; till it was published, the only sources we possessed for the events related were the biography of Philip III., by Guillaume de Nangis (*Grandes Chroniques de France*, edit. P. Paris, chaps. xix., xxiii., xxiv.), Guillaume Guiart's *Branche des Royaux Lignages*, and the chronicle of the Prince of Viana. The slightest reference to historians who have dealt with that episode in the annals of the thirteenth century will sufficiently prove the high value of the metrical chronicle, for which we are indebted to Guillaume Anelier. M. Francisque Michel supposes (not without reason) that Garci Lopez de Roncevaux, treasurer of King Charles III. of Spain, was alluding to our troubadour, when in his *Annales del Reyno de Navarra* (vol. iii. p. 414), he says that he abstains from giving an account of the civil war of Pampeluna, because it was a long one, and that the details of it were enumerated in books preserved at Pampeluna itself, and elsewhere. The reader will observe further that the history of Navarre, at that time, is the history of a country almost entirely French. The Prince of Viana, just now alluded to, speaks of the population of Saint Cernin and Pampeluna as consisting of Frenchmen who had come from Cahors; and the names of most of the burgesses mentioned in the poem belong to the southern provinces of France. With reference to the language, it may be designated as Provençal, strongly modified by the introduction of Spanish words and phrases; and, what is extremely curious, it offers the closest resemblance with the poem on the Crusade against the Albigenses, already noticed in this volume. The structure of the lines, their distribution into stanzas, the metre—in short, every detail of composition is alike. Finally, the poem is full of interesting details on the arms, equipment, navy, etc., of the fifteenth century—details which M. Francisque Michel has well illustrated and explained in his notes. Thus, we know that the ships engaged by Saint Louis for the sixth Crusade belonged to the Venetians, and the deed of agreement for the purpose has been preserved in Duchesne's *Hist. Franc. Scriptores.* Thus again, the skill of the Navarrese archers and cross-bowmen alluded to by Guillaume Anelier is amply confirmed by the author of the metrical romance of Gérard de Roussillon.

It has often been remarked as a subject of regret that French literature should boast of no composition such as the historical plays of Shakespeare, and that no writer of genius should have ever stepped forward to carve out tragedies from Monstrelet, Froissart, and Joinville, as the author of "King Henry V." did from Holinshed. Be the cause what it may, the fact subsists, and the few French historical plays which the Middle Ages have left us cannot lay claim to the slightest spark of genius. The *Complainte et Jeu de Pierre de la Broce*, written on the episode of the disgrace of Philip the Bold's favourite minister, is rather a metrical dialogue than anything else; and all the interest it possessed for the Parisians of the thirteenth century arose from the fact that it denounced, to the indignation of the mob, an unpopular statesman. If we have alluded to dramatic works in connection with this part of our subject, it is because the history of Saint Louis found two writers to arrange it for public performance, and these compositions are sufficiently founded upon fact to deserve the title of metrical chronicles. The former may be described, indeed, as "une véritable chronique découpée en dialogues," composed by an author whose name has not been handed to us. It dwells especially upon the events of the Crusade, eschews the allegorical personages and incidents which mediæval poets indulged in so freely, and allows nothing to imagination. The second play composed on the life of Saint Louis is by Gringore, a well-known author, who flourished during the first half of the sixteenth century, and to whom we shall refer, further on, more particularly. It is written in octosyllabic lines, and subdivided into eight parts or books, treating respectively of the following incidents:—1. The early years of the king. 2. The attempts made against the crown by the great vassals. 3. The wars of the Emperor of Germany against the pope and the King of France. 4. The first Crusade in which Saint Louis was engaged. 5. The king's return to France. 6. The king's careful administration of justice. 7. The same subject, illustrated by the account of two sentences of condemnation pronounced, the one against a blasphemer, and the other against the Lord of Coucy. 8. The second Crusade and the king's death. The play winds up with an epilogue, relating three miracles due to the intercession of the king.

If we now endeavour to ascertain the sources which Gringore consulted whilst writing his *Vie Monseigneur Saint Loys*, we shall find that he made use especially of the Golden Legend of Jacopo de' Voragine, and of the French *rédaction* of the chronicles of Saint Denis, about which we shall presently have more to say. Gringore has, no doubt, grouped the facts with a view to a certain amount of stage effect, but he does not adulterate or misrepresent them; and it would be a curious, and by no means an unprofitable study, to compare his voluminous play with the narrative given by the prose annalist of the abbey of Saint Denis.

In order to finish at once what we had to say about the Crusades, we shall mention Philip Mouskes, or Mousket, a French writer, who occupied the episcopal see of Tournay in 1274. The metrical chronicle composed by that author, and which extends over thirty thousand lines, is not very remarkable as an exhibition of literary talent, but it is curious on account of the historical facts which the author has preserved, and which confirm the statements given in the works of professed chroniclers. Philip Mouskes entitles his poem a chronicle, and, in the introductory lines, he declares it as his express purpose—

> "Des rois de *Franche*[1] en rime mettre
> Toute l'estoire et la lignée."

His authority, he adds, is the collection of histories preserved in the abbey of Saint Denis. The greater part of his work, however, belongs almost exclusively to the realms of fable, and appears borrowed mainly from the old *chansons de geste* and the chronicle of the pseudo-Turpin. Beginning quite *ab ovo* with the Rape of Helen by Paris, Philip Mouskes takes us down as far as the year 1242; and the earlier part of his work, from the election of Baldwin to the throne of Constantinople, is the one on which he chiefly rests his

---

[1] *Franche* is the Picard and Flemish way of writing *France.*

pretensions to be called an historian. It has been printed separately, first by Ducange, as an appendix to his edition of Villehardouin, and by M. Buchon.

Louis IX. may be said to have closed the era of the Crusades. Nothing but the influence of so holy a character, so distinguished a prince, could have led against the enemies of the cross a society already tainted by scepticism, and more careful of its comforts than of the claims of religion. After his death, the appeals made from time to time on behalf of the Christians in Palestine remained unsuccessful; nothing soon remained of those principalities, once so flourishing, which the old Crusaders had founded in the Archipelago and in Asia Minor; nor even did the name survive of that ephemeral kingdom of Jerusalem, for the establishment of which the nations of Europe had, for the space of nearly two centuries, spent so much blood, so much money, so much heroism.

The historians whom we have been reviewing treat the subjects of which they have to inform us with the gravity of writers who feel conscious that the task undertaken by them is an important one, and that they are providing for the instruction of posterity. It is amusing, by way of a contrast, to see a chronicler selecting the satirical and comical side of the picture, and eager only to entertain the public and to express his own political and social ideas.

Such is exactly the line adopted by an anonymous writer, whom we may designate, as his editor M. N. de Wailly does, by the title of *Le Ménestrel de Reims*, and whose singular narrative has recently been published by the *Société de l'Histoire de France*. We have seen that the old metrical romances and *chansons de geste* were designed to be sung by the *trouvères* and wandering minstrels in the form of episodes, each one choosing the parts which suited him best, and which were most likely to captivate his audience. What is quite novel is to find history treated in that fashion, and chapters of prose composition recited (without any musical accompaniment, of course), just as poetry had been, and still was, during the thirteenth century. Now, this is just the peculiarity belonging to the *récits* of the Rhemish minstrel; the work is a collection or series of short chapters beginning with the death of Godefroy de Bouillon, and ending at that of Saint Louis in 1860. The Crusades, the histories of France, Germany, and England, are reviewed in this extraordinary work, which has sometimes been honoured with the name of chronicle, but which has not the slightest claims to historical accuracy. It is quite clear, 1. That the minstrel, more anxious to secure the applause of his hearers than to give us well-authenticated facts, was, above all, led by the desire of pandering to the satirical tendencies of the time; and the grotesque way in which he launches against the avarice of the court of Rome and the college of cardinals proves exactly the reverse of what he meant to establish, viz. that the papacy was then hopelessly degraded. 2. The minstrel must not be held responsible for the numerous errors and misstatements contained in his work; he followed to a great extent the data of popular tradition, and several of the episodes which he relates can be found either in the compilation known under the name of *Chronique de Flandres*, or in other works of the same kind. After borrowing largely from others, our minstrel, in his turn, was subjected to the same treatment by later historians. Thus, the *Chronique Normande* of Pierre Cauchon, as far as the first three chapters are concerned, is an abridged reproduction of the minstrel's narrative. From what we have just stated, it seems singular that the *récits* should have been printed as part of a series of historical works; but it is interesting to see how prejudice, ignorance, or a kind of political bias, can lead an author to disfigure what we would suppose to be the best known facts; and the traditional severity of Louis IX., whenever the Church was attacked, or even made the subject of satirical remarks, must have been sometimes very lax, if he tolerated the buffoonery which our anonymous minstrel indulged in before the people gathered together to listen to his pseudo-historical effusions.

CHAPTER XI.

THE "CHRONIQUES DE SAINT-DENIS"—FROISSART.

WHILST the records of the Crusades were thus committed to writing by Villehardouin, Joinville, and Robert de Clari, another great work, intended to be the national history of mediæval France, was gradually getting into shape, thanks to the industry of the monks of Saint Denis. England boasts its chronicles of Saint Alban's, an important series of documents throwing so much light upon the events of the country during the Middle Ages; in like manner, the famous establishment of which the King of France was always *ex officio* the *avoué*, where the oriflamme was kept, and which contains in its vaults the remains of a long race of monarchs—the abbey church of Saint Denis—had its studious monks, who were busily engaged in compiling the history of their native land, both from the old traditions which had been handed down to them in the *chansons de geste* and other documents, and from their own personal observations. It is now successfully demonstrated that the *Grandes Chroniques* cannot be ascribed to an earlier period than the beginning of the reign of Philip the Bold, who succeeded to the throne in 1270. Undertaken at his command—nay, even, perhaps, by the order of Saint Louis, his father— the chronicles were drawn up in the first instance by a monk of Saint Denis, named Primat, under the direction of Matthieu de Vendôme, abbot, and regent of the kingdom. The original narrative, concluding with the death of Philip Augustus (1223), was completed in 1274, when Primat, accompanied by his superior, had the honour of submitting it to Philip the Bold. As we have already hinted, the *Chroniques de Saint Denis* cannot pretend to be anything but a compilation. M. Paulin Paris, in his excellent edition of the work, has carefully enumerated all the sources from which the narrative was borrowed; they include Aimoin, Eginhard, Suger, Rigord, Gulielmus Brito, Guillaume de Nangis, and the first continuator of that annalist, and are therefore mere translations from Latin texts, interspersed here and there with facts borrowed from other sources, but so inconsiderable in point both of number and importance, that they hardly deserve mentioning. Continued successively by different writers whose names are now unknown, but who seem to have all been, as was the first translator and compiler, monks of Saint

Denis, the chronicles were thus carried on as far as the reign of King John. From 1310 to the death of Philip de Valois, in 1350, the work ceases to be a translation, and has all the characters of an original production; still, however, it must be ascribed to a *religieux* of the royal abbey, who wrote his share of the chronicles before the battle of Poitiers (1356).

For a considerable time the *Grandes Chroniques* ended with the death of Philip de Valois; several manuscripts belonging to the reign of King John or of Charles V. prove this beyond a doubt—some of them concluding as they do with the word *amen*, whilst others, still more explicit, state: *ce fenissent les Chroniques de France*. At last Charles V., one of the best known and most illustrious of French kings, and who owed the surname of "the Wise" to his intelligent love of the arts of civilization, as well as to the character of his government, entrusted to the Chancellor of France, Pierre d'Orgemont, the task of continuing the work left unfinished by the monks of Saint Denis, and of writing the annals of a glorious and happy reign. That Pierre d'Orgemont is responsible for all the portion comprised between 1350 and 1377 is quite certain; it is extremely probable that he went on as far as the death of Charles V., in 1380. Continued till the year 1461, the *Chroniques de Saint Denis* were published in 1476, under the title *Chroniques de France depuis les Troyens jusqu'à la Mort de Charles VII.;* they became extremely popular, and, being regarded almost in the light of a national monument, they served as the source from which Nicole Gilles, Gaguin, and the other early French historians derived their information. The part treating of the reign of Charles VII. was written by Jean Chartier, brother of Guillaume Chartier, Bishop of Paris, and of Alain Chartier, the most celebrated French poet of the fifteenth century. Named historiographer of France in 1437, and subsequently precentor of Saint Denis, "qui étoit," says Dom Félibien, "une des premières dignités de l'abbaye," Jean Chartier lost no time in beginning his task as a chronicler; but we are bound to say that very few have done so wretchedly a work which, in competent hands, might have been made exceptionally interesting, considering the political events which marked the reign of Charles VII. Chartier is dull and inaccurate, slovenly in his composition, and absolutely regardless of chronology. The value of his work, as M. Vallet de Viriville (his recent editor) remarks, consists entirely in its being a kind of official record, a *Moniteur* given under authority, and registering only what the king wished to commend to the attention of the public. It has preserved, besides, a number of authentic documents of the most valuable kind, the great portion of which cannot be found anywhere else.

Whilst the *Grandes Chroniques de Saint Denis*,

thus gathering, as time went on, fresh materials, came to assume the proud position of an official record, compiled (so to say) *cum privilegio*, independent authors added their share to the stock of historical information, and left, on the stirring events of the thirteenth century, memoranda which are still profitably consulted. Let us name Adam de la Halle, surnamed *Le Bossu d'Arras*, although he indignantly repudiated a sobriquet which it seems he did not deserve :—

"On m'apele *bochu*,[1] mais je ne le suis mie."

Having left his native town in order to seek his fortune in Paris, Adam de la Halle attached himself to Robert II., Count d'Artois, nephew of Saint Louis, and son of Robert I. In 1282, he went to Naples, in the company of the Duke d'Alençon, whom Philip the Bold was sending to Charles of Anjou, King of Naples, for the purpose of assisting him in punishing the authors of the Sicilian Vespers. Our *trouvère* composed on that occasion a short metrical history of 378 lines, entitled *C'est du Roi de Sézile*. He died about the year 1286.

The poem known by the name of *La Branche des Royaux Lignages* belongs to the same epoch; it is the production of a native of Orleans, Guillaume Guiart, who, in common with so many others, professes to have taken as the ground-work of his compositions—

---

[1] *Bochu*, Picard for *bossu*.

> "The certain chronicles,
> That is to say, the true words,
> The memoirs of which I have transcribed
> At Saint Denis, evening and morning,
> From the Latin original,
> And which I have translated into good French,
> And then arranged imto rhyme."[1]

The portion of the *Grandes Chroniques* translated by Guillaume Guiart, is the history of Philip Augustus for which we are indebted to Gulielmus Brito; but the French poet continued it as far as the year 1306, and the part which is really his own work deserves special notice, because it records several events which Guiart himself witnessed. He had taken an active share in the war waged by Philip the Fair against the Flemings; he was present at the battle of Mons-en-Puelle, and at the attack of the Haiguerie, where he was disabled. The poem, begun in 1304, whilst the author was recovering at Arras from the wounds he had received in the campaign, is dedicated to Philip the Fair. As a sequel to it, the reader can take up the metrical chronicle of Godefroy de Paris, an author about whose biography nothing certain is known, but who lived during the reigns of Philip IV., Louis X., Philip V., and Charles IV.

---

[1] "Les certaines croniques,
C'est-à-dire paroles *voires*,[1]
Dont j'ai transcites les mémoires
À Saint Denis, soir et matin,
À l'exemplaire du Latin,
Et à droit Français ramenées
Et puis en rimes ordenées."

[1] *Voires* = *vraies*.

The thirteenth century was the culminating point of mediæval institutions and of feudalism; with the fourteenth we see the growing power of the crown, the influence of the legists, and the foundation laid of that system of centralization which was destined to become the characteristic feature of the government in France. Froissart and Monstrelet stand by themselves as the chroniclers of that epoch, and even the heavy, prosy work of the latter leaves far behind the useful, but somewhat dull, labours of the monks of Saint Denis.

Sir Walter Scott's appreciation of Froissart has often been quoted; it is so true that we cannot resist the pleasure of transcribing it once again: " His chapters inspire me with more enthusiasm than even poetry itself. And the noble canon, with what true chivalrous feeling he confines his beautiful expressions of sorrow to the death of the gallant and high-bred knight, of whom it was a pity to see the fall, such was his loyalty to his king, pure faith to his religion, hardihood towards his enemy, and fidelity to his lady-love! Ah! benedicite! how he will mourn over the fall of such a pearl of knighthood, be it on the side he happens to favour, or on the other. But, truly, for sweeping from the face of the earth some few hundreds of villain churls, who are born but to plough it, the high-born and inquisitive historian has marvellous little sympathy."

Jean Froissart (1337–1410) was a native of

Valenciennes. Destined from his childhood for the Church, he put off as long as he could the period of his ordination, for the purpose of enjoying the pleasures which were then within the reach of a young man of fashion and of taste. Dancing, hawking, music, dress, sports of every kind, engaged his attention much more than the study of theology, and he tells us very honestly, in one of his poems, that throughout his whole life he preserved a fondness for the diversions which had given so much charm to his youth. Fortunately, intellectual pleasures had also for him a peculiar kind of fascination; he was eager for travels and adventures, he had all the gifts of a shrewd and careful observer, and he noted down diligently all the events of any importance which either came under his own cognizance, or which he became acquainted with through the report of trustworthy witnesses. Like most young men of his times, he attached himself to the household of a person of importance, in whose service he might hope to obtain both preferment and honour. Robert de Namur was his first master, and at his request he undertook to write the history of the wars which were then desolating Europe. He then became clerk of the chapel of Philippa of Hainault; he visited Scotland (1364), followed the Prince of Wales to Bordeaux (1366), the Duke of Clarence to Italy (1368), and on his return to Flanders, his native country, was presented to the cure of Lestines (1369). We cannot imagine a man of Froissart's temperament settling quietly down to the duties of a village clergyman, and ending in retirement a life which had been marked by so much action. His next master was Wenceslaus of Luxemburg, Duke of Brabant, who took him as his secretary and chaplain, and at whose death he obtained a clerkship (1384) of the chapel of Guy de Chatillon, Count of Blois. This nobleman was wise enough to appreciate Froissart's tastes, and to encourage that passion for travelling which had already produced such brilliant results in the first part of the chronicle presented by the Rector of Lestines to the queen consort of Edward III. Assisted by the Count of Blois, Froissart visited Touraine, Blaisois, Berry, and Bearn; he stopped several times in Paris, journeyed as far as Holland, and went once more to England, where he met with the most cordial reception. On the death of his patron, the Count of Blois (1397), he retired to Climay, in Flanders, and spent the last fourteen years of his life in comparative quiet.

The chronicle of Jean Froissart extends from 1328 to 1400, and treats of the events which took place not only in France, but in England, Scotland, Ireland, Flanders, Spain, and the other countries of Europe. There exist three different drafts (*rédactions*) of this work, each represented by a certain number of manuscripts, and corresponding to the different epochs in the author's life. The first *rédaction*, composed at the time when Froissart was enjoying the friendship and patronage of Robert de Namur, is often a mere transcript of another chronicle compiled by Jean le Bel, Canon of Liège; it must be ascribed to the period included between 1369 and 1373. It breathes the strongest partiality for England, and is characterized by a brilliancy of touch, a *verve*, a spirit particularly striking. The descriptions of the battles of Crécy and of Poitiers, as this *rédaction* presents them to us, are masterpieces which have never been equalled. When, at a later period of his life, Froissart attempted to give another account of these memorable engagements, he fell far short of that animation, that freshness, which stamp his earliest compositions.

Time went on, however, and our chronicler became chaplain to the Count of Blois, and the favourite poet of Wencelaus of Luxemburg, Duke of Brabant. Thus circumstanced, Jean Froissart began to see from a totally different point of view the political events, which he had originally related under the *prestige* of the flattering reception he had met with at the court of the enemies, or at any rate the rivals, of France. This difference is particularly noticeable in the description of the battle of Poitiers; and it is interesting to see how the same events have been successively appreciated, according to the prejudices and impressions of the two conflicting parties.

The third *rédaction*, posterior to the year 1400, is

remarkable especially, from the philosophical style in which it is written. Here Froissart appears no longer as a mere chronicler; he endeavours to trace events to their true causes, and his account of the manners, laws, and institutions of the various people whose history he relates, is striking for its depth and accuracy. He judges the English especially with an amount of harshness which could scarcely have been expected from the enthusiastic writer who gave so anti-Gallican a version of the battle of Poitiers; but this final draft, we must not forget, was composed after the tragic end of the unfortunate King Richard II., and Froissart, when he wrote it, was still mourning, no doubt, over the death of a monarch who was son of the Black Prince, and grandson of the chronicler's earliest friend, the good Queen Philippa of Hainault.

The episode about the elevation of Arteveld and the Flemish revolution exemplifies perfectly well the way in which the three *rédactions* have been successively prepared by Froissart. In the first, he merely reproduces the text of Jean le Bel, without either addition or suppression. In the second, he still retains as his groundwork the narrative of the Canon of Liège, but he improves upon it; and, amongst other developments, he explains the origin of the troubles of Flanders with the greatest impartiality, the deepest political insight, and an amount of discrimination which is almost incredible. The third draft allows nothing to remain of Jean le Bel's description; all the details are Froissart's own, and the particulars he presents to us have an unmistakable character of originality.

Froissart's chronicle is of the highest importance as a biographical and geographical *répertoire;* it may be considered as a kind of international temple, where all the grand feudal families of Europe are represented, and where our aristocracy can find its title-deeds. No writer excels him in describing the bustling scenes which took place around him. Gifted with a real passion for observing, knowing, and relating all that was worth attention, we fancy we can see him travelling from spot to spot, making friends everywhere by his agreeable manners, his lively temperament, his talent as a poet, and availing himself of the *otium cum dignitate* which he enjoyed, for the purpose of taking notes of all the deeds of valour and of chivalry which were performed throughout the battle-fields of Europe. The reader must not seek in the pages of Froissart for anything like the spirit of patriotism; he was the historian of chivalry, not of one single nation, and provided he could record the catastrophes of tournaments, battles, or such other dazzling exploits, his motto was—

"Tros Rutulus ve fuat, nullo discrimine habebo."

There are two good English translations of Froissart, the one written by Lord Berners being particularly valuable, not only for its fidelity, but for the *naïveté* and picturesque character of its style. Born about the year 1474, Sir John Bourchier (Lord Berners) did good service to King Henry VII., and was made by Henry VIII. chancellor of the exchequer for life. He held the important post of lieutenant of Calais and of the marches, when he died at Calais in 1532. Alderson, who published (1812) an edition of Lord Berners' *Froissart*, has the following remarks :—" The language is at once nervous, yet plain ; elegant, yet impressive ; it is very often affecting, but never tame. Notwithstanding his sentences, from their length and involution, are sometimes, though rarely, difficult of immediate comprehension, Lord Berners' style, on the whole, may be considered as giving us a very favourable specimen of the power and compass of the English language in the early part of the sixteenth century."

We have thought that our readers would be interested by a comparison between Froissart's original text and the translation of Lord Berners ; we therefore subjoin, as a specimen, the account of the Lollard insurrection :—

INSURRECTION DES LOLLARDS.

1381.—En ces tretiés durans et parlemens faisans, avinrent en Engletière très grans *meschiés*[1] de rebellions et esmouvement de menu peuple, par lequel fait Engletière en fu sus le point que de estre toute perdue sans recouvrer ; ne onques roiaulmes, ne païs n'en fu en si grant péril, ne aventure, comme il le fu en celle saisson ; et

---

[1] *Meschiés*, from *mès* = *mis* and *cheoir* (Lat. *cadere*).

pour la grant aise et abondance de biens où li menus peuples d'Engletière gratoit et vivoit, s'esmut et esleva ceste rebellion, eussi que jadis s'esmurent et eslevèrent en France li Jaque-Bonhomme qui y fissent moult de maulx et par quels incidensses li nobles roiaulmes de France a esté moult grevés.—1357.

Che fu une merveilleuse cose et de povre fondation, dont ceste pestillensse commencha en Engletière ; et pour donner exemple à toutes manières de bonnes gens, j'en parleray et le remonstreray selonc ce que dou fait et de le incidensse j'en fuy adont[1] infourmés. Uns usages est en Engletière (et ossi est-il en plusieurs païs) que li noble ont grant francisse sus leurs hommes et les tiennent en servage, c'est à entendre que il doient de droit et par coustume labourer les terres des gentils hommes, quellier les grains et amener à l'ostel, mettre en la grange, batre et vaner, et par servage les fains fener et amener à l'ostel, la busce[2] copper et amene à l'ostel, et toutes telles corvées ; et doient cil homme tout ce faire per servage as signeurs, et trop plus grant fuison[3] de gens a en Engletière que ceilleurs, et en sont li gentil homme et li prélat ou doient estre servy ; et par espécial en la conté de Kent, d'Ersexs, de Sousexs et de Beteforde en y a plus que ens ou demorant de toute Engleterre.

HOWE THE COMONS OF ENGLANDE REBELLED AGAYNST THE NOBLEMEN.

1381.—In ye meane season whyle this treate was, ther fell in England great myschife and rebellion of mouyng of the comon people, by which dede England was at a poynt to haue been lost without recouery ; ther was neuer realme nor countrey in so great aduentur as it was in that tyme, and all bycause of the ease and ryches that the comon people were of whiche moued them to this rebellion, as somtyme they dyd in Fraunce, the whych dyd moche hurt, for by suche incidentes the realme of Fraunce hath been greatly greued.

It was a marveylous thing and of poore foundacion that this myschife began in Englande ; and to gyue ensample to all maner of people, I wyll speke therof as it was don, as I was enfourmed, and of the incidentes therof. Ther was an vsage in England, and yet is in diuerse countreys, that the noble men hath great franches ouer the comons, and kepeth them in seruage, that is to say, their

---

[1] *Adont = donc.*   [2] *Busce = bûche.*   [3] *Fuison = foison.*

Decay of Chivalry. 171

tenauntes ought by custome to laboure the lordes landes, to gather and bring home theyr cornes, and some to threshe and to fanne, and by seruage to make theyr hey, and to heaw their wood and bring it home; all these thynges they ought to do by seruage; and ther be mo of these people in Englande than in any other realme: thus the noblemen and prelates arre serued by them, and specially in the countie of Brendpest,[1] Sussetter,[2] and Bedford.

A chronicler of the twelfth century informs us that, on one occasion, certain knights, having conquered a castle in Syria, gave up the plan they had originally formed of pursuing the miscreants, in order to look for the gold which, according to report, lay hidden under the foundations of the fortress they had obtained possession of. However, through a just visitation of God, the castle gave way, and fell to the ground, burying them amidst its ruins. It was the same with chivalry, that great and memorable institution, as with these knights. It sank under the weight of its faults, and corruption was its ruin. As soon as, from being courteous, it became covetous, gold rose in esteem, and honour proportionately declined. Money grew to be the moving principle of the new generation of knights, and the *auri sacra fames* prevailed where disinterestedness and generosity had formerly reigned supreme. These symptoms of decay are apparent in the chronicles of Froissart, and examples might be easily multiplied to prove it. We shall select one almost at random; and, as our first quotation was borrowed from the trans-

---

[1] Kent and Essex. [2] Sussex.

lation of Lord Berners, we shall turn for the following to the modern version of Colonel Johnes:—

"Amerigot Marcel was besieging the castle of Mercœur, in Auvergne, on behalf of the English. He and his men took up their lodgings early in a small wood near the castle, where they remained until sunset, and the garrison had retired into the castle. While the governor, whose name was Gérardon Buissel, was at supper, the English, who knew well what they had to do, affixed their ladders, and entered the castle at their ease. Those passing through the courts saw others climbing over the walls, and instantly cried out, 'Treason! treason!' Gérardon, on hearing this, had not any hope of saving himself but through a private passage, which led from his apartment to the great tower, which served as the dungeon of the castle. Thither he instantly retired, taking with him the keys of the gates, and shut himself in, whilst Amerigot and his companions were otherwise employed. When they discovered that the governor had retired into the great tower, which they were unable to take, they said they had done nothing, and repented greatly having enclosed themselves, for the gates being fastened, they could not get out. Amerigot, having mused a little, came to the tower, and, addressing the governor, said, 'Gérardon, give us the keys of the castle gate, and I promise you we will leave it without doing any mischief to the castle.' 'Indeed,' replied Gérardon, 'but you will carry off all my cattle. How can I believe you?' 'Give me your hand,' answered Amerigot, 'and I swear to you on my faith that you shall not suffer the smallest loss.' Upon this he, like a fool, came to a small window in the tower, and offered his hand for him to pledge his faith on; but the moment Amerigot got hold of it, he pulled it to him, squeezing it very hard, and called for his dagger, swearing he would stick his hand to the wall unless he gave him all the keys.

"When Gérardon saw himself thus caught, he was stupefied, as indeed he had reason, for Amerigot would not give up his hand without nailing it to the wall, unless he received the keys. With his hand, therefore, he gave the keys, for he had them near him. 'Now see,' said Amerigot to his companions, when he had got the keys, 'if I have not well cheated the fool. I am equal to many such feats as this.' They opened the tower gate, and, being the masters, put out of the castle the governor and all who were in it."

Froissart speaks to us of the knights of Germany and of the banks of the Meuse, who are "good warriors, provided they are suitably paid, but who will not do any service if money is not forthcoming." In the south, towards Bearn and Gascony, the same lust for gold is apparent, and is denounced by our historian in the strongest terms. "The Gascons," says he, "are never, for thirty years running, steadily attached to one lord. . . . Such are the Gascons; they are very unsteady." Turn to Brittany, you find exactly the same complaint. The Bretons often forgot the honourable names which had shed so much lustre over their land; they considered war as merely an opportunity for marauding and plunder. Princes did not trust Gascons; knights looked upon themselves as lost if they fell into the hands of the Germans; the inhabitants of the good cities, the commons and the peasants, dreaded one Breton soldier as much as twenty Germans or twenty Gascons. Together with the most thorough contempt of plighted troth and solemn engagements, perjury and lying stepped in, deceit took the place of courage, and generosity made way for hatred and treachery. The episode of the murder of Clisson is a notable instance of the decay of chivalry; the assassin was the Duke of Brittany, the son of the illustrious Duchess of Montfort, of whom it was said that she had the heart of a woman and the courage of a lion. He restored, indeed, his adversary to liberty in the first instance, at the earnest entreaty of the Lord of Basvalan, after having treacherously enticed him to the ducal castle of Ermine, near Nantes; but he soon regretted the act of generosity, and sent Pierre de Craon to contrive the murder of Clisson in the streets of Paris.

The pages of Froissart teem with the exploits of the freebooters and soldiers of fortune who, under the name of the *Grandes Compagnies*, laid waste the whole of France. Geoffrey Tête-noire, Briquet, Meschin, Perrot de Savoie, Antoine le Nègre, Talebart Talebardon—such were the plebeian names which frightened French children in the nursery, just as the Black Douglas was the terror of English infants. One of the most savage amongst them was the English Hawkwood (*Falco in Bosco*), who stormed Rome, and who, as well as his companions, put off till his death the moment for making his peace with the pope.

So melancholy a state of things had succeeded to the chivalry of Roland, King Arthur, the Cid, and Joinville. No wonder that Froissart, on finishing his chronicle, indulged in thoughts of the gloomiest kind on the revolution which had taken place throughout Europe, and on the dissolution of a society whose principles of existence were courage, generosity, and the strictest regard to honour. "Flayers," "butchers," "hammerers," inherited the rich succession of glory left by the knights of old. What was to be the result of such a disorganisation? The Vicar of Lestines could not, of course, foresee the advent of modern society, the substitution of the monarchical principle instead of feudalism, and the growing power of the *bourgeoisie;* hence his expressions of regret and discouragement. In the mean while, the urgent question was how to get rid of all those adventurers who, like a swarm of locusts, were eating up the resources of France.

Duguesclin stepped forward, took command of them, and led them into Spain.

As a general conclusion, we would just say that, in point of style and of brilliant colouring, Shakespeare alone can be placed on the same line with Froissart.

CHAPTER XII.

MONSTRELET AND HIS CONTINUATORS.

As we pass on from Froissart to the chroniclers who immediately followed him, we find ourselves in the midst of a literary atmosphere entirely different from that wherein the early mediæval annalists moved so freely and so gracefully. History is rising by degrees to the position of a science, and the naïve, uncritical sketches of the old school make way for writings more philosophical and more ambitious in their style and composition. When we consider that upwards of *thirty* chronicles belong to the former half of the fifteenth century, to the epoch extending between Froissart and Philippe de Commines, we shall see at once that important events were taking place, and that the political world was affording to thoughtful observers food for serious meditation. The reputation which Froissart acquired contributed, no doubt, to swell the ranks of historians; and many a writer was fired by the ambition of rising to the popularity enjoyed by the brilliant painter of chivalry and of mediæval civilization. *Indiciaries*, as they are called, or historiographers henceforth are the necessary appendage of every noble household; each king, each prince, each baron, has not only his chaplain and his court fool, but his official annalist. Some of these are scholars of no despicable pretensions; most are gentlemen holding posts of trust, and often engaged in important diplomatic transactions.

The principal feature which characterizes the historians of the epoch we are now considering, is that, according to their political sympathies, they are French or Burgundians. Froissart had, as we have seen, adopted no distinctive badge, and joined no special nationality. His successors do exactly the reverse, and make no secret of their party spirit. Another trait deserving to be mentioned here is the frequent introduction of state-papers, speeches, and official documents in the body of the narrative. The literary effect of the composition is sadly marred thereby; but the work acquires, of course, greater weight, and claims more attention. Even when *pièces justificatives* are not copied *in extenso*, and clumsily tacked on to the tedious and drowsy memoirs, we see that the archives and muniment-rooms of cathedrals, town corporations, and baronial residences, have been assiduously consulted and searched for illustrative matter. The style, too, is frequently elaborate and pretentious; and the approaching influence of the Renaissance is perceptible in the display of an erudition equally ill-timed and puerile. Finally, whilst the biographies of lords and kings, losing their personal character, too often become mere panegyrics or even codes of morality, the *bourgeoisie* steps in, and from the ranks of the third estate shrewd observers appear, who, keeping records of passing events, and taking notes of all that they had the opportunity of witnessing, show themselves the worthy predecessors of Tallemant des Réaux or Pierre de l'Estoile.

We have now arrived, in fact, at the time when chivalry is in its decay, and when mediæval institutions are making way for a new order of things. Enguerrand de Monstrelet and his continuators have the sad task of chronicling the events which marked an epoch when France had apparently reached the brink of destruction, and when, a prey to enemies both from within and without, and torn by religious schism and political anarchy, the unfortunate country seemed to be in the last convulsions of death. Charles VI. then occupied the throne; after having been for a period of six years under the surveillance of his uncles, he had married the infamous Isabel of Bavaria, and his mind, which had never been strong, completely forsaking him at last, the kingdom was given over to the rapacity of the queen, and the ambition of the Dukes of Orleans and of Burgundy. The former of these princes was murdered in the streets of Paris (November 24, 1407), by ruffians hired for the purpose by the Duke of Burgundy, who openly dared to justify the assassination. Somewhat to account for this crime, if not to vindicate it, it was stated that the profligate Orleans had had the effrontery to introduce the Duke of Burgundy into a cabinet, which he said was adorned with the portraits of all his mistresses, amongst which that of the Duchess of Burgundy occupied a prominent place. Valentine Visconti, Duchess of Orleans, died of grief without having been able to avenge her husband (1408); but her son, Charles, married the daughter of the Earl of Armagnac, and that nobleman excited a large number of partisans, in the south and west provinces of France, to take up the cause of his son-in-law against the Duke of Burgundy. This prince, in his turn, united himself with Henry of Lancaster, who had become King of England by the murder of Richard II., and he called to arms the provinces of the north and east. The result of this terrible conflict was the civil war of the *Armagnacs* and the *Bourguignons*, and to the pages of Monstrelet we must turn for a narrative of the events which marked the strife.

Born about the year 1390, Enguerrand de Monstrelet belonged to a noble family of Picardy, or of Flanders, and attached himself to the fortunes of the Duke of Burgundy, through whose influence he became Provost of Cambray and *Bailli* of Walincourt; we need not be astonished, therefore, at finding that his work is deeply characterized by Burgundian sympathies, and that its statements of the views and motives of the Armagnacs must be received with extreme caution. He died July 20, 1453. His chronicle begins in 1400, takes us down to the year 1444, and has been continued in succession by several writers as far as 1516. He gives us a broad, general history of the epoch which has occupied his attention, and there is no doubt that, compared with the brilliant sketches of Froissart, his narrative is singularly tame, considered from a merely literary point of view. The *pièces justificatives* quoted by him *in extenso*, in support of the facts he relates, mar the effect of the narrative, and give to it an appearance of prolixity, which makes it wearisome to the general reader; but, on the other hand, the almost uniform accuracy of the details amply compensate for any amount of literary shortcomings. The following extract from Dacier's memoir, published in the transactions of the French *Académie des Inscriptions et Belles-Lettres* is a very fair and satisfactory description of Monstrelet:—

"If the numerous imperfections of Monstrelet are not made amends for by the beauty of his style, we must allow that they are compensated by advantages of another kind. His narration is diffuse, but clear, and his style heavy, but always equal. He rarely offers any reflections, and they are always short and judicious. The temper of his mind is particularly manifested by the circumstance that we do not find in his work any ridiculous stories of sorcery, magic, astrology, or any of those absurd prodigies which disgrace the greater part of the historians of his time. The goodness of his heart also displays itself in the traits of feeling which he manifests in his recitals of battles, sieges, and of towns won by storm; he seems then to rise superior to himself, and his style acquires strength and warmth. When he relates the preparations for, and the commencement of, a war, his first sentiment is to deplore the evils by which he foresees that the poorer ranks will soon be overwhelmed. Whilst he paints the despair of the wretched inhabitants of the country, pillaged and massacred by both sides, we perceive he is really affected by his subject, and writes from his feelings. . . . It appears that benevolence was the marked feature of his character, to which I am not afraid to add the love of truth."[1]

Dacier alludes to the "numerous imperfections" of Monstrelet. One of the most noteworthy of these imperfections is the frequent recurrence of chronological mistakes, which disfigure his pages, as well as those of Froissart; and what deserves particularly to be noticed, to avoid falling into errors, is, that each of these chroniclers, when passing from the history of one country to another, introduces events of an earlier date, without even mentioning

---

[1] *Mémoires de l'Acad. des Inscript.*, xliii. 535, transl. in Johnes's translation, I. xxviii.

it, and intermix them in the same chapter, as if they had taken place in the same period; but Monstrelet has the advantage of Froissart in the correctness of counting the years, which he invariably begins on Easter Day, and closes them on Easter Eve.[1]

Another drawback must be mentioned here—the frequent disfiguring of proper names, more especially foreign ones, which are often so mangled that it is impossible to decipher them. Ducange had corrected between one thousand and eleven hundred on the margin of his copy of the edition of 1572, and these corrections appear, of course, in the edition published by the *Société de l'Histoire de France*.

Finally, we should not forget to notice the very unequal proportions assigned by the annalist to the various episodes he brings before his readers. Whenever he has to relate facts concerning Flanders or Picardy, he goes into the most trivial circumstances, and preserves the most stupid details; on the other hand, he frequently apologizes for the brevity of his narrative, when discussing events bearing upon the history of France, and which led to political results of the gravest character. Rabelais, who often shows so much shrewdness and critical acumen in the midst of his coarseness, has aptly described Enguerrand de Monstrelet as "more slobbering than a mustard-pot"

---

[1] Dacier, *ubi suprà*, xxvi., xxvii.

(*plus baveux qu'un pot à moutarde*). There can scarcely be any doubt whatever that Monstrelet is the most remarkable of a series of annalists, who, natives of Flanders or of Picardy, had been attracted to the court of Burgundy by the protection of the duke, Philip the Good, an enlightened patron of art and literature, and who attached themselves to his fortunes, and to those of his son, the celebrated Charles the Bold. We shall name the most remarkable amongst them.

Jacques du Clercq, born in 1420, died during the second half of the fifteenth century; his chronicles, which extend from 1448 to the death of Philip the Good (1467), give us a narrative, almost day by day, of the events of every kind which took place in Flanders, both at court and elsewhere. Of all the histories of that epoch, his is the one where the people occupy the largest share; and the number of details he introduces on private and domestic life, the amusing and characteristic anecdotes which make up the main substance of his memoirs, are extremely important towards an acquaintance with the history of society during the early part of the century.

Olivier de la Marche (? 1426–1502) is distinguished by other qualities, which make him as valuable as Monstrelet and as Du Clercq, though in a different manner; and we may say that these three historians supplement each other. Du Clercq generally expresses himself with much *naïveté*; his work is neither a piece of special pleading nor a bill of indictment, and, Burgundian as he is, he does not hesitate to give us a faithful description of the scandalous maladministration produced by the unpardonable *nonchalance* of Duke Philip. His ignorance of the history of foreign countries is amusing; but when he treats of events which have taken place, either in France or in Flanders, he is singularly accurate. Olivier de la Marche resembles Du Clercq in point of style, and there it would be difficult to decide which of the two is the weaker; laden with provincialisms, diffuse and obscure, the narrative in both historians drags its weary length along, unrelieved by the slightest quality of harmony or elegance. Olivier de la Marche is useful for military history, and he describes chiefly the jousts, tournaments, combats, and engagements which took place at the court of Burgundy between 1435 and 1492. He is remarkably sincere, and from that point of view many sound critics prefer him even to Philippe de Commines.

George Chastellain, celebrated equally as a poet and a chronicler, was born in 1403, at Alost in Flanders, and died at Valenciennes in 1473. After having followed for some considerable time the military profession, and travelled in France and in England, he joined the court of Philip the Good, who named him his historiographer. Charles the Bold conferred upon him the order of knighthood. The chronicle composed by Chastellain extended originally from 1419 to 1474; all the part included between 1422 and 1451 is, however, lost. The disputes between Lonis XI. and Charles the Bold, together with the principal events more or less referring to it, form the theme of our author's researches. Aiming at exceptional literary perfection, and carried along by the desire of being considered as an artist in point of style, Chastellain never loses the opportunity of indulging in his taste for verbiage; he dilates the slightest speeches, even the conversations of the *dramatis personæ*, in the most tedious and wretched manner, and the reflections which the events suggest to him are uniformly put in the shape of oratorical outbursts, in which he apostrophizes either the princes, his contemporaries, or France, or even himself. We must acknowledge, at the same time, that he paints admirably the artful and treacherous policy of Louis XI., and the violence of Charles the Bold.

If Monstrelet is liable to the accusation of being too much of a Burgundian by his political sympathies, the charge is still more applicable to Lefèvre de Saint-Rémy, of whom we have now to say a few words. Born at Avesnes (in France, department of the Somme) about 1394, he became king-at-arms of the Order of the Golden Fleece, and died at Bruges, June 10th, 1468. The memoirs of Jacques Lefèvre de Saint-Rémy, extending from 1407 to 1436, are chiefly plagiarized from Monstrelet; and may be regarded as a kind of abridgment of the older chronicle. The portion included between 1407 and 1411 is a mere transcript, often disguised in a somewhat clumsy manner. The next division of the work (1411–1422) presents all the characters of an exact copy, entire chapters being reproduced without the slightest alteration, whilst the few changes introduced are of the slightest possible nature. Sometimes Saint-Rémy leaves out episodes mentioned by Monstrelet; occasionally, on the other hand, he adds a few details, and he condenses all the illustrative documents, giving only their purport, instead of reproducing the original text. The third portion of the chronicle we are now noticing (1422–1428) still presents to us Saint-Rémy in the character of a copyist, but with less servility than before; he now describes certain facts otherwise than Monstrelet had done, whether he appears in the character of a condenser, or, on the contrary, indulges in minute descriptions. Finally, the concluding part (1428–1436) deserves to some extent to be regarded as an original composition. Here Saint-Rémy gives his own version of the events related by Monstrelet, adding new particulars and suppressing still more. We can see that he has been an eye-witness of some of the incidents he narrates, and that he has taken a prominent share in not a few of them. For this period of eight years, his memoirs are a valuable *résumé* of the history of France. We have said already that Saint-Rémy is much more prejudiced still than the very partial and one-sided Monstrelet. Thus, when he copies from his predecessor, he suppresses carefully the few passages unfavourable to John, Duke of Burgundy; thus again, before relating the murder of that prince on the bridge of Montereau, he writes a preamble in which he openly accuses the dauphin of having premeditated the assassination. The affection which Saint-Rémy entertains for the English is never concealed, and the French are certainly those with whom he sympathizes least. Monstrelet always gives the name of *king* to the dauphin immediately after the death of Charles VI.; Saint-Rémy never styles him but as dauphin till the day of the actual coronation. Monstrelet designates the Duke of Bedford as the *soi-disant* (self-styled) regent, whenever he does not call him by his title— Bedford; with Saint-Rémy, the duke is uniformly *the regent*. Let us conclude this notice by observing that some critics have erroneously considered Monstrelet and Lefèvre de Saint-Rémy as independent authorities, whose evidence should bear distinct and separate weight; whereas, for the greater part of his memoirs, Saint-Rémy, as we have already seen, is nothing but an echo of the more exact and more complete Monstrelet.

The excellent edition of Mathieu d'Escouchy's memoirs, published by M. Dufresne de Beaucourt for the *Société de l'Histoire de France*, enables us to give a few trustworthy particulars of a writer whose merits are, in every respect, far superior to those of Monstrelet, and who belongs to the same group of Burgundian sympathizers. Born about the year 1420, at Quesnoy-le-Comte, in the province of Hainault, Mathieu de Coucy (de Coussy or d'Escouchy) continued the chronicle of Monstrelet as far as the 27th of July, 1461. He held the important post of Provost of Péronne for several years, and seems to have been a man of the most troublesome and litigious nature, always appearing before the law courts either as defendant or as plaintiff, often taking the law into his own hands, assaulting his neighbours, and righting himself *vi et armis*, when he could not obtain in a legitimate manner the redress to which he fancied himself entitled. In this respect, there cannot be imagined a greater contrast than that which exists between the vindictive, turbulent, spiteful provost, and the impartial, grave, dignified annalist, writing under the inspiration of genuine modesty, and revealing a moral perception which is really most remarkable. The memoirs of Mathieu d'Escouchy are not of equal value, but portions of them are original, and relate facts which we would vainly look for elsewhere; thus the description of the battle of Saint-Jacques, so justly praised by M. Michelet;[1] the account of the festivities which took place in Scotland on the occasion of the marriage of James II.

---

[1] *Hist. de France*, v. 251, *note:* "C'est l'historien contemporain; il a parlé aux combattants même."

with Mary of Gueldres. With reference to this event, Pinkerton has the following remark:—"In the barrenness of materials for the reign of James II., the information of that writer is invaluable, and yet has been unknown to all our historians." The chapters devoted to the establishment of the *compagnies d'ordonnance*, to the trial of Brézé, to the battle of Castillon, to Jacques Cœur, are also well worth the reader's attention. On the other hand, many instances might be named where d'Escouchy's narrative is the mere reproduction of documents which he had borrowed from various sources, and which he gives us in common with other contemporaries. Thus, several relations of feats of chivalry may be found in Olivier de la Marche and in the chronicles of Jacques de Lalaing; thus again, the descriptions of the vow of the pheasant, and of the funeral of Charles VII., are only the transcript of official documents, the text of which can be found elsewhere. The history of the campaign of Normandy is taken from the herald Berry's *Recouvrement de la Normandie*. Mathieu d'Escouchy was on terms of friendship with many of the officers who took part in that expedition, and so he could aspire to something better than the position of a mere copyist. As M. de Beaucourt well observes, whenever he copies he does so intelligently, and has often observations of his own wherewith to supplement those of other chroniclers. He in general only describes those things which he has actually witnessed, and frankly acknowledges his ignorance whenever there is occasion for doing so; he may commit blunders, but it is in honest good faith. The introductory words of his prologue are remarkable from this point of view: "In order to avoid committing blunders, as is my duty, and according to my power, I have in the present treatise followed my subject without partiality or favour; and I have always made diligent inquiries one year before putting down anything in writing."[1] Every page shows this praiseworthy aim at being strictly impartial. We meet constantly with sentences like the following:—" Et me fut dit sur ceste matière;" "Comme il me fut certifié;" "Selon ce qui me fut rapporté." If we compare d'Escouchy with Monstrelet, we cannot help being struck by the fairness of the former's appreciation, and by the impartiality with which he holds the balance between the King of France and the Duke of Burgundy. As a writer he is infinitely superior to Froissart's continuator, and sometimes rises to the brilliancy and picturesqueness of Froissart himself; in short, for an accurate knowledge of the last seventeen years of the reign of Charles VII., no work can replace the

---

[1] "Pour *eschiever*[1] de commettre faulte, à mon devoir et pooir, en ce présent traictié ay porsievy ma matière sans partialité ny favour aucune à l'une des parties plus que à l'autre; et me suis toujours infourmé diligamment ung an auparavant que aye riens mis ne couchié par escript."[1]

[1] *Eschiever = esquiver.*

chronicle of Mathieu d'Escouchy. M. de Beaucourt has given several instances of the high moral tone, the delicate touch, and the lifelike sketches, which make the remarkable work so pre-eminently interesting; we shall quote a few by way of specimen:—

On flatterers:—" People of wicked note, through whose influence princes are often in great dishonour and damage." [1]

On the death of Charles VIII.:—" There were in this kingdom great cries and lamentations, for during his time he had wisely and powerfully kept and governed his aforesaid people in peace and prosperity." [2]

On Margaret d'Anjou:—" She was often irritated and grieved because she saw and knew pretty well the wretched government of her lord and husband; in the sight of the people she bore these grievances patiently, but when she was alone, she often made great lamentations and piteous complaints." [3]

On the tragic end of the Duke of Gloucester:—

---

[1] "Gens de meschant estat, dont aucunes fois les princes se trouvent en grand deshonneur et domaige."

[2] "Y ot en icellui royaueme de grans cris et lamentacion, car en son temps avait bien et sagement et grandement tenu et gouverné son dit pœuple en paix et prospérité."

[3] "Souventes fois estoit en grant haine et dolleur de ce que elle véoit et assez congnoissoit le petit gouvernement de son seigneur et mary . . . lesquelles choses à la veue des pœuple elle portoit paciamment, mais quant elle estoit à son privé, souvent faisoit de grans lamentacions et piteuses complainttes."

"The wheel of fortune showed him one of its revolutions, as it very often does to many, and of various conditions."[1]

The following narrative of Talbot's death brings out in strong relief the literary merits of Mathieu d'Escouchy:—

"The next day, several heralds and officers from the English side came to the aforesaid field, amongst whom was the herald of the aforesaid Talbot, who had put on his coat-of-arms; they requested that permission and leave might be granted them to seek and look for their master. Talbot's herald was asked whether he would recognize his master if he saw him; thinking that Talbot was alive and a prisoner, he answered that he would like to see him. Thereupon he was led to the place where the aforesaid Lord Talbot was dead, and on the ground; and when he saw him there, some one said, 'See if this is your master.' Then he changed colour, but yet he could not at once decide; for Talbot was much disfigured on account of the scar he had on his face; and since his death he had been lying there, the whole night and the day following, in consequence of which he was much changed. Nevertheless, the herald knelt down, saying that he would immediately know the truth. Then he thrust into the dead man's mouth one of the fingers of his right hand, in order to feel

---

[1] "La roe de fortune luy monstra ung de ses tours, comme elle fait moult souvent à pluseurs et de divers estatz."

on the left side for a tooth which he knew to a
certainty that Talbot had lost; he found as he
had suspected, and immediately, still being on his
knees, as I have said, he kissed him on the mouth,
saying, 'My lord and master, my lord and master,
is it you? I pray God that He may forgive you
your sins. I have been your officer-at-arms for
forty years or more; it is time that I should
surrender my post to you.' Then, making piteous
wailings and lamentations, and crying bitterly, he
took off his coat-of-arms, and placed it on the
corpse of his master."[1]

---

[1] "Le lendemain, furent audit champ pluseurs heraulx et officiers
d'armes du partie des Anglois, entre lesquelz estoit le hérault dudit
Seigneur de Talbot, qui avoit vestu sa cotte d'armes; lesquels firent
requeste de avoir licence et grace de quérir et *cherquier*[1] leurs
maistres. Auquel hérault de Talbot fut demandé, se il véoit son
maistre, se il le recongnoisteroit; à quoi respondit joyeusement,
cuidant que il fut vif prisonnier, que voullentiers le verroit. Et sur
ce fut mené du lieu où ledit Seigneur de Talbot estoit mort et sur le
pavais; et quant il le vit illec, on lui dit : 'Regardez se c'est vostre
maistre.' Lors lui changa la coulleur, sans de prime face en faire
le jugement, car il estoit fort deffait par la *trenche*[2] qu'il avoit ou
visage, et sy avoit esté depuis sa mort toutte la nuit et le lendemain
jusques à ceste heure, par quoy il estoit fort deffais. Néant mains
il se mist à genoulx, et dit que incontinent il en saveroit la vérité; et
lors lui boutta l'an des dois de sa main destre en la bouche, pour
quérir au costé senestre ung dent *maceler*[3] qu'il savoit de certain
qu'il avoit perdu, lequel il trouva ainsy comme il entendoit; et
incontinent qu'il ot trouvé, lui estant à genoulx comme dit est, le
baisa en la bouche, disant ces mos : 'Monseigneur mon maistre,
monseigneur mon maistre, ce estes-vous! Je prie à Dieu qui vous
pardoinst vos meffais. J'ay esté vostre officier d'armes xl. ans ou

---

[1] *Cherquier* = *chercher*.   [2] *Trenche* = *blessure*.
[3] *Maceler* = *machelière*.

After Mathieu d'Escouchy, when we open the chronicle of Pierre de Fénin, we feel as if we were falling very low indeed in the domains of historical composition. Born in the province of Artois, and belonging to the first half of the fifteenth century, Fénin has written the history of the events which took place in France from 1407 to 1422. The wars between the houses of Orleans and of Burgundy are the subjects of his book, and the Dukes John and Philip are the most prominent personages of his narrative. Indeed, as the latest editor of Fénin's memoirs has observed, it seems as if the history of France was a mere appendage to that of the Dukes of Burgundy. The great drawback of the work we are now noticing is that, generally speaking, it merely reproduces Monstrelet, or the sources from which Monstrelet compiled his own chronicle. There are, however, a certain number of facts given by Fénin which we would uselessly look for in contemporary writers; and although the style, as a rule, is slovenly and poor, yet when he has to describe a feat of arms, the siege of a town, or the scenes of a battle-field, he sometimes contrives to be animated, and even eloquent. We may also notice that his appreciation of distinguished historical characters is often remarkably shrewd and correct. Thus, describing the state

---

plus, il est temps que je le vous rende,' en faisant piteux cris et lamentacions et en rendant l'eaue par les y ung très piteusement. Et lors devesti sa cotte d'armes et ce mist sus son dit maistre."

of moral prostration from which the unfortunate King Charles VI. was suffering at the time of the siege of Paris, he says, "The king was satisfied with worse things, and with everybody, whether Bourguignons or Armagnacs, and he cared little how matters went."[1] The following character of Charles VII. cannot fail to strike the reader by its accuracy:—"He was a very handsome prince, affable to all, and compassionate to the poor; but he did not arm himself willingly, and if he could have done without war, he would not have cared."[2]

The memoirs of Pierre de Fénin do not deserve to be ranked in the same place as those of Mathieu d'Escouchy or of Monstrelet, but they still possess an importance of their own, and the Burgundian proclivities, which distinguish all the chroniclers of Northern France at that time, are here reduced to an almost insignificant minimum.

The publications of the *Société de l'Histoire de France* include on the reigns of the first four Valois kings, a volume which must be briefly mentioned here. It is the production of an anonymous author, who lived during the latter half of the fourteenth century, and who, according to all probability, was a clergyman and a native of Normandy. The *Chronique des Quatre Premiers Valois* is written

---

[1] "Le roy estoit de tout content, et de Bourguignons et d'Ermignas, et peu luy chaloit comme tout allast."

[2] "Il estoit de sa personne moult bel prince et biau parleur à toutes personnes, et estoit piteux envers povres gens; mais il ne s'armoit mie vollentiers, et n'avoit pour chier la guerre, s'il s'en eust pu passer."

in a clear and easy style, but without much vigour, except when the annalist has to describe the vicissitudes of a campaign and the excitement of the battle-field. It does not add any great amount of information to what we gather from Froissart, the *Chronique de Saint Denis*, and the continuators of Nangis; at the same time, it brings before us a number of details which the anonymous clerk seems to have alone observed and noted. The final incidents of the Jacquerie, the events which brought to an end the rebellion of Etienne Marcel, are the principal episodes here illustrated; and on those various points we must say that the *Chronique* helps us to supply desiderata left by other contemporary historians. There is also the account of a curious expedition made in England by some adventurers from Picardy, together with the revenge taken by the English. The Hundred Years' War, commenced in 1336, was then raging, and a number of attacks, forays, invasions, and skirmishes of greater or less importance were constantly taking place, some of which are recorded by one annalist, while the others are recorded elsewhere. Thus it is that the numerous historians belonging to the fifteenth century must *all* be studied, whatever may be their relative importance; for it often happens that, from amongst the dull, lifeless details registered in an apparently insignificant volume, we find one entry which enables us to establish a doubtful point of chronology, or to identify an imperfectly known character.

CHAPTER XIII.

THE RELIGIEUX DE SAINT DENIS—THE CHRONICLE OF DU GUESCLIN—THE CHRONICLES OF LOUIS OF BOURBON.

IT appears extraordinary, at first, to find on the Burgundian side such a numerous and powerful array of historians; but we must bear in mind that the Armagnacs were associated in the thoughts of the Paris *bourgeoisie* with the rapacity of the court, the immorality of the French aristocracy, and the misery of the nation. The Burgundians had, no doubt, been guilty of crimes; but still, on the whole, they seemed to have preserved the traditions of good government, and therefore we see the duke, Philip the Bold, and his son, John the Fearless, supported by the University of Paris, the Hôtel de Ville, and the magistracy. A revulsion of feeling took place later on, it is true, but it was when John appealed for support to the Cabochiens and to the mob, and finally betrayed the kingdom into the hands of the English. The influence of the University of Paris, and the important part it played in the civil wars of the fifteenth century, are especially evident in the Latin chronicle which is generally known under the name of *Chronique du Religieux de Saint Denis,* and which was published by M. Bellaguet, together with a French translation, in the year 1839. The author of this work is still unknown; he had written a history of the reign of Charles V., with the view of setting before the unfortunate successor of that monarch a pattern for imitation, little suspecting, as M. de Barante remarks, that the sceptre so cleverly wielded by *Charles le Sage* was doomed to fall into the hands of *Charles l'Insensé.* The former compilation has been lost, and the one we are now noticing gives us only the reign of Charles VI. It is a series of annals, and not a history strictly so called; the events are registered as they occurred, and we are led to the conclusion that the honest religious, writing by the express orders of his superior, was merely accumulating materials for the great national monument we have already attempted to describe—the *Grandes Chroniques de Saint Denis.* As a matter of fact, the portion of the *Grandes Chroniques* which treats of the reign of Charles VI., so far at least as its early years are concerned, is nothing but a transcript of the *Chronique du Religieux.*

We have said that the present compilation is anonymous. Le Laboureur, who has made free use of it in preparing his own history of Charles VI., tells us that two of the monks of Saint Denis were at that time particularly conspicuous for their learning and their literary talents: the one was Guillaume Barrault, belonging to a family having decided Burgundian sympathies; the other, Benoit Gentien, doctor of divinity, one of the most illustrious members of the University of Paris. It seems probable, notwithstanding Le Laboureur's assertion, that if the religious is to be identified with one of these personages, the claims preponderate in favour of Guillaume Barrault, and it would be difficult to speak too highly of his impartiality. "Quand il parle," says the historian, "des exactions du Duc d'Orléans, on dirait qu'il est Bourguignon; quand il donne le détail des pratiques et des funestes intelligences du Duc de Bourgogne avec des assassins infâmes, et avec la canaille de Paris, on croirait qu'il est Orléanais."

A number of passages from the chronicle we are now noticing might be quoted, to show that the author was an eye-witness of the events which he relates. Thus, he was at the port of Sluys when the king, after having collected together all the preparations for an attack upon England, awaited impatiently the arrival of the Duc de Berri, whom he urged, by repeated messages, not to allow the opportunity to slip for carrying out so momentous an enterprise: "Mihi et universis residentibus in castris et de rerum statu sciscitantibus asserebant ducem ipsum nihil amplius affectare," etc., etc. Such are the very words of the annalist.

In 1393, the same Duke de Berri ordered him to make an exact memorandum of what was taking place at the Lelinghen conferences, for the purpose of entering these details in his chronicle. He was present at the siege of Bourges in 1412; two years later, we find him sharing the tent of the Sire d'Aumont, oriflamme-bearer, who took compassion upon him, amidst the disorder and the wretchedness of the expedition conducted by the King of France against the Duke of Burgundy.

On the other hand, we notice that, either designedly or from want of accurate information, the *Religieux de Saint Denis* omits several important facts, and as part of the ground which his narrative covers is also occupied by Froissart, it is interesting to compare the statements of the two historians with one another. Thus, the monk, describing the death of the Count d'Armagnac before Alexandria (July 25, 1391), distinctly says that he was made a prisoner, and that he died from the eight wounds which he had received during the action. If, on the contrary, we are to credit Froissart's account, the Count d'Armagnac was struck down by apoplexy, captured by a Lombard squire, and taken into Alexandria, where he breathed his last during the night, without having been able to utter a single word.

The Hundred Years' War presents to our notice several distinguished historical characters whose courage and patriotism still live in the grateful recollections of all Frenchmen, and whose exploits have been recorded in biographical poems which remind us of the old *chansons de geste*. Let us name, amongst others, the well-known Bertrand Du Guesclin, the hero of a metrical narrative extending over thirty thousand lines, and which deserves our attention, as well for its literary merits, as for its historical importance. The name of the stalwart Constable of France is spelt in ten different manners; there seems to be an almost equal variety in the orthography of the poet's appellation, and this fact has been the origin of endless blunders. No wonder that *Cimelier*, *Cuvelier*, and *Tueiller* should have been thought to be three distinct personages, whereas they are really one and the same individual. The poem composed by Cuvelier (such seems to be the right designation) may be regarded as the last specimen of a long series of semi-historical, semi-fictitious epics, beginning with the *Chanson de Roland*, and forming the poetical and popular annals of mediæval times. From it, as branches from a tree, have sprung a number of chronicles unequal in point of artistic talent, and in which history is singularly blended with fiction. A time came, however, for all the old *chansons de geste* when poetry was replaced by prose, and when the wonderful anecdotes about the warriors and knights of mediævalism, instead of being sung by the minstrels to the accompaniment of harp or cittern, were merely related by the fireside in modest *sermo pedestris.* The chronicle of Cuvelier shared this fate, and led to the appearance of works such as *Le Livre des Faiz de Messire Bertrand du Guesclin, Les Prouesses et Vaillances du Preux et Vaillant Chevalier Bertrand du Guesclin,* etc., etc.; all having their origin in the same monorhyme poem, the accurate title of which is *Le Roumant de Messire Bertran du Glayequin, jadis Chevalier et Connestable de France.*

Cuvelier's romance is not only a history of Du Guesclin, but, in point of date, the earliest French account we have of the war about the succession to the dukedom of Brittany, the expedition into Spain, and the campaign against the English invaders. It may not be uniformly trustworthy, but it has over other narratives the decided advantage of being almost contemporaneous with the events related, and in this respect it must be preferred to Froissart, whose brilliant chronicles *as a whole*, were published only during the last years of the fifteenth century, subsequently to the composition of the poem we are now examining.

We have just named Froissart; Dom Morice, who has written a history of Brittany and made considerable use of Cuvelier, thus draws the parallel between the two annalists: "Tueiller [read *Cuvelier*] has the same defects as Froissart; he seldom gives the dates of the episodes he describes, nor does he observe the chronological order throughout his narrative. His work requires a great deal of comments and explanatory notes." We may examine the *Roumant de Bertran du Glayequin* either as an historical document, or as a picture of society during one of the most interesting epochs in the Middle Ages. The first thing that strikes us is that the author, who was not himself a Breton by birth, says very little about the native country of the illustrious captain, and takes a very disinterested and impartial view of the great quarrel which broke out between Charles de Blois and Jean de Montfort. Here, again, he compares most advantageously with Froissart, as far as the accuracy and the fulness of his statements is concerned. The expedition into Spain occupies half the chronicle; it is decidedly the weakest part of the work, if we look at it from the point of view of literary composition, and here Cuvelier presents curious and interesting analogies with Ayala and the other Spanish historians who have discussed the same events. Froissart is disappointingly brief; our poet, on the other hand, goes into details, and if many of the facts he introduces contain an amount of exaggeration, the fictitious element can always be easily distinguished; and the impression we preserve is that, if the author is not uniformly accurate, he is, at any rate, strictly honest.

To sum up the above remarks, we may say that Cuvelier's work is neither a general history, nor a biographical memoir; it participates in the nature of both classes of writings, and this indecision on the part of the author tells unfavourably upon the book. The facts are put together without any connection with each other; they are frequently presented in a mutilated form, not in their natural sequence, but according to the caprice of the poet, unsystematically, almost at random, and just as they appear useful by way of contrast. The defects are still more glaring, if we consider the *romaunt* as a biography; for, in the first place, a great number of circumstances in Du Guesclin's career are entirely omitted, and, in the second, Cuvelier does not take the trouble of explaining the meaning of certain incidents, or the influence they had on contemporary history. He merely selects such episodes as seem to him most amusing, most *romantic;* and here the *littérateur*, the artist, endeavours to outshine the historian.

To the same epoch belongs the *Chronique du Bon Duc Loys de Bourbon*, published for the *Société de l'Histoire de France* by M. Chazaud. Louis II., Duke de Bourbon, son and successor of Peter I., who was killed at the battle of Poitiers, took an important share in the events of the fourteenth century. Born August 4, 1337, he belonged to the band of hostages sent to England (1360) as securities for the ransom of King John; he resided for the space of eight years in this country, and on his return to France he founded a new order of knighthood, under the designation of the *Shield of Gold*. The Duke de Bourbon earned considerable reputation for courage and generalship in the wars against the English, both in Brittany and in Guyenne; he was one of the four princes of the blood appointed as guardians of King Charles VI. (1380), he fought at the battle of Rosebecke (1382), and took the command of the Crusade summoned in 1390 against Tunis. He died at Moulins in 1410.

The chronicle we have now to consider gives us the complete biography of Louis de Bourbon. The author describes himself as *Jehan d'Orreville, Picard, nommé Cabaret, pouvre pèlerin.* Having undertaken to "compiler et descripre les œuvres d'armes et chevalerie, vertus, bonnes meurs, belle vie et bonne fin" of so illustrious a prince, he feels a modest distrust of his own powers, and he deplores the "insuffisance de son petit *engin*[1] et de son rude langage." Fortunately, in this extremity, help comes to him from the right quarter, and Jehan de Châteaumorand, an ancient companion in arms of the Duke de Bourbon, volunteers to relate to the historian the biography of his friend; therefore, after having taken down his notes and written from them the first draft of his work, Jehan d'Orreville will have merely to revise and correct it, arrange it in chapters, and clothe it in language best calculated to fix the reader's attention. We thus see that, although Jehan d'Orreville actually committed the biography to writing, he was merely

---

[1] Lat. *ingenium*.

the amanuensis of Châteaumorand, to whom belongs the honour of recording the *belle vie et bonne fin* of the illustrious Duke de Bourbon. With reference to Châteaumorand himself, we must turn for information either to Froissart or to Boucicaut. The combined evidence of these two historians shows him to have been not only a brave soldier, but a distinguished statesman and diplomatist. He took a prominent part in what could already be styled the *Eastern question*, and was appointed by King Charles VI. to accompany Jacques de Helly, for the purpose of negotiating with Sultan Bajazet the final liberation of the prisoners made at Nicopolis. When Boucicaut returned to France in charge of the Emperor Manuel-Palæologus, Châteaumorand was left behind to defend Constantinople. He, whom Froissart describes as a "chevalier pourveu de sens et de langage, froid et attrempé de toutes manières," was certainly worthy of composing the biography of a prince whose interests he maintained both at the council board and on the battle-field, and he is entitled to a distinguished place in the annals of the fourteenth century. Born about the year 1355, he lived long enough to see the appearance of the maid whose courage and patriotism rescued France from utter destruction.

The chronicle of the "good Duc Loys" was, if not composed, at any rate put into shape and subdivided into chapters in 1429. Châteaumorand was then about seventy-five years old, and age had, no doubt, somewhat obscured his recollection of things long gone by. D'Orreville does not seem to have consulted other witnesses, or borrowed from other sources of information. The only annalist whom he names is Froissart, to whose description of the battle of Rosebecke he refers the reader anxious for further details on this episode. As his sole object is to write the biography of the Duke de Bourbon, the other heroes in the stirring drama are mentioned by him merely incidentally, and so far as they are brought into contact with the duke. He writes, above all, to leave to posterity an amusing, instructive, and profitable book. Accordingly, he never troubles himself to verify the dates or statements for which he is indebted to Châteaumorand's conversation, and he takes as his models the chronicles of Du Guesclin and of Boucicaut, rather than the brilliant pages of Froissart, or the somewhat ponderous style of Christine de Pisan. It follows, from what has just been said, that the chronology of the present work, the geographical indications, and even the proper names of persons, require to be verified and in most cases corrected; nor can we much wonder at this circumstance, when we remember that D'Orville wrote down memoirs, not of what he had seen himself, but of the events related to him by a knight who had overstepped the limit of threescore years and ten, and whose memory could not be as good in 1429 as it was in

1380, when, at the siege of Châteauneuf de Randon, he fought side by side with Constable du Guesclin. D'Orreville, or his *collaborateur*, Châteaumorand, shares with Froissart an enthusiastic admiration for the nobility, whom he considers as the true sinews and the glory of the country. We must also note, by way of literary merit, an amount of genuine eloquence which we do not generally find in compositions belonging to the class of official panegyrics or professed *éloges*. One short extract will suffice to give an idea of D'Orreville's style; it is taken from the thirth-eighth chapter, where is described the interview between the Dukes d'Anjou and de Bourbon on the one side, and Du Guesclin on the other. It is well known that, in the year 1378, the King of France obtained from the parliament a decree of confiscation of the duchy of Brittany; the nobles of that province immediately revolted, and Du Guesclin, who had vainly attempted to reduce the county of Rennes, and had been accused of treachery by the king, finally refused to carry on the war against his *compatriotes*, and sent back to Charles V. his sword, resigning at the same time his office as constable.

"Thereupon the King of France, Charles, thought better of it, and wished to mend matters; he accordingly sent the Dukes d'Anjou and de Bourbon into Brittany, for the purpose of appeasing the constable's wrath. They went to Pontorson, and sent for the constable, who came readily. And

when he had arrived, the Duke d'Anjou said,
'Constable, my lord the king sends us to you, both
myself and my fair cousin of Bourbon, because of
the displeasure you have felt at certain words
which he has addressed to you, to the effect that
you were siding with the Duke of Brittany, as he
was given to understand. Now, you should be
very pleased and joyful at hearing that the king
believes none of these reports. Here is the sword
of your office; take it back again—the king orders
you to do so—and come along with us.' The
speech of the Duke d'Anjou being ended, the good
constable answered, 'My most dread lord, I thank
you very humbly for the words you tell me, and
for informing me that the king does not believe
the reports spread about me; for which I thank
the king, notwithstanding the great rumour which
has arisen. And I wish the king to know that
I have served him well and loyally, as a gentleman
should do, and I have never been guilty of treason
towards him. For, if I should serve the Duke of
Brittany, who is against him, I should be a traitor
towards him, who is the greatest king alive, and
the small amount of honour I have earned in this
world, I would not lose for any consideration
whatever. And tell the king that I rate my
honour higher than all the lordships and goods
he could give me, and that I certify unto him.
I thank you for the sword you have brought back
to me; I shall not take it: bestow it upon any

one whom he may please to appoint. For, in order to give no room for suspicion, both to him and to all others, I am going to Spain, and I give you my word that I shall remain no longer in this kingdom.'"[1]

The interview referred to above occurred in 1379; a year had scarcely elapsed, when the body of the valiant constable found its last resting-place in the vaults of the abbey of Saint Denis.

---

[1] "Sur ce le Roi de France, Charles, se advisa, et voult réparer la chose, et envoya les Ducs d'Anjou et de Bourbon en Bretaigne, pour apaiser le Conestable du courroux qu'l avoit; lesquels allèrent à Pontorson, et là mandèrent le conestable, qui à eulx vint voulentiers. Et estre là venu, dit le Duc d'Anjou: 'Conestable,' fait-il, 'monseigneur le roi nous envoie à vous, moi et beau cousin de Bourbon, pour ce que vous avés esté mal content d'aucunes paroles qu'il vous a mandées, c'est assavoir qu'on lui avoit donné à entendre que vous teniez la partie du Duc de Bretaigne, et devez bien estre lie et joyeux, quand telles choses vous mande, les quelles le roy ne creut oncques. Véez-cy l'espée d'honneur de vostre office: reprenez-la, le roi le veult, et vous en venez avecques nous.' Les paroles finées du Duc d'Anjou respondit le bon conestable: 'Mon très redoubté seigneur, je vous remercie humblement des paroles que me dictes, et des paroles que vous m'avez aussi dit, que le roi ne les creut oncques, dont je remercie le roi, non obstant le grant bruit qu'on a couru. Et veuil bien, monseigneur, que le roi saiche que je l'ai servi bien et loyaument, comme preu d'homme et ne lui fis oncques trahison; car si je servoie le Duc de Bretaigne, qui est contre lui, je seroie traistre envers lui, qui est le plus grant roi qui vive, et ce puc d'honneur que jai conquis en ce monde, je ne le vouldroie pas perdre, pour quelque chose qui vive. Et dictes au roi que j'aime plus mon honneur que toutes les seigneuries et biens qu'il me pourroit donner, et cela je lui certiffie. Si vous regracie de l'espée que vous m'avez apportée. Je ne la reprendrai point, baillez la à ung aultre qui lui plaira. Car pour le oster de souspeçon et lui et tous autres, je m'envois en Espaigne, et vous jure, par ma foi, que jà mais en ce royaume je ne demourerai."

We cannot terminate this brief notice without drawing the attention of our readers to the fact that, despite the numerous blunders which we have alluded to above, the *Chronique du Bon Duc Loys* is not unfrequently more reliable than the brilliant narrative of Froissart. This point is satisfactorily demonstrated by M. Chazaud in the notes to his excellent edition, who gives as an instance the episode of the capture of the Duchesse de Bourbon at Belleperche, in 1372 (d'Orreville), or 1369 (Froissart). At any rate, if we wish to study the work of D'Orreville, we should compare it closely with the accounts given by Christine de Pisan, and Froissart, and the anonymous historian who composed the memoirs of Boucicaut.

CHAPTER XIV.

"LE LIVRE DES FAICTZ DE BOUCICAUT"—JOUVENEL DES URSINS — THE COUSINOTS — PIERRE COCHON AND HIS "CHRONIQUE NORMANDE."

A PROVERB was current in France during the fourteenth century, to the effect that—

> "Quand vient à un assault
> Mieulx vault Saintré que Boussiquaut;
> Mais quand vicat à un traicté,
> Mieulx vault Boussiquaut que Saintré."

Patriotism, military skill, and also diplomatic genius were hereditary in the Le Maingre family. Jean le Maingre, surnamed *Le Brave*, and as Bransôme says, *par esbatement*, was Marshal of France, and an intimate friend of Jean de Saintré; the peculiar merits ascribed to him in the couplets quoted above caused him to be appointed as one of the negotiators of the treaty of Bretigny, in 1360. The Boucicaut with whom we are more specially concerned here was Jean II. le Maingre.

Placed by Charles V. as a companion to the dauphin, afterwards Charles VI., he showed the most decided disposition for warlike pursuits; he was only twelve years old when he made his first campaign under Du Guesclin, and the brilliant service he rendered to France on the field of battle caused him to receive the staff of Marshal of France at the early age of twenty-five. Chivalry was on the wane, and the noble institution which had done so much for the good of mediæval civilization was gradually losing all the qualities which render it still attractive in the work of Friossart. Boucicaut may be considered as the model of the genuine knight; like the *Loyal Serviteur*, he maintained unimpaired the best traditions of chivalry, and certainly he cannot be taxed with remissness as a warrior. We find him at the battle of Rosebecke (1382), where he distinguished himself amongst the most intrepid; his next exploits are in the ranks of the Teutonic knights against the Lithuanians. On his return from Germany, sent into the comtat d'Avignon for the purpose of putting an end to the schism, he takes possession of Pope Benedict XIII. The fondness for adventures of a warlike character then took Marshal de Boucicaut to Hungary, where he was made a prisoner at the battle of Nicopolis (1396). Having escaped from the terrible massacre of his companions, by the clever and generous interposition of the Count de Nevers, our hero was sent into Bithynia as a captive, and on payment of a heavy ransom he obtained his liberty during the course of the same year. The Greek emperor, Manuel-Palæologos, was at that time sorely pressed by the Sultan Bajazet, who, after conquering the Hungarians, was bent upon finishing the ruin of the empire of Constantinople; he despatched as an ambassador Theodoros Cantacuzene, to apply for assistance from the King of France. Boucicaut started immediately with a few troops; he drove back the invaders, fortified Constantinople, healed the divisions which had contributed to weaken the imperial family, and, as a reward for his services, received from Manuel the title of Constable of the Greek Empire. This exploit very soon led to another. Whilst defending Constantinople, Boucicaut had gained the affection of the Genoese, whose commercial establishments he had saved from destruction. Weary of anarchy, the republic of the Genoese had, some years before, placed itself under the French rule, but no governor had yet succeeded in establishing his authority; Charles VI. was accordingly requested to delegate Boucicaut for that important post. The marshal administered from 1401 to 1409 a nation remarkable for its fickleness and dislike of all restraint. Obliged, in 1409, to go to Milan on a diplomatic errand, the Genoese took advantage of his absence, rose to arms, and massacred the French garrison. The last occasion which the unsettled state of Europe afforded to our hero for the display of his undoubted talents as a warrior was the battle of Agincourt; sharing the fate of so many of his countrymen, he was made a prisoner, and taken to England, where he died, in 1421.

The *Livre des Faictz du Bon Messire Jean le Maingre, dict Boucicaut*, takes the reader from 1368 to 1408. "It seems that, weary of the painful scenes of which France had been the theatre since the accession of Charles VI., the anonymous historian endeavoured to divert his thoughts from the horrors of civil war, by relating the exploits and singular adventures of a knight who spent out of France the best part of his life, and filled the world with the fame of his consummate courage." The author of *Le Livre des Faictz* is gifted with a brilliant imagination; he is deeply read in classical literature, and his style, thus formed in the best school, is singularly free from the defects which are so characteristic of his contemporaries. Following the destinies of the gallant marshal, he relates in detail the various exploits in which he was engaged, but carefully avoids touching upon the unfortunate condition of France, satisfied, when obliged to do so, with a few allusions of the most insignificant nature. The biography of Boucicaut, therefore, throws no light whatever upon the reign of Charles VI., the anarchy which succeeded to a long minority, and the terrible conflicts between the Armagnacs and the Bourguignons; its only importance consists in its being a record of the relations of France with other countries, and the biography of a gentleman who, as the anonymous author wittily remarks, deserved to be called *le philosophe de combat*, just as the philosophers of old were surnamed *chevaliers de sapience*. The first edition of the *Livre des Faictz* was published in 1620, by Theodore Godefroy, a distinguished historian and lawyer, to whom we are indebted for many works of the same kind, such as the chronicles of Juvenal des Ursins, Jean d'Auton, Seyssel, Jaligny, the history of Bayard, and that of Artus III., Duke of Brittany.

We have just named Juvenal des Ursins; it is time that we should say a few words on his character, both as a politician and as an historian. Like the Boucicauts, the Jouvenels, Juvenels, or Juvenals numbered two generations of distinguished men. Jean Juvenal, born about the year 1360, died on the 1st of April, 1431. He was successively councillor at the Châtelet, advocate in the court of Parliament, provost of the merchants (mayor of Paris), king's councillor, and chancellor of the dauphin, Duke of Guienne. Driven from Paris by the Burgundian party, he became president of the Parliament of Poitiers, and afterwards of that of Toulouse. Jean II. Juvenal added to his name that of *des Ursins*, pretending to be derived from the Orsini family at Rome. Born in Paris, November 23, 1388, he died at Reims, July 14, 1473; and during the course of his long life he took a very prominent part in the events of the time, both in Church and State. He held the following offices: *Avocat général* at the Parliament of Poitiers (1425), Bishop of Beauvais and peer of France (1431), Bishop of Laon (1444), Archbishop of Reims (1449). The history of Charles VI., composed by Juvenal des Ursins, is a very important work, and has always been considered as an excellent authority for the epoch of which it treats. The archbishop had at his disposal a number of documents for the narrative of those events in which he had not actually joined, and there is no doubt that he procured information of the most valuable kind from his father, whom he often names in his work, and who had, both as a councillor and as chief magistrate of the city of Paris, been actively employed during the disturbed reign of Charles VI. Godefroy remarks in his preface that Juvenal des Ursins is always careful to state nothing but the truth, and to be strictly impartial in his account of the civil wars between the Burgandians and the Armagnacs:—"As Froissart and Monstrelet incline towards the Burgundians, suppressing what might be quoted in condemnation of their party, so the present history gives, on the contrary, the evidence in favour of the just and lawful quarrel of those who were styled *Orléanais* or *Armagnacs*. The author, at the same time, never forgets the notable judgments of God upon those (however exalted their rank, and to whatever party they belonged)

whose actions followed an evil course, and who, moved by ambition, avarice, revenge, and other like passions, have been the cause of the misfortunes which followed. That is the reason why the author would not be known. In one place he even gives us to understand that he was born in the diocese of Châlons, and that he was a subject of the Duke of Burgundy." If we turn to the passage alluded to by Godefroy, we find the following statement:—
" Some said that he who has written on these transactions, and from whom have been derived the things said above, was an Armagnac. He has throughout told the exact truth. He had almost always been a servant of the late Duke of Burgundy; but when he saw that the son of the duke wished to place the kingdom in the hands of the English, he abandoned the service of that son, and returned into his own native country, namely, the diocese of Châlons, where he has continued to write with as little imperfection as he could, according to what was related to him."[1] Papirius Masson, alluding to Juvenal des Ursins, says : Cujus libros aliquot ad Carolum Regem, nondum editos evolvimus, plenos sapientiæ, et singularis erga rempublicam animi." Scævole and Louis de Sainte-Marthe, in their *Histoire Généalogique de la Maison de France*, likewise bear witness to the accuracy of Juvenal des Ursins, adding, " Il est d'autant plus digne de foi, qu'il a été témoin oculaire de la

---

[1] pp. 376, 377.

ce plupart de qu'il écrit." The history of Charles VI. is written in a very interesting and simple style; the author does not fall into those pedantic habits which were so dear to most of the authors of the fifteenth century. The Renaissance movement was at hand; a taste for classical literature had spread all over Europe, influencing for good the few whose mind was sufficiently well balanced to avoid pedantry, but spoiling, in all the others, whatever talent and imagination they possessed. Juvenal des Ursins escaped the contagion. His work is extremely readable, and he has shaped his way most dexterously between the affectation of the professed scholar and the pompous verbiage of a lawyer. The history of Charles VI., beginning with the 13th of September, 1380, and ending in 1422, comprises the whole reign of that monarch.

Godefroy's edition gives, by way of appendix, several interesting documents which illustrate the same epoch in the history of France, and amongst these a fragment of a chronicle extending from 1402 to 1455, and generally supposed to have been written by Gilles le Bouvier, who occupied the office of herald under the title of *Berry*, and during the reign of Charles VII. "Whereas," he says, "in the year 1402, the kingdom of France had reached the highest pitch of honour, and therein could be found the greatest amount of riches and power, as much in princes, prelates, knights, merchants, clerks, and common people, as in everything else, I resolved that, according to my small abilities and in proportion as I could understand, I would see all the high deeds which might happen henceforward in the aforenamed kingdom, and betake myself where the largest assemblies and most important transaction would take place. Then, I would make it my business to write, or have some one write for me, so far as I could best understand, eveything that had happened, whether good or bad." Berry's chronicle, composed in a very interesting manner, is distinguished by its impartiality, and forms the natural supplement to the longer work of Juvenal des Ursins.

We must mention likewise another curious document referring to the history of the reigns of Charles VI. and Charles VII. It is the *Journal d'un Bourgeois de Paris*, edited for the first time by Godefroy, together with the memoirs we have just been noticing, and which has found its place in all the large collections of autobiographies.

Two works appear to be here put together under the same title. The former, beginning with the year 1409, takes us as far as 1431; the latter then steps in, and follows the course of events to the year 1449. *Bourgeois* No. 1 was, according to all probability, a Paris *curé* and a doctor of divinity; *bourgeois* No. 2 modestly proclaims himself *l'un des plus parfaits clercs de l'université*. All that can interest a Parisian contemporary of the Cabochians and the Flayers is related, and the dismal catalogue gives us a slight idea of all the miseries, both public and private, which made of French life at that time one long tragedy. Riots and famine, plunder and massacres, hangings at Montfaucon, depreciation of the coinage—the list is so appalling that it sickens us to look at it. " Hélas ! " exclaims the *bourgeois*, " je ne cuide mie que depuis le roi Clovis France fut aussy désolée et divisée comme elle est aujourd'huy. . . . Le royaume de France va de mal en pis, et peut on mieulx dire *la terre déserte* que la terre de France." We regret to say that our two annalists are very unpatriotic ; their wishes are entirely on the side of the English, and the second especially repeats against Joan of Arc the calumnious imputations which passed current in the camp of the Duke of Bedford. Mixed up with well-authenticated details, there are many anecdotes of doubtful origin ; and the fancies, wishes, and imaginings of the Parisian populace are faithfully reproduced.

We possess a third journal of the same kind. The third *bourgeois* was a contemporary of Francis I., and therefore does not come within the scope of the present work. Our Parisian fifteenth-century clergymen have not yet been identified. All we know is the extreme character of their political sentiments. Rabid Burgundians, they never lose an opportunity of expressing their opinions, and inveighing in the strongest possible manner against the Armagnacs. They are two amongst the large company of chroniclers who took Monstrelet as their guide, but who do not equal him in point of talent. The *Journal* amply justifies its title; it is merely a succession of short, dull entries, extending, as we have said, from 1409 to 1449. Finally, Salmon, secretary to King Charles VI., has left memoirs, which are full of interest, on the first half of the fifteenth century; subdivided into fifty-five chapters, they contain historically an account of the author's travels in Italy and in England, where he had been sent on diplomatic errands. Salmon was perfectly acquainted with the causes of the feud which had broken out between the Burgundians and the Armagnacs, and he explains them better, perhaps, than any of his contemporaries.

There are few episodes in the whole history of France so touching as that of Joan of Arc. The genius of Schiller and the talent of Southey have thrown the garb of poetry around one of the noblest characters which our neighbours can boast of, and have made us forget the misrepresentations of Shakespeare and Voltaire's shameful ribaldry. M. Michelet's touching chapters and M. Wallon's excellent monograph are, no doubt, the best modern sources for the history of the Maid of Orleans; but if we want to turn to original documents, and to accounts given by contemporary writers, we should consult the *Procès de Jeanne d'Arc*, published by the *Société de l'Histoire de France;* the

Mystère du Siège d'Orléans, which forms part of the *Collection de Documents Inédits;* and Cousinot's *Chronique de la Pucelle*, an excellent edition of which was given, a few years ago, by M. Vallet de Viriville. We shall notice these various works in succession, beginning with the one mentioned last.

It is more than two hundred years since the learned Godefroy printed, in his *recueil* of historians of the reign of Charles VII., a work composed by an author whose name he had not been able to identify, and which he introduced to the reader in the following manner: "Autre histoire d'un auteur inconnu contenant partie du règne du même Charles VII., savoir depuis l'an 1422 jusques en 1429. Dans laquelle se voient diverses circonstances curieuses et particularités mémorables . . . surtout de la Pucelle d'Orléans, du surnom de laquelle cette histoire est communément appeleé." Reprinted by Roucher, M. Buchon, and M. Quicherat, this chronicle exercised the ingenuity of many critics; and M. Quicherat, after a long and attentive study, ascertained that it was borrowed, almost word for word, from another compilation still *inédit*, and entitled *Les Gestes des Nobles Françoys*, which was known to be written by a certain Cousinot. It was reserved for M. Vallet de Viriville to tear completely asunder the veil which still hung over the *Chronique de la Pucelle*, and the results at which he has arrived may be briefly stated as follows.

Guillaume I. Cousinot, Cousinet or Cosinot, distinguished as a barrister, was in the year 1406 councillor of the Duke of Burgundy in the Paris Parliament, at the time when the kingdom was rent asunder by the civil war, and apparently fated to perish for ever. During the next year, Louis d'Orleans having been murdered by order of John the Fearless, Petit, as every one knows, made a public justification of that crime. But soon, at the request of Valentine de Milan, dowager Duchess of Orleans, a new assembly was summoned at the Louvre, on the 11th of September, 1408. There, by the medium of Maître Guillaume Cousinot, "notable avocat au parlement," says Juvenal des Ursins, she defended her husband, and appeared in her turn as plaintiff against the Duke of Burgundy. Cousinot thus took a prominent part on the Armagnac side, and exposed himself to the hatred of the Burgundians. He occupied posts of considerable trust, discharged with much courage and patriotism the most arduous duties during the civil wars, and was rewarded for his services, in 1439, by his nomination as *président à mortier* in the Parliament of Paris. He was still living in 1422. The *Gestes des Nobles Françoys* composed by Guillaume I. Cousinot is nothing else, so far as the opening chapters are concerned, but a very succinct *résumé* of the *Grandes Chroniques de Saint Denis*, and other old historical documents. When we come to the reign of King John (1350), the work assumes a character of greater originality; the details increase in number, sketches of a certain importance take the place of dry and dull indications, and the account given us of the reign of Charles VI. clearly shows that the author was a witness of the events which he relates, and therefore quite competent to pass judgment upon them. Seven years of the reign of Charles VII. are described in the work. Here the *Gestes des Nobles Françoys* becomes a regular journal, the incidents being duly entered as they take place. We need scarcely tell our readers that, when he describes the tragic episodes of war between the Armagnacs and the Burgundians, Cousinot takes no trouble to conceal his political sympathies; quite the reverse. He is always temperate and calm in his sentiments; he never allows party spirit to carry him beyond the limits of the strictest impartiality; but, at the same time, he takes care to bring prominently forward all the acts capable of interesting the reader in favour of the Orleans family. We often find even events of a purely domestic nature assuming the proportions of historical episodes, and, to quote M. Vallet de Viriville, Guillaume Cousinot stands forth as a retainer of the house of Orleans, wearing honourably its colours and its coat of arms. But events hurry on; the hour of deliverance has struck for France, and La Pucelle appears on the banks of the Loire to raise the siege of Orleans. The narrative of Cousinot then assumes an entirely new character; it is a long, detailed, consecutive memoir, reproducing illustrative documents of an official nature: thus, the famous letter in which Joan of Arc summoned the English to depart from the land which they had so long occupied, and to recross the Channel. The *Geste* takes us to the 6th of July, when Charles VII. besieged Troyes, and it then stops abruptly, without giving us even the result of the campaign.

The *Chronique de la Pucelle*, as we have already hinted, is borrowed from the *Gestes des Nobles Françoys*, and was written by another Guillaume Cousinot, nephew of Guillaume I. Born about the year 1400, Cousinot de Montreuil, as he is generally called, rose to become one of the most important personages of his time. We find him secretary to the king, *maître des requêtes*, and privy councillor. In 1442 he was nominated senior president to the *Conseil Delphinal*, which soon assumed the title of Parliament of Grenoble. From 1438 to 1444 he discharged, in the capacity of royal commissioner, a number of important duties of an administrative nature; he then became the principal agent of the negotiations between France and England, proving himself equally capable of serving his country on the field of battle and at the council board. Cousinot's extraordinary abilities were thoroughly appreciated by Louis XI., who employed him upon the most delicate public affairs; and he lived to take a part in the States-

General assembled at Tours (1484), where his experience and skill proved of great assistance in the course of the deliberations. The work known by the title of *Chronique de la Pucelle* was composed by Guillaume II. Cousinot, and is the amplified continuation of the *Gestes* which we have been just now examining. It embraces the first seven years of the reign of Charles VII., and takes us as far as the month of September, 1429, a little later on than the *Geste*. Written in a much higher style than the compilation upon which it is based, it differs from it, besides, in various important particulars. Thus, when Guillaume I. describes the beginning of the reign of Charles VII., he merely alludes to the faults of that monarch; to the scandalous *insouciance* of his advisers; to the intrigues, follies, and misdeeds of the worthless favourites whom he had honoured with his confidence. This was, perhaps, to be expected from an author who, writing in the year 1429, was obliged to use extreme caution, and to avoid every statement which might give offence in high quarters. Guillaume II., on the contrary, being relatively unfettered, could accumulate details; and, accordingly, his narrative of the same facts is full of the most valuable and important revelations. The *Chronique de la Pucelle* is a journal of the sittings of the privy council; it explains, with the fullest details and the most remarkable shrewdness, the complications of politics, the affairs of the kingdom, and the moral causes which led to this or that special result. The account of Joan of Arc's arrival at Orleans is a mere reproduction of the narrative contained in the *Gestes*, for the simple reason that Guillaume I. had been an eye-witness of that event, and that, consequently, he was best qualified to describe it. On the other hand, the episode of *La Pucelle's* examination at Poitiers is one of the original parts in the *Chronique*, because Guillaume II. was present when it took place. His evidence, therefore, is extremely important here, and it cannot be adequately replaced by a reference to other contemporary memoirs. The *Chronique* and the *Gestes*, as a matter of fact, supplement each other, and give us, on the early part of the reign of Charles VII., a mass of particulars, the authenticity of which is fully borne out by comparison with independent sources. We have already observed that the work of Guillaume I. might almost be considered as a *domestic* chronicle—as a memoir of the house of Orleans. The majority of chronicles composed during the fifteenth century are, in like manner, *personal* works, if we may use such an expression—that is to say, family records or biographies in the strictest sense of the word; and it has, therefore, sometimes been supposed that the *Chronique de la Pucelle* was indebted for its title to the fact that it had been written under Joan of Arc's dictation. This hypothesis, however, is absolutely destitute of all solid foundation.

Before terminating this notice, we must say that Guillaume II. composed, in addition to the *Chronique de la Pucelle*, another work of still greater importance, alluded to by Lacroix de Maine and other authors, but which seems to have hopelessly disappeared. No traces of it, at any rate, can now be found in any public or private library.

Before examining the valuable collection of documents published by M. Quicherat under the title of *Procès de la Pucelle*, we must say a few words of a small chronicle which is generally printed as a sequel to the memoirs of the Cousinots, and which deals with the history of France during the fifteenth century, from the Burgundian point of view. We mean the *Chronique Normande* of Pierre Cochon. Very little is known about the writer, except that he was a native of Normandy, and that he died about the year 1434. His chronicle begins with the year 1181, and its first part is taken almost entirely from Monstrelet. When we come, however, to the middle of the fourteenth century, we find ourselves in the company of an eye-witness; and here the work has the importance belonging to contemporary evidence. Cochon re-echoes the popular passions of the time; a member of the University of Paris, he has endorsed with the utmost enthusiasm and bitterness the Burgundian sympathies of that body, and his memoirs read almost like a political pamphlet. John the Fearless is his hero. He defends his conduct, takes up his quarrel, and stands boldly by him up to the dastardly murder of the Duke of Orleans in the Rue Vieille du Temple; here a sense of shame makes him hesitate, and we are bound to add that the sight of his native country invaded by the English wakes up in him sentiments of patriotism to which he had not accustomed us. Pierre Cochon was a clergyman, and throughout his chronicle the interests and privileges of the Church occupy a prominent part. The memoirs which he has left us may be divided into two sections: the former, of a local character, deals exclusively with the history of the city of Rouen, and the latter treats of the general history of France. It has been noticed that Cochon is provokingly silent on the trial of La Pucelle and her melancholy death; and M. Vallet de Viriville ingeniously remarks that, whilst his feelings as a Frenchman prevented him from expressing approbation of so ill-judged a measure, his delicate position in a town then occupied by the English obliged him to say nothing which might irritate the invaders. We need scarcely say that Pierre *Cochon* must not be mistaken for Pierre *Cauchon*, Bishop of Beauvais, who tried and condemned Joan of Arc. They belonged to different provinces, and, in spite of an apparent similarity of names, they had in common no family ties whatever. The chronicler's name is not, we grant, a very dignified one;

Cauchon, on the other hand, is derived from the Latin *calx*, which, in the dialect both of Normandy and of Picardy, has produced *caucu* = *chausse*, and *cauchon* = *chausson*.

CHAPTER XV.

THE MAID OF ORLEANS—"MYSTÈRE DU SIÈGE D'ORLÉANS"—JEAN DE WAVRIN—CHRISTINE DE PISAN.

WE now come to the voluminous work of M. Jules Quicherat, *Procès de Condamnation et de Réhabilitation de Jeanne d'Arc*, a publication the study of which is indispensable for those who wish to be thoroughly acquainted with the life of the Maid of Orleans. The learned editor has not only collected all the documents referring to both trials, but also the allusions, testimonies, and evidence of every description to be found in the annalists and historians of the fifteenth century, French, Burgundians, and foreigners. His bibliographical account is as complete as possible, and there are few *causes célèbres* on which we possess such an amount of valuable information. The documents bearing upon the first trial, the trial of condemnation, are given in the first volume, and we can see, by studying these pieces, the futility of the proofs on which the sentence was delivered. When, during the reign of Charles VII., a fresh inquiry was instituted for the purpose of revising and annulling the original one, public opinion had forestalled the decision of the king, and in the mind of most impartial judges the condemnation was deemed null, both on account of the absence of a civil judgment, and also because the usual formalities had not been carried out. As early as the year 1440, we find the following passage in a small poem entitled *Le Champion des Dames*, which was dedicated to the Duke of Burgundy, the very prince who caused Joan of Arc to be delivered over to the English. One of the characters having maintained that *Outrecuidance* (conceit) had ruined the maid, and that Reason had caused her to be burned at Rouen, *Franc-vouloir* (free-will) answers:

> "Your arguments do not avail much
> Against the innocent maid,
> Or that of the secret judgments
> Of God upon her she should feel any the worse;
> And it is right that every one should agree
> To give her honour and glory,
> For her most excellent virtue,
> For her strength and her victory."[1]

---

[1] "Guères ne font tes arguments
Contre la Pucelle innocente,
Ou que des secretz jugements
De Dieu sur elle pis on sente;
Et droit est que chacun consente
À lui donner honneur et gloire
Pour sa vertu très-excellente,
Pour sa force et pour sa victoire."

Martial d'Auvergne, another contemporary poet, rightly described, in his *Vigiles de Charles VII.*, the trial as an iniquitous one, because the same persons were both judges and plaintiffs :

> " Lui firent ung tel quel procès
> Dont les juges estoient partie."

It is not our business here to go through the various circumstances of the trial of rehabilitation ; they have been fully described by M. Wallon in his history of Joan of Arc, and the reader who cares to examine the case for himself, can easily do so with the help of the documents published in the second volume of M. Quicherat. There is no doubt, and the learned editor is the first to acknowledge it, that the trial of condemnation shows a far greater amount of skill than the other one. The manner in which the documents are arranged and commented on, the lucidity of the discussion, the classing and selecting of the witness, are extremely remarkable. But, on the other hand, in the inquiry which led to the rehabilitation, no real care was needed. There were few witnesses to examine, no contradiction to expect, no arguing worth the name ; in fact, the result was known beforehand.

The documents referring to the rehabilitation of the Maid of Orleans occupy the second and third volumes of M. Quicherat's work ; the last two are taken up by *testimonia*, bibliographical tables, and information of every kind on the principal events in the life of the heroine.

Amongst the numerous publications issued by the French Government in the *Collection des Documents Inédits*, we must notice a kind of mystery or dramatic poem entitled *Le Mystère du Siège d'Orléans*. We mention it here because it is important both from an historical and a literary point of view. Under its primitive shape, it seems to have been performed publicly as early as the year 1435, on the anniversary of the raising of the siege, and again in 1439. The *rédaction* we possess, however, in which it is not difficult to trace the collaboration of several authors belonging to different epochs, should be ascribed to the year 1456. It is a very extensive development of the original text, and, as the title itself sufficiently proves, it must be regarded as a veritable historical compilation, intended to render the festival more attractive by the addition of dramatic performances, and, at the same time, to keep up amongst the good people of Orleans the spirit of patriotism. The *Mystère* was represented, with more or less excisions and in various forms, during the latter half of the fifteenth century. Like most of the monuments of the mediæval stage, it has very little artistic merit to boast of, and the 20,529 lines of which it consists are, to all intents and purposes, a metrical gazette or chronicle recording the chief episodes of the siege. King Charles VII. is introduced imploring the assistance of the Almighty, but ready, at the same time, to retire from a desperate contest, and feeling that the taking of Orleans by the English must carry along with it the submission of the whole kingdom. The intercession of the Blessed Virgin, and the prayers of Saint Euvertus and Saint Aignan, formerly Bishops of Orleans, obtain the welcome assurance that France shall be delivered from the English invaders. God declares that the French are bearing the just punishment of all their misdeeds—

> "And I wish them to be warned
> That they shall be severely punished." [1]

At the same time the archangel Saint Michael is instructed to start immediately for Domrémy—

> "Which is situated in the land
> And lordship of Vaucouleur," [2]

in quest of the maid through whose instrumentality the deliverance of the realm is to be brought about. Alain Chartier, in his *Quadriloge Invectif*, had already lectured the various orders of the State on their vices, and on that neglect of duty which, during the reign of Charles VI., had well-nigh brought France to ruin. The anonymous author of the *Mystère* takes up the same strain; but he then introduces Joan of Arc, and gives us the narrative

---

[1] "E vueil que on les admoneste
Que pugniz seront grandement."
[2] "Qui est situé en la terre
Et seigneurie de Vaucouleur."

of her exploits down to her triumphal entry into Orleans after the battle of Patay.

Respecting Jean de Wavrin, another contemporary of Monstrelet, we cannot do better than borrow a few particulars from the interesting and exhaustive preface written by the late Sir Thomas Duffus Hardy for the edition of the *Chroniques d'Angleterre*, published in the Master of the Rolls' series of *Chronicles and Memorials*.[1]

"Like his more widely known contemporary, Enguerrand de Monstrelet, Wavrin was born of a noble and ancient family; but a blot was equally on the escutcheon of both. As regards our author, he tells us this fact in a manner clearly indicating how little he viewed such a circumstance as reflecting discredit upon his name; and perhaps few will be found at this day to esteem him the less on that account. . . . He thus describes himself: ' I, John de Wavrin, knight, Lord of Forestel, illegitimate son of your grandfather, Monseigneur Robert de Wavrin, formerly knight, and lord of the lands and seignories of Wavrin, Lillers, and Malannoy.' " We have no certain indication of the year of Jean de Wavrin's birth, but we may assign it roughly to the end of the fourteenth century, somewhere about 1394. He was brought up, like most young men of noble family, to the profession of arms; and by referring to the list of names given by Sir T. D. Hardy in the notes to his introduction, we

---

[1] Preface, page xviii.

find that several of the Wavrins distinguished themselves during the Middle Ages on the battlefield. One of them was killed at the siege of Ptolemaïs in 1169; another was taken prisoner at Bouvines, with his three sons; Robert de Wavrin was present at the battle of Poitiers in 1356; Froissart mentions a Sire de Wavrin amongst the knights slain at Rosebecke; "le Seigneur de Wavrin et son fils" died for their country at Agincourt; finally, Philippe de Wavrin took part in the battle of Montlhéry.

It appears that our Seigneur de Forestel was advanced in age when he undertook to appear before the public in the capacity of a chronicler. His arm was no longer strong enough to mind the sword, but it had still sufficient vigour to use the pen; and in his prologue he gives as an excuse for writing, that he is incapacitated for the busy duties of the soldier's profession: "Feeling within me that old age is approaching, and that I can no longer follow the profession of arms, nor prosecute long voyages, as I did aforetime with you" (his nephew Waleran), "and in the company of many other princes and knights, which now, through the good pleasure of our Lord God, I have quitted, without blame or reproach."

The epoch of Jean de Wavrin's death is as difficult to determine as that of his birth. We shall quote another passage from Sir T. D. Hardy's introduction: "His chronicle, as it is at present known to us, concludes somewhat abruptly at the end of chapter xxxii., with Edward's letter to the men of Bruges, dated the 29th of May, 1471; but the relation of the taking, by the King of Portugal, of the city of Azille, in Africa, by assault on the 24th of August, 1471, is given by Wavrin in chapter xxiv. The portion of this narrative which follows from chapter xxiv. is based upon, and, as regards the principal portion, is closely translated from, a contemporary English narrative of the 'arrivall of Edward IV. in England, and the finall recouerye of his kingdomes from Henry VI., A.D. mcccclxxj.' Wavrin, it is conjectured, wrote two accounts of the progress of King Edward IV. in recovering his crown; one immediately upon the news of Edward's victories reaching the court of the Duke of Burgundy, and the second after he had become acquainted with the English narrative. The earlier relation appeared in the first edition of his sixth and last volume; the subsequent account was intended to take the place of the former in the revised edition, the materials for which he was preparing when overtaken by death. He did not, probably, survive very long the period of Edward's recovery of the crown of England. Assuming the time of his birth to be satisfactorily referred to about the year 1394, he may be said to have died an octogenarian, in or about 1474." [1]

The chronicle of Jean de Wavrin is entitled

---

[1] pp. xxi., xxii.

Recueil des Croniques et Anchiennes Istoires de la Grant Bretaigne, à présent nommée Engleterre. It was originally intended to be comprised in four volumes, each volume being subdivided into six books, and each book comprising an unequal number of chapters. Referring the reader to the very full and minute analysis given by Sir T. D. Hardy (introd. xlix.–li.), we need only say here that the fourth volume of the chronicles, as designed in the first instance, ends with the death of King Henry IV. in 1413, and was probably compiled between the years 1445 and 1456. The fifth volume, written later on by Jean de Wavrin as a continuation of the previous work, takes us to the year 1443, when the inhabitants of Dieppe were succoured by the Dauphin Louis, son of King Charles VII. It relates the history of the Maid of Orleans, and of her great undertaking for the deliverance of her native country from the English. The sixth and last volume, as it was originally published, bore the following title, *En ce Livre sont Escriptes les Guerres Advenues en France, en Angleterre et en Bourgoine depuis l'an 1444 jusques en l'an 1471.* As we have already hinted, it was revised for a second edition, the author inserting at the commencement a long account of the expedition despatched against the Turks in 1444. This armament, fitted out partly at the expense of Philip, Duke of Burgundy, was under the command of Waleran de Wavrin, so far, at least, as the duke's contingent was concerned.

With reference to the sources from which Jean de Wavrin has taken the materials of his chronicle, we may name Matthew Paris and the *Brut*, for the early part of the history of England; where the *Brut d'Engleterre* ceases, Froissart becomes the principal authority, although the narrative of the great annalist is not strictly followed, even when, according to all probability, he has supplied the information. Sometimes the narrative is abridged, sometimes episodes are transposed, occasionally other sources are consulted. Here we find great anxiety to invoke the authority of Froissart, and to leave him the responsibility of the events described; further on, Wavrin, on the contrary, repudiates Froissart altogether, and would appear as the original narrator of the facts he unfolds before us. Monstrelet and Lefevre de Saint-Remy have also been consulted by our chronicler, but with a liberty which must exonerate him from the charge of being a mere plagiarist; and, finally, he acknowledges his obligation to the *Chroniques de Saint Denis*. Respecting the sixth volume, where Jean de Wavrin describes contemporary events, and which is, therefore, the most important part of his work, Sir T. D. Hardy considers it as being really a second and revised edition of the continuation of Monstrelet's chronicle.

As late as the sixteenth century Clément Marot said—

> "D'avoir le prix en science et doctrine
> Bien mérita de Pisan la Christine."

This praise is somewhat above the mark, but still there is no doubt that the elegant authoress to whom we are indebted for the *Livre des Faictz et Bonnes Mœurs du Roi Charles V.*, was a person of remarkable talent, and the historical work we have just mentioned entitles her to a distinguished place in our volume. Very few biographical details have been preserved on Christine de Pisan, and all our information is derived from the scanty particulars she has herself furnished in her various writings. She was born at Venice, about the year 1363. Her father, Thomas de Pisan, councillor of the republic, and a man of considerable intellectual attainments, was invited by King Charles V. to come over to France in the quality of a court astrologer, and he arrived in Paris in 1368, together with his daughter Christine, who was then about five years old. They were both extremely well received at the Louvre, and, thanks to the protection of a powerful monarch, a career of prosperity seemed to be opening before them. Brought up at court as a young lady of rank, Christine soon displayed talents of no common order. Her accomplishments of various kinds, joined to the high and lucrative position which her father enjoyed at court, attracted a number of suitors.

Thomas de Pisan, however, gave the preference to a young man named Etienne du Catel, a native of Picardy, but who, although of good family, had no fortune. Through the influence of his father-in-law, he obtained the office of notary and secretary of the king, and the circumstances of the Pisans seemed especially brilliant, when the death of Charles V. inflicted upon them the first blow. Together with his protector, Thomas soon lost his influence; the greater part of his salary was suppressed, and the remainder paid at irregular intervals. He was no longer young, and the combined effects of infirmities, age, and sorrow, brought him to the grave. Etienne du Catel followed him very soon, leaving Christine with three children, a young widow of twenty-five, comparatively destitute and helpless. Her talents, however, had procured for her a number of distinguished friends. The Duke of Milan, the Earl of Salisbury, Henry of Lancaster, wished to attract her to their respective courts, but she preferred residing in France. Philip, Duke of Burgundy, took her eldest son into his service, and commissioned her to write the life of King Charles V. She had finished the first book of this work when the duke died. Notwithstanding her reputation as an authoress, and the support of her patrons, she was far from being in affluent circumstances. Charles VI. at last presented her with a sum of two hundred livres. The date of her death is still unknown, and it is a remarkable fact that a person so superior in every respect, and who at one time enjoyed such great and well-deserved popularity, should occupy in biographical dictionaries so insignificant a place.

On the 1st of January, 1403, Christine de Pisan had offered to the Duke of Burgundy, as a New Year's present, her book entitled *Le Livre de Mutacion de Fortune.* Philip was so struck with the talent and learning displayed by the authoress in her sketch of the various revolutions which have affected the history of the world, that he requested her, as we have already said, to take up as her next subject the biography of King Charles V. She consented, and the protection of the duke was useful in enabling her to consult all the documents, charters, and official pieces she stood in need of. The persons who had lived in the intimacy of the late king, or who had taken a part in the affairs of the State, were directed to give her all the assistance she might require ; and, thus amply furnished with materials, she wrote a work which is all the more valuable because its authenticity is beyond a doubt.

The *Livre des Faictz* is divided into three books. The first of these, entitled *Noblesse de Courage,* describes the education of Charles V., his manner of living and of travelling when he had ascended the throne, the order established in his palace, his patience, humility, chastity, and temperance. Christine also gives us curious particulars on the expenses of the royal household, and the minutiæ of court life.

The second book bears the title *Noblesse de Chevalerie*, and has for its subject the king's foreign policy, the wars he had to make, and the principal military events which occurred during his reign. Several chapters are devoted to notices of the king's brothers, and of other princes of the blood royal.

The third volume, treating of *Noblesse de Sagesse*, tells us first the science and arts which Charles had more specially cultivated; it dwells upon the prudence manifested by him in all his actions, and in support of this statement it quotes a number of memorable sayings. We have next a description of the visit made to Paris by the emperor Charles IV.; the election of Pope Clement, the death of the queen, that of the king, are duly registered, etc., etc. It is a matter of regret that Christine should have adopted an artificial order, instead of following the chronological one, and that she should have written her work in the strain of a panegyric; but the merit of the composition is not much affected by these drawbacks, for the most superficial acquaintance with the history of France during the reign of Charles V. will enable the reader to classify the events recorded in the three divisions of the book. As for the style, it is certainly far too heavy for our taste. Formed upon a close study of classical writers, it lacks the *naïveté* which delights us so much in Joinville, and that easy, graceful flow which is so characteristic of Froissart; but a vein of deep feeling runs through all her works, more than compensating for any redundancy of style, and she deserves a high place, side by side with Alain Chartier, Gerson, and the other patriotic writers, who maintained the dignity of France in the midst of the most terrible distresses, and who endeavoured to show that a speedy return to the path of duty, on the part of all the orders of the State, would be the best means of retrieving the past and preparing for the future.

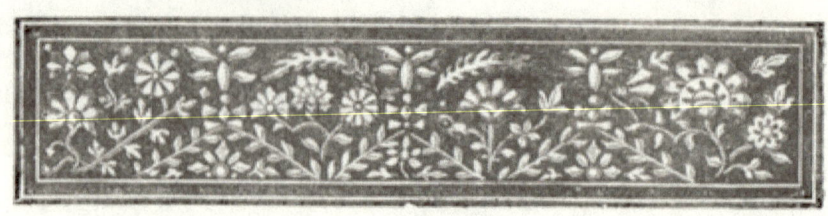

CHAPTER XVI.

THOMAS BASIN—PHILIPPE DE COMMINES—JEAN DE TROYES AND THE "CHRONIQUE SCANDALEUSE."

THE history of the reigns of Charles VII. and of Louis XI., composed by Thomas Basin, Bishop of Lisieux, was for a long time ascribed to a certain Belgian writer, named Amelgard, who lived during the fifteenth century. This opinion, endorsed by Labbe, Duchesne, and Dom Martène, who quoted long extracts from the work, seemed to recent critics, at any rate, open to controversy; for it was somewhat curious that a humble priest of Liège should have been favoured by Charles VII. with several private interviews, that at the suggestion of the king he should have composed an apology of the Maid of Orleans, and that he should have resided at one time in Trèves, and at another in Utrecht. Then, was it not extraordinary that a Liégeois should apply to his own fellow-countrymen the epithets "stulti" and "temerarii"? How-

ever, the history in question continued to pass as
the work of Amelgard, till a Flemish writer,
Antoine Meyer, author of the *Annales Flandriæ*,[1]
found out the mistake. He made great use of the
Latin history of the reigns of Charles VII. and
Louis XI., quoting long passages from it, sometimes transcribing whole chapters, and always with
expressions of most unqualified praise. At first he
merely describes him as an anonymous writer, about
whom all he knows is that he enjoyed the fami-
liarity of Charles VII.; further on, he designates him
by the title of Bishop of Louvain; then the Bishop
of Louvain is transformed into a Bishop of Lisieux,
and finally the name Thomas Basin is given in full.
It is useless to explain here by what train of circumstances, by what process of identification, the
real authorship of the work was ascertained. Suffice
it to say that a number of facts perfectly inex-
plicable on the supposition that the writer was a
Liégeois clergyman of the name of Amelgard, now
became quite clear; many an expression destitute of
all significance under the pen of a Flemish priest,
assumes an important meaning when written by
the Bishop of Lisieux; and, to mention only one
fact, it is perfectly consistent that a Norman prelate, associated by virtue of his dignity to the
deliberations and discussions of the provincial
assemblies, should have been a councillor and
adviser of Charles VII., trusted with the honour-

---

[1] Antwerp, 1561.

able duty of writing an apologetic memoir on La Pucelle, and sent by the King of France on certain political missions.

Thomas Basin was born at Caudebec, in 1412. His talent, learning, and shrewd common sense, backed by a certain amount of ambition, soon contributed to help him on the road to ecclesiastical promotion. He began by a canonry at Rouen; he was then named lecturer on canon law at the University of Caen; and, finally, the see of Lisieux having become vacant, he was presented to it by the unanimous votes of the cathedral chapter. His bull of institution bears date October 11, 1447, being the first year of the pontificate of Nicholas V., and the twenty-sixth of the reign of Henry VI., by the grace of God King of England and of France. Basin was obliged to act with the utmost caution in his new dignity; the tide was beginning to turn against the English, but they still held possession of Normandy, and the Bishop of Lisieux saw himself compelled to disguise, as carefully as he possibly could, his patriotic sympathies. He had good reason to hate the invaders; the misfortunes by which his family had been visited were all due to them, and he ascribed to them the calamities under which France had been suffering for nearly a century. He openly declared for Charles VII. as soon as he was able to do so, and was rewarded with a nomination to the office of councillor. We cannot enter here into the detail of the causes which led

Basin to join the League of the *Public Good* against Louis XI.—these causes have been very accurately described by M. Quicherat;[1] suffice it to say that the radical measures introduced by the new king seemed to the Bishop of Lisieux dangerous for the safety of the realm. Two things especially offended him, viz. the law against hunting, and the decree ordering all the cathedral churches, parishes, and religious communities to send in a statement of their revenues and properties, whatever might be their origin and nature. At all events, Basin, in the first place, was prohibited from appearing at court; he then was sentenced to exile, deprived of his see and of his temporalities. Then it was that he retired to Louvain, where he lectured on law, and afterwards to Utrecht. Sixtus IV. named him Archbishop of Cæsarea, *in partibus*. He died at Utrecht, December 30, 1491.

The work of the Bishop of Lisieux with which we have to do is the history of Charles VII. and of Louis XI., erroneously ascribed, as we have already stated, to Amelgard. M. Michelet calls it "une satire de Louis XI.," and Legrand describes the author as "très envenimé contre Louis XI." The portion referring to this monarch seems to have been composed between 1471 and 1472; that is to say, at the very time when the disgraced bishop, concealed at Trèves, was endeavouring to avoid the wrath of the offended king. It must be acknowledged that he

---

[1] *Bibl. de l'École des Chartes*, 1re série, vol. iii.

was not then in a position to write impartially and calmly. M. Quicherat observes of him that he was "an upright, sincere, intelligent man, but his captious spirit prevented him from viewing events and appreciating characters with clearness, and his feelings were so easily moved that he could scarcely help being sometimes unfair." From the very beginning of his book, you can see at once this peculiar disposition of his mind, in the expression of hatred with which he visits indiscriminately all the English commanders, and the dissatisfaction he shows in describing the timid reforms introduced by Charles VII. This tone of universal condemnation increases a hundredfold when the reign of Louis XI. comes under notice, and when our author has to appreciate administrative changes of a far more sweeping character. As M. Quicherat observes, he is so eager to blame everything, to find fault with every one, that he scarcely allows himself time to narrate the incidents of the reign. Nothing is excused by him; Louis XI., for him, is merely a ruthless tyrant, destitute of every quality, without wit, without even eloquence, utterly unable to discriminate character, and to judge those with whom he has to do, or who are appointed to play a part in the carrying out of his government. At the same time, we must do Thomas Basin the justice to say that he hardly ever trusts merely to public rumour when he states facts; when he has not been an eye-witness, or when he could rely for information neither upon eye-witnesses nor upon official documents, he preferred being silent. His appreciations are generally untrustworthy; his facts are always well authenticated and reliable.

With Louis XI. the era of mediævalism definitively closes, and modern history begins. More than any other prince, perhaps, he contributed to found the French monarchy. Unfortunately, his government was one of violence and of dissimulation. Amongst the charges which history has justly brought against him, and for which there is no excuse whatever, we may name the deaths of Guyennec, Armagnac, and Nemours; the punishment of Cardinal Balue; his treachery in the case of the citizens of Liége; his want of faith when required to perform the conditions of treaties which he had signed with his own hand. The state of prosperity in which he left France may be adduced on the other side of the question. He obtained of John II. of Arragon the cession of Roussillon and Cerdagne; the betrothal of the dauphin procured to him Franche Comté and Artois; he confiscated Burgundy; the succession of René of Anjou brought to him that province, Maine, and Provence, in addition to eventual rights on the kingdom of Naples, which, unfortunately, led to a long period of disastrous wars. At home his levelling disposition destroyed the power of the nobles, and the principle he acted upon, of allowing nothing to birth and all to merit, justifies us in considering him as the representative of the modern system in politics and administration. Unfortunately, intellect with him was another term for duplicity and perfidy, and his endeavours to consolidate the national unity were carried out *per fas et nefas*. If the maxim so extolled by a certain class of statesmen, that the end justifies the means, be sound, then the appreciation of Duclos is a correct one: " Louis XI. fut également célèbre par ses vices et ses vertus, et tout mis en balance, c'était un roi." Commines, too, would have spoken the truth when he says: " Encore fait Dieu grand grâce à un prince, quand il sçait le bien et le mal, et par espécial quand le bien l'emporte, comme au roi nostre maistre dessus dit." But history is bound to deal more sternly with a character such as Louis XI., and, whilst acknowledging the successful results of his policy, we cannot approve of the means by which that policy was carried out.

The dexterity with which the wily monarch managed to extricate himself from all the apparently overwhelming difficulties by which he was beset during the course of his reign, had excited the admiration of some statesmen who, even then, were inaugurating that immoral system which we may call "the politics of accomplished facts." Philippe de Commines, originally the adviser of the Duke of Burgundy, abandoned his master in 1472, and attached himself to Louis XI., who rewarded him handsomely for his defection. Named successively a councillor, *Sénéchal* of Poitou, Lord of Argenton and of other estates, Commines rendered to the King of France the most important services. Born in 1445 at the castle of Commines, in Flanders, he died in 1509. At the beginning of the reign of Charles VIII., he espoused the cause of the Duke d'Orleans, and was for eight months in one of those iron cages with which Cardinal Balue had seemed so painfully acquainted. "Plusieurs les ont maudites," says he, speaking of those cages, "et moi aussi qui en ai tâté sous le roi d'à présent." Charles VIII. employed him in several negotiations, but Louis XII. did not avail himself of his services. During the period of comparative retreat which marked the latter years of his life, he wrote his memoirs, which are, no doubt, extremely remarkable for the common sense they display, but which are composed from the stand-point of a very easy, elastic code of political morality. The work of Commines extends from 1464 to 1483, and from 1488 to 1494. It was published for the first time in 1524, with the following title: *Cronique et Hystoire Faicte et Composée par feu Messire Philippe de Commines;* but this edition includes only the first six books of the memoirs, and ends with the death of Louis XI. The remainder appeared in 1528, as the *Chroniques du Roy Charles Huytiesme.* Absorbed by the study of effects and causes, full of admiration for successful intrigue, Commines is in his glory when he can follow three or four political combinations which are unfolding themselves simultaneously. If he holds in his hand all these diplomatic threads, which cross one another, divide, meet again, and yet never get confused, his joy is boundless. "Et se menoient tous ces marchés," he exclaims, "en un temps et en un coup." Sometimes the reader perceives that Commines had occasional scruples of conscience respecting the actions of his royal master; but these qualms are soon quieted by the thought that, after all, "Louis XI. étoit un des plus sages hommes et des plus subtils qui aient regné en son temps;" and that "au fort, en nul n'y a mesure parfaite en ce monde." It is only fair to add that Commines was no friend to despotism. In several passages of his memoirs he expresses his admiration of the English form of government (iv. i., v. 19); and he thus exposes the secret thoughts of those who would not consent to the summoning of the States-General for fear of curtailing the authority of the crown: "Ces paroles servoient et servent encore à ceux qui sont en autorité et crédit sans en rien l'avoir mérité, et qui ne sont propices d'y être, et n'ont accoutumé que de flageolet et fleuretter en l'oreille, et parler de choses de peu de valeur, et craignent les grandes assemblées, *de peur qu'ils ne soient connus, ou que leurs œuvres ne soient blasmées.*"

It is impossible, however, to give an adequate idea of Commines as a writer and historian without transcribing at least one extract from his admirable memoirs, and we have selected, by way of specimen, the following striking paragraph:—

"Is there any king or prince that hath power to levy one penny upon his subjects besides his domains, without leave or consent of those that must pay it, unless it be by tyranny and violence? A man will say that sometimes a prince cannot tarry to assemble his estates, because it would require too long time. Whereunto I answer that if he move a war offensive, there needeth no such haste: for he may have leisure enough at his own pleasure to make preparation. And further, he shall be much stronger, and much more feared of his enemies, when he moveth war with the consent of his subjects, than otherwise. Now, as touching a war defensive, that cloud is seen long before the tempest fall, especially when it is foreign war; and in this case good subjects ought not to complain, nor refuse anything that is laid upon them. Notwithstanding such invasion cannot happen so suddenly, but that the prince may have leisure at the least to call together certain wise personages, to whom he may open the causes of the war, using no collusion therein, neither seeking to maintain a trifling war upon no necessity, thereby to have some colour to levy money. Money is also necessary in time of peace to fortify the frontiers, for the defence of those that dwell upon them, lest they be taken unprovided;

but this must be taken measurably. In all these matters the wisdom of a sage king sufficeth; for if he be a just prince, he knoweth what he may do, and not do, both by God's law, and man's. To be short, in mine opinion, of all seniories in the world that I know, the realm of England is the country where the commonwealth is best governed, the people least oppressed, and the fewest buildings and houses destroyed in civil war, and always the lot of misfortune falleth upon those that be authors of the war.

"Our king is the prince in the whole world that hath least cause to allege that he hath privileges to levie what him listeth upon his subjects, considering that neither he nor any other prince hath any power to do so. And those that say he hath, do him no honour, neither make him to be esteemed any whit the mightier prince thereby; but cause him to be hated and feared of his neighbours, who for nothing would live under such a government. But if our king, or those that seek to magnify and extol him, should say: 'I have so faithful and obedient subjects that they deny me nothing I demand, and I am more feared, better obeyed, and better served of my subjects than any other prince living; they endure patiently whatsoever I lay upon them, and soonest forget all charges past;' this, methink (yea, I am sure), were greater honour to the king than to say: 'I levie what me listeth, and have privileges so to do, which

I will stoutly maintain'"   (Danett's translation, fo. 1596).[1]

[1] "Y a il roy ne seigneur sur terre qui ait povoir, oultres on domeine, de mettre ung denier sur ses subjectz, sans octroy et consentement de ceulx qui le doibvent payer, sinon par tyrannie ou violence? On pourroit respondre qu'il y a des saisons qu'il ne fault pas attendre l'assemblée; et que la chose seroit trop longue à commencer la guerre et à l'entreprendre. Ne se fault point tant haster, l'on a assez temps : et si vous dis que les roys et princes en sont trop plus fors, quant ils entreprennent du conseil de leurs subjectz, et en sont plus crainctz de leurs ennemys. Et quant se vient à soy deffendre, on voit venir ceste nuee de loing, especiallement quand c'est d'estrangiers : et à cela ne doibvent les bons subjectz rien plaindre ne refuser : et ne sçauroit advenir cas si soubdain où l'on ne puisse bien appeler quelques ungz et personnaiges telz que l'on puisse dire : 'Il n'est pas faict sans cause,' et en cela ne user point de fiction, ne entretenir une petite guerre à voulenté et sans propos, pour avoir cause de lever argent. Je sçay bien qu'il fault argent pour deffendre les frontieres et les environs garder ; quant il n'est point de guerre, pour n'estre point surprins ; et le tout faire moderement : et à toutes ces choses sert le sens d'ung sage prince : car s'il est bon, il congnoist qui est Dieu et qui est le monde, et ce qu'il doibt et peult faire et laisser. Or, selon mon advis, entre toutes les seigneuries du monde, dont j'ay congnoissance, où la chose publicque est mieulx traictee, où regne moins de viollence sur le peuple, et où il n'y a nulz ediffices abbatus, ny desmolis pour guerre, c'est Angleterre ; et tombe le sort et le malheur sur ceulx qui font la guerre.

"Nostre roy est le seigneur du monde qui le moins a cause de user de ce mot: 'J'ay privilege de lever sur mes subjectz ce qui me plaist,' car ne luy ne aultre ne l'a : et ne luy font nul honneur ceulx qui ainsi le dient pour le faire estimer plus grant, mais le font hayr et craindre aux voisins, qui pour riens ne vouldroient estre soubz sa seigneurie : et mesmes aucuns du royaulme s'en passeroient bien, qui en tiennent. Mais si nostre roy, ou ceux qui le veulent louer et agrandir, disoient : 'J'ay des subjetz si trés bons et trés loyaulx qu'ilz ne me refusent chose que je leur sçaiche demander, et suis plus crainct, obey et servy de mes subjectz que nul aultre prince qui vive sur la terre, et qui plus patiemment endurent tous maulx et

Mr. Hallam's appreciation of the distinguished writer whom we have just been examining may be quoted here, as remarkably correct: "The memoirs of Philip de Commines . . almost make an epoch in historical literature. If Froissart, by his picturesque descriptions and fertility of historical *invention*, may be reckoned the Livy of France, she had her Tacitus in Philip de Commines. . . . He is the first modern writer . . . who in any degree has displayed sagacity in reasoning on the characters of men, and the consequences of their actions, and who has been able to generalize his observation by comparison or reflection. . . . An acute understanding and much experience of mankind gave Commines this superiority; his life had not been spent over books; and he is consequently free from that pedantic application of history which became common with those who passed for political reasoners in the next two centuries."

One of the most valuable sources for the history of Louis XI. is the chronicle of Jean de Troyes, generally known by the title of *Chronique Scandaleuse*. It includes the narrative of events between 1460 and 1483, and the earliest edition of it has neither date nor author's name on the title-page. Lacroix du Maine, in his *Bibliothèque Française*, published in 1584, alludes to "Jean de Troyes,

---

toutes rudesses, et à qui moins il souviengne de leurs dommaiges passez,' il me semble que cela lui seroit grant ioz (et je dis la verité), non pas dire : ' Je prens ce que je veulx et en ay privilege ; il le me fault bien garder.' '·

historian François du temps de Louis XI." He then goes on to say, " Il a écrit la chronique du dit roi, laquelle est vulgairement appelée *La Chronique Scandaleuse*, à cause qu'elle fait mention de tout ce qu'a fait le dit roi, et récite des choses qui ne sont pas trop à son avantage, mais plutôt à son deshonneur et scandale." Notwithstanding this declaration, it will be evident to any one who takes the trouble of reading Jean de Troyes, that there is nothing whatever in his work to justify the description of *Chronique Scandaleuse*, and we must conclude, with Sorel and other critics, that the title was given by some publisher for the purpose of exciting curiosity and securing a sale. Brantôme, in his *Éloge de Charles VIII.*, alludes to a history of Louis XI., which was in the king's library, and which Francis I. would never allow to be printed, on account of its satirical character. That is, in all probability, the real *Chronique Scandaleuse*, and it would be curious to find it out and publish it.

With reference to the biography of Jean de Troyes we absolutely know nothing. Grosley, in his *Mémoire sur les Troyens Célèbres*, suggests that he may have been the son of that other Jean de Troyes who, according to Juvenal des Ursins, played an important part in the political disturbances which marked the reign of Charles VI., and who held the post of grand master of the artillery under Charles VII. The old relations of the father with the municipal body of Paris procured for the son the office of registrar (*greffier*) to the Hôtel de Ville. As Jean de Troyes, speaking of the sister of Louis XI., Joan of France, calls her his *trés redoutée dame*, it has been conjectured that he belonged to the household of that princess.

"Jean de Troyes," says Sorel, "is an honest *bourgeois*, who speaks very openly. We find in his work curious remarks on what took place in those days, such as you might expect from a man who knew the surface and outside of things, without having ever penetrated to their motives and circumstances." This very fact gives a great deal of interest to the memoirs of Jean de Troyes, which should be read immediately after those of Commines. The adviser of Louis XI. exposes the policy of the monarch, unravels his intrigues, and explains the secret causes of the events he relates. The registrar never dreams either of going to the bottom of political occurrences, or of accounting for them; he merely states them just as the king wished them to be known by the Paris *bourgeoisie* and by the common people. If we take, for instance, the well-known episode of the interview at Péronne, in 1468, Jean de Troyes gives us an account of the journey of Louis XI. as an ordinary thing; you would not suppose from his narrative that the king, a dupe of his own artifice, has imprudently placed himself at the discretion of the Duke of Burgundy, and that he has been his prisoner. The agreement signed at Péronne appears in the *Chronique Scandaleuse* as having been freely signed by Louis, who of his own accord decides upon joining Charles the Bold in an expedition against the inhabitants of Liége. When we have studied, in the pages of Commines, the real course of events as they actually occurred, we are interested in seeing how the king wished them to be known by his subjects, and the colouring he put upon them for the purpose of concealing both the dangers which had threatened him, and the humiliation which he had been obliged to put with. The memoirs of Jean de Troyes are full of particulars which he alone gives; they contain a number of details illustrating the habits, feelings, and domestic life of the Parisians; they make us acquainted with the political sympathies of the capital of France, and it is not too much to say that no work gives us a deeper insight into the history of Paris about the end of the fifteenth century. The great drawback to the narrative of Jean de Troyes is that the worthy registrar seldom speaks from actual observations. He is rather a collector of gossip, and therefore his statements are not always reliable; at all events, they require to be compared with those of Philippe de Commines and other writers. We must spare room for a couple of extracts from the *Chronique Scandaleuse*.

The first refers to the death of Charles the Bold,

Duke of Burgundy. On that subject Jean de Troyes is better informed than Philippe de Commines; and after describing the battle, the losses of the Burgundians, the pursuit of the Swiss, etc., he informs us that "on Monday, which was Twelfth Day (A.D. 1476), the Count de Campobasso met with a page that was taken prisoner, belonging to the Count de Chalon, who was with the Duke of Burgundy in the battle. This lad, upon examination, confessed the Duke of Burgundy was killed; and the next day, upon diligent search after him, they found him stripped stark naked, and the bodies of fourteen men were in the same condition, at some distance from each other. The duke was wounded in three places, and his body was known and distinguished from the rest by six particular marks, the chiefest of which was, the want of his upper teeth before, which were beaten out with a fall; the second was a scar in his throat, which was occasioned by the wound he received at the battle of Montlhéry; the third was his great nails, which he always wore longer than any of his courtiers; the fourth was another scar upon his left shoulder; the fifth was a fistula in his right groin, and the last was a nail that grew into his little toe. And, upon seeing all these abovementioned marks upon his body, his physican, the gentlemen of his bed-chamber, the Bastard of Burgundy, Messire Olivier de la Marche, his chaplain, and several other officers that were taken prisoners by the Duke of Lorraine, unanimously agreed it was the body of their lord and master, the Duke of Burgundy."

The second quotation describes the muster of troops made by Louis XI. in 1467:—

"On the fourteenth of September, the king, who had ordered the Parisians to make standards, published a proclamation commanding all the inhabitants from sixteen to threescore, of what rank or condition soever, to be ready to appear in arms that very day in the fields; and that those who were not able to provide themselves with helmets, brigandines, etc., should come armed with great clubs, under pain of death; which orders were punctually obeyed, and the greater part of the populace appeared in arms, ranged under their proper standard or banner, in good order and discipline, amounting to fourscore thousand men; thirty thousand of which were armed with coats of mail, helmets, and brigandines, and made a very fine appearance. Never did any city in the world furnish such a vast number of men, for it was computed there were threescore and seven banners or standards of tradesmen, without reckoning those of the court of Parliament, exchequer, treasury, mint, and Châtelet of Paris, which had under them as many or more soldiers than what belonged to the tradesmen's banners. A prodigious quantity of wine was ordered out of Paris, to comfort and refresh the vast body of men, which took up a vast tract of ground; extending themselves from the Lay-stall between St. Anthony's gate, and that of the Temple as far as the Town-ditch, upwards to the Wine-press; and from thence, along the walls of St. Antoine des Champs, to the Grange of Reuilly; and from thence to Conflans; and from Conflans, back again by the Grange aux Merciers, all along the river Seine, quite to the royal bulwark over against the Tower of Billy; and from thence, all along the Town-ditch on the outside, to the Bastille and St. Anthony's gate. In short, it was almost incredible to tell what a vast number of people there were in arms before Paris, yet the number of those within was pretty near as great."

CHAPTER XVII.

MOLINET—GUILLAUME DE VILLENEUVE—BOUCHET—JEAN MASSELIN.

MOLINET is not the first French mediæval author who combined the talent of a poet with that of a chronicler; Froissart's *joli buisson de Jonèce* is well known, and George Chastellain has left a volume of songs. We do not mention, of course, Robert Wace, Benoit de Sainte-Maure, and the numerous array of annalists who were *poet-historians* rather than *poets* and *historians*. Jean Molinet was born in a village of the Boulonnais, and he died at Valenciennes in 1507. After the death of his wife, he took orders, and obtained a canonry in the collegiate church of Valenciennes. He was the historiographer to the house of Burgundy, and subsequently librarian of Margaret of Austria, who governed the Netherlands on behalf of her father, the Emperor Maximilian I. It is chiefly as a poet that Molinet was appreciated by his contemporaries, and if we would form a just idea of the absurd character of his style, we cannot do better than turn to the satirical description which Rabelais gives of it in chapter liv. of the *Gargantua*. Never was criticism so thoroughly deserved, and the following specimen, which we take almost at random, will furnish an accurate idea of his *Temple de Mars, Complainte de Constantinople*, etc., etc. :—

> "Molinet[1] is neither without fame, nor without name.
> He has his sound, and, as you see, his voice.
> His sweet pleading pleases more than does your tune ; . . .
> For wind often comes to the small windmill."[2]

Amongst his historical works we would name the historical stanzas which he added to those of Georges Chastellain, entitled the *Recollection des Merveilles Advenues en nostre Temps*. This poem is a kind of review of the principal events which happened during the fifteenth century, such as the invention of printing, etc. Molinet thus alludes to the new process devised for multiplying the productions of the human mind :—

> "I have seen a great number
> Of printed books
> In order to draw to study
> Poor, impecunious people.

---

[1] *Molinet*, diminut. of *moulin*, old French *molin*, "a windmill" (low Latin, *molinus*).

[2] "Molinet n'est sans bruyt, ne sans nom, non.
Il a son son, et comme tu vois, voix.
Son doulx plaid plaist mieulx que ne faict ton ton ; . . .
Car soubvent vent vient au Molinet net."

> Thanks to these new fashions,
> Many a scholar will have
> A book of *decrees*, Bibles, and codes,
> Without giving much money."¹

The only work of Molinet which in the slightest degree justifies the reputation he enjoyed is his chronicle, which extends from the year 1474 to 1506, and is introduced by two prologues, having respectively the following mottoes:—"*Fundata est domus Domini super verticem montium*," and "*Militi est vita hominis super terram*." The *domus Domini*, we need hardly say, is the house of Burgundy, "la très illustre et réfulgente maison," as he designates it; and all the resources of metaphorical language, the whole Latin vocabulary, with its various combinations and associations, are employed for the purpose of describing the virtues, both civil and political, of the various princes and princesses who, from the days of Charles V., King of France, have ruled over the destinies of Burgundians. The royal family is described as a "liligerous orchard" (*vergier liligère*), and the Duke of Burgundy is praised for the energy he displayed in subduing "the *mu*-

---

[1] " J'ay veu grand multitude
De livres imprimés,
Pour tirer en estude
Povres mal argentés.
Par ces nouvelles modes
Aura maint escollier
Decret, Bibles, et codes,
Sans grand argent bailler."

tins rebellans, the *rebelles mutinants*, the *traffiqueurs séduisants*, and the *séducteurs traffiquants*." A whole work of considerable length, written in that style, is sufficiently tedious. When he is not hurried along by the vivacity of the narrative or the interest of historical descriptions, Molinet launches forth into the most incongruous platitudes, written in a ridiculously pompous style; and his faults as an author are all the more deplorable because he can relate a touching episode or sketch a war-picture with considerable vigour.

The last two books of Philippe de Commines contain a history of the reign of Charles VIII.; but the author, as we have already hinted, had incurred the king's displeasure in the early part of his reign, for having joined the faction of the Duke of Orleans, and he had even spent eight months as a prisoner in one of the iron cages of the castle of Loches. We are not surprised at finding, therefore, that he says nothing whatever about the States-General held at Tours, or about the regency of Madame de Beaujeu. Sent afterwards to Venice during the Italian expedition, and not having witnessed the greatest part of the events which occurred in consequence of that war, he merely describes the negotiation with which he was entrusted. Now, whilst, in his narrative of the mission to Venice, he displayed a foresight and a skill which deserve the highest praise, we cannot help, on the other hand, being struck by the unfairness he shows in his appreciation of a young monarch full of honour and of kindness, but whom he could not forgive what he regarded as an act of tyranny, although it was really an act of justice. For the reign of Charles VIII., then, Philippe de Commines is an insufficient authority, even so far as the expedition to Naples is concerned; and we must complete the details he gives us by referring to the memoirs of Villeneuve, who explains the consequences of the invasion, and the disasters which befel the French army.

Nothing certain is known about Guillaume de Villeneuve, except that he accompanied Charles VIII. to the kingdom of Naples, and was one of the officers intrusted with the difficult task of protecting the French conquest when the monarch had recrossed the Alps. It might have been expected that the yoke of France would not be patiently borne by the Italians, and that, at the very first opportunity, a rebellion would break out. Two months after his arrival at Naples, Charles VIII. received from Philippe de Commines an ominous letter, informing him that a formidable league of the sovereigns of Europe had been organized against him, for the purpose of stopping his retreat from Italy, and of reducing France to its original limits. Charles accordingly marched back towards the Apennines, leaving 4000 men, under the command of Gilbert de Montpensier, besides the small forces which garrisoned the chief towns. Villeneuve shut himself up in the castle of Trani, fully resolved to die rather than surrender. Betrayed by his own soldiers, he was taken prisoner and detained at Naples, where he wrote the memoirs of the campaign in which he had taken a prominent part. He subsequently recovered his liberty, and was named by Charles VIII. master of the royal household. The memoirs of Villeneuve contain local descriptions which can be found nowhere else; they are the only historical record of an authentic character describing the fatal results of the French expedition of 1494. The Italian campaign promised to be merely a brilliant military promenade, where the only trouble would be that of nominating governors, quartering the troops, and collecting the taxes; the result proved far otherwise, and the victory of Fornovo, decided as it was, had no other consequence but that of facilitating the retreat of the French.

The *Panegyrique du Chevalier sans Reproche* is mentioned here because, although it takes us as far down as the reign of Francis I. (far beyond the limits of our subject), it discusses likewise the events of the reign of Louis XI. The *Chevalier sans Reproche* is none other than Louis de la Trémouille, governor and lieutenant-general of Burgundy, who, born September 20, 1460, was killed at the battle of Pavia, February 24, 1525. Sent into Brittany at the head of an army by Madame de Beaujeu, the regent, he defeated the Duke d'Orléans (afterwards Louis XII.) at the battle of Saint Aubin du Cormier, and made him prisoner (1488); he went through the campaign of Naples with Charles VIII., helped Louis XII. to conquer the Milanese (1500), and failed completely in an expedition organized against the kingdom of Naples (1503). We next find him at the battle of Agnadel (1509), and at that of Novara (1513), where he was beaten by the Swiss, with whom he was obliged to conclude, at Dijon, an ignominious treaty. He was also present at the battle of Marignan (1515).

The author of the *Panegyrique* is a certain Jean Bouchet, born at Poitiers in 1476, and who, despite his great taste for literature, practised as an attorney (*procureur*) in his native city, as his father had done before him. He appears to have been very young when he attached himself to the fortunes of the La Trémouille family, and when Louis XII. died at Pavia, he resolved upon raising, as far as he could, a monument to the memory of a benefactor who had always honoured him with special marks of kindness. Bouchet was fifty years old then, and the *Panegyrique*, far from betraying signs of old age, is, on the contrary, characterized by an amount of imagination which is frequently quite juvenile. The title of the work must not lead us to suppose that it is written in a tone of adulation, or as a declamatory memoir; Bouchet always remains, notwithstanding his political fervour, within the bounds of truth. He describes briefly the military exploits and political labours of La Trémouille, placing on his lips very appropriate remarks, and characterizing most accurately his courage and his prudence. The chief interest, however, of these memoirs is the picture they give of domestic life, of a nobleman's home in the France of the fifteenth century, and of the relations which then existed between a landlord and his dependents. The great defect of Jean Bouchet is one which he shared with all those amongst his contemporaries who aspired to the honour of being considered scholars, viz. a passion for classical allusions, and for the traditions of Greek and Latin mythology. The chief deities of Mount Olympus appear in his pages: Minerva cautions the young hero against the seductions of love; Juno gives him lessons on political science; and Mars, of course, teaches him all the mysteries of the art of war. Some of the speeches ascribed to these fictitious characters contain very accurate and shrewd observations; but, on the whole, they produce a disagreeable effect, and throw upon the composition an air of unreality which detracts from the merits of the volume.

We have seen that the memoirs of Guillaume de Villeneuve and of Jean Bouchet have a fragmentary and, if we may so say, a special character. The volume we are about to notice is of a totally different nature; it treats of interests which affected the whole of France, and the administration of the kingdom in its various branches forms the topic of Jean Masselin's interesting journal.

We have only the scantiest possible details of Jean Masselin, and we shall borrow them from M. Bernier's biographical notice. The name of Masselin occurs nowhere previous to the month of May, 1468, when we find it on the capitular registers of the cathedral of Rouen, to which he was attached as a canon. Received doctor in civil and ecclesiastical law, Masselin enjoyed the reputation of being a learned and distinguished man— *egregius vir et scientificus,* says a chronicler ; and, as such, he was habitually selected by the chapter to be their spokesman on great occasions.

Louis XI. died August 30, 1483. He left France full of abuses and of irregularities, which it was absolutely necessary to destroy. Was a lad of thirteen governing under the authority of a woman, Madame de Beaujeu, capable of facing the difficulties of the situation ? It was thought not. The States-General were summoned at Tours ; and the causes which led to their convocation are duly and minutely set forth in the journal we are now introducing to our readers. All the provinces of the kingdom sent representatives ; the bailiwick of Rouen deputed Jean Masselin, official of the archbishop, together with Georges de Clere, knight, Jacques de Croismare, and Pierre Daguenet. Jean Masselin was present at the States-General during the whole time of their meeting—that is to say, from January 5, 1484, to March 14 of the same year. His journal contains the fullest particulars on his parliamentary career, and a contemporary, alluding to the part he took in the proceedings of the Assembly, says, "Ut summus orator, ante reges et principes elegantissimus pro bono publico fecit orationes." Four years after the meeting of the States-General, Jean Masselin was named Dean of Rouen, and he died, from the consequences of a short illness, in the night of the 26th to the 27th of June, 1500.

It does not appear that our hero composed any other work besides the remarkable memoirs he wrote on the transactions of the Assembly at Tours. This journal had long remained unpublished, but it had been often consulted and turned to excellent use by historians, who were unanimous in regarding it as one of the most curious monuments left to us by the fifteenth century. The edition prepared for the *Collection des Documents Inédits* by M. Adhelm Bernier is in every way worthy of the series to which it belongs.

There is no doubt that Jean Masselin, as M. Picot remarks,[1] deserves a distinguished place amongst the greatest political orators which France can boast of. The States-General, which might have been productive of so much good by the introduction of necessary reforms, ultimately failed, through the weakness of some of the deputies and the venality of others. But Masselin identified himself from the very first with those who asserted the

---

[1] *Histoire des États Généraux.*

right of the nation to discuss, vote, and assess the taxes; and "his independent eloquence made him the natural interpreter of the States whenever the deputies showed any amount of courage." One of his most noteworthy speeches is the one which he delivered on the 20th of February, and in which he discussed the various items of expenditure to be met by the taxes. According to him, there are not more than four kinds of necessary expenses: 1. The king's household; 2. the salaries of the judges and magistrates; 3. the maintenance of the army; 4. the various pensions granted by the Crown. "All these matters," observed Masselin, "are so intimately connected together, that not one of them can be treated separately; if money is squandered upon one of them, the others must necessarily suffer. The deputies, therefore, have a right to insist on examining these four points together; but, in the first place, it is indispensable that they should possess an accurate statement of the income resulting from the royal domains, and from the aids of every kind paid into the king's exchequer, for it is impossible that the budget of expenses should be fixed without a knowledge of what the revenue amounts to." Our readers cannot fail to notice the boldness of the step thus taken by Jean Masselin, and the important precedent it created. For the first time, the States-General had in their hands all the elements of the financial problem, and they had wrested from the king's *entourage* the real power, by obtaining the control over the exchequer. So decided, so unheard-of a procedure was regarded as scandalous; obstacles were thrown in the way of a solution, and the returns claimed by the deputies were so manifestly false, that, rather than be put to the long and useless task of correcting these returns, the States-General, on the motion of one of the members, determined upon proposing that the country should pay, for the space of two years, the annual sum which was raised at the end of the reign of Charles VIII. After that epoch, the States were to be again summoned, and a final resolution taken. In support of this *mezzo termine*, Jean Masselin made a speech which M. Picot justly describes as a *magnifique résumé*. It shows what an amount of good sense, knowledge of public business, and true patriotism was to be found in that gathering of men, till then unknown, who had come forth from their chapter-houses. their guild-halls, and their mansions, to carry on together the important work of administrative reform.

The few remarks we have thus made show the great value of Masselin's journal towards an accurate knowledge of France during the fifteenth century. The only regret we feel is that a monument of the same kind should not exist for all the other assemblies of the States-General.

CHAPTER XVIII.

LEGISLATIVE MONUMENTS—LAWS OF THE BARBARIANS—THE FEUDAL SYSTEM AND THE "COUTUMES"—PUBLICISTS.

AFTER the notice we have given of M. Adhelm Bernier's publication, we need scarcely tell our readers that a study of mediæval history would be incomplete if we did not endeavour to form some slight idea of the legislative enactments made at various epochs, and which, modified from time to time according to the vicissitudes of the kingship and the progress of the feudal system, contributed to make up the body of French law. To the Merovingian epoch belong the Salic law, the Ripuarian code, and that of the Burgundians. Respecting the first of these monuments, which we must consider as a tarif of compensations and not as a real code, we may say briefly that, according to the opinion of a distinguished legist, M. Pardessus, the text which has reached us is the Latin translation of a document originally composed in the German language. But, further, we do not even possess the editions supposed to have been drawn up by the order of Clovis; and the fact that the sentences of which the Salic law consists vary in number from sixty-five to a hundred, according to the manuscripts, is explained by the circumstance that Clovis himself and his successors added fresh enactments to those originally laid down. Charlemagne was the last Frankish king who issued a revised edition of the Salic law; if, indeed, this name is not more appropriately reserved for the body of customs preserved traditionally amongst the various tribes, rather than to a written document which has very little indeed of a legislative character.

The Ripuarian code is so far similar to the Salic law that it consists chiefly of penal sentences (eighty-nine or ninety-one, according to the manuscripts), but differs from it because it is less uncouth in its form, and has retained considerable traces of Roman legislation. As its name indicates, it was compiled for the use of the Frankish tribes which, instead of penetrating into Gaul at the time of the general invasion, remained quartered on the banks of the Rhine (*ripuarii*). Drawn up for the first time by Theodoric I., King of Austrasia, at Châlons-sur-Marne, between the years 511 and 534, it was successively revised by Childebert, Clotaire, and Dagobert I.; Charlemagne himself, towards the beginning of the ninth century, introducing into it important alterations and additions.

Gregorius Turonensis, alluding to Gondebaud, king of the Burgundians, remarks, *Burgundionibus leges mitiores instituit, ne Romanos opprimerent.* This code of laws, known generally by the name of *Loi Gambette*, was issued in 468, and is, in fact, an attempt to soften down and *humanize*, if we may employ this expression, the rude and savage customs of the Teutonic invaders. It is the only monument of legislation connected with these tribes which enforces the rights of hospitality, and punishes those who are guilty of refusing food and shelter to the poor traveller.

We now come to the *capitularies*, about which so many mistakes have passed current, and have been accepted even by professed historians. It will be best, on this subject, to quote M. Guizot's own words: "The capitularies (*capitula*, small chapters) are the laws or legislative measures of the Frankish kings, Merovingian as well as Carlovingian. Those of the Merovingian are few in number, and of slight importance; and amongst those of the Carlovingians, which amount to 152, sixty-five only are due to Charlemagne." A German writer, H. Klimrath, tells us that the capitularies were kept at the imperial chancery, and that copies of them were distributed amongst the officers and prelates who having taken part in the various legislative assemblies, had to promulgate and make known the resolutions there adopted. Hence there exist various sets of capitularies, more or less complete according as the persons who had them transcribed had been present or not at these public deliberations. Not only did the dignitaries of the empire, lay or ecclesiastic, form these collections, but also private individuals who had been struck by the insufficiency of the *recueils* preserved at the various episcopal palaces. Thus Ansegise, abbot of Fontenelles and of Flavigny, composed, in 827, a work offering a methodical arrangement of the capitularies of Charlemagne and of Louis le Débonnaire. This code was so celebrated that it was quoted by Louis le Débonnaire himself in the laws he promulgated subsequently to the year 827. Charles the Bold also referred constantly to it. Another compilation, made in 845 by Benedict, surnamed the Levite, a deacon of the Church of Mentz, obtained likewise great popularity. It contains, however, besides the capitularies of Charlemagne and his predecessors, a mass of enactments derived from other sources, such as conciliar canons, decretals, texts of Scripture, extracts from the Fathers of the Church, etc.; and is generally regarded as inferior to the work of Ansegise, so far as authenticity is concerned.

The variety of subjects discussed in the capitularies is extremely striking, and some of them seem hardly to fall within the scope of a code or a distinctive law. If we attempt a rough classification of the sixty-five capitularies which belong properly to Charlemagne, we find the following result: these enactments make up together 1151 articles, subdivided into 87 treating of moral legislation, 130 of a penal character, 110 dealing with civil cases, 85 bearing upon religious topics, 305 on canonical details, 73 of a domestic nature, and 12 on miscellaneous subjects. The first edition of the capitularies was published in 1545, at Ingolstadt, by Amerbach. The best one was that of Baluze (1677, 2 vols. folio), until Pertz gave to the world his splendid *Monumenta Germaniæ Historica*, the thirteenth volume of which contains a much more complete text of all the laws edicted, both by the Merovingian and the Carlovingian kings.

The *formulæ* of Marculphus should also be consulted; the author lived during the seventh century, and compiled his work about the year 640. The Teutonic legislation is the basis on which these acts have been drawn up; and they are subdivided into two books, the former being consecrated to the royal charters (*cartæ regalis*), that is to say, treating of public enactments, whilst the latter, taken up by the *cartæ pagenses* comprises the acts and laws of a private nature, affecting the inhabitants of the several *pagi*. The original *formulæ* collected by Marculphus are followed by an appendix of a more recent date. It will be useful, perhaps, if we name here the best editions of these various works:—SALIC LAW: Pardessus, *Commentaire sur la Loi Salique*, Paris, 1843, 4°. RIPUARIAN LAW:

Walther, *Deutsche Rechtsquellen*. LAW OF THE VISIGOTHS :—Haenel, *Rex Romana Wisigothorum*, Leipsig, 1869, folio. LAW OF THE BURGUNDIANS : Bluhme, *Lex Burgundiorum*. The conciliar canons have an equal importance, for we must always bear carefully in mind that, in those days, political society was deeply leavened by the influence of the Church. The Councils of Agde (506), of Orleans (511), and of Yenne (Epaône, 577), judged from this point of view, deserve to be closely studied ; and the last, in particular, shows in the most striking manner the catholic character of the reign of Sigismund. The second Council of Tours (506), the fourth of Valence (584), and the fourth of Mâcon (585), are not less instructive with reference both to the internal organization of the Church, and to its connection with the State. We might dwell at much greater length on the ecclesiastical legislation of the Middle Ages, and on its extreme worth as a treasure-house of information, but we must be satisfied with referring the student to M. Guizot's lectures on civilization, and to Father Sirmond's *Concilia Antiquæ Galliæ* (Paris, 1629, folio), where the texts of the various conciliar enactments will be found.

The charters and official acts of the Merovingian epoch are scanty (Pardessus, *Diplomata, Chartæ, Epistolæ, Leges*, Paris, 1843–1863, 7 vols. folio), but the indications they contain are of the highest value. Finally, the student will discover ample means of verifying the assertions of historians and annalists in M. Le Blant's splendid *recueil* of epigraphic monuments (*Inscriptions Chrétiennes de la Gaule*, 3 vols. folio, Paris, 1856–1865).

With the Capetian dynasty we come to the Feudal system properly so called, the legislative history of which is contained in the *coutumes* and the *coutumiers*. The reader must here be cautioned against an error which is often committed, and which consists in mistaking the collections of feudal laws and enactments (*coutumes*) with the explanations, discussions, and commentaries published at various times on those texts (*coutumiers*). The last-named work—that is to say, the scientific arrangement and treatment of the feudal laws—is of a relatively modern date. In 1250, or about that time, Pierre de Fontaines, formerly *bailli* of Vermandois (1253), composed, under the title of *Conseil à un Ami*, a commentary on the laws of Ile-de-France, and of the district subjected to his administration. Undertaken, it appears, at the suggestion of Saint Louis, this work was never finished; it is interesting, however, as showing the transition from the old Germanic legislation, even in civil cases, to the usages of canon law.

The *Établissements de St. Louis*, the *Assises de Jérusalem*, and the *Coutumes du Beauvoisis*, are the most remarkable monuments of feudal legislation, and a slight acquaintance with them is indispensable towards a satisfactory knowledge of French mediæval history. With reference to the first mentioned of these three compilations, we may notice that the word *établissement* was not applied exclusively to it; in the thirteenth century all decrees of a general character received the name of *établissement (stabilimentum)*, and if the work we are now alluding to is the only one now known by that name, it is simply because its superior merits have left all the others in oblivion. Although published under the guarantee, so to say, of Saint Louis, the *Établissements* are posterior to the reign of that monarch, and are the work of a legist whose name has remained unknown. The character of this work is a constant endeavour to reconcile two principles according to all appearances incompatible; and in trying to interpret feudalism from the point of view of canon law, the writer is led to exaggerate the pretensions of the Crown in opposition with the prerogatives of the nobles. On the other hand, the *Établissements* lay down very clearly the rights which belonged undoubtedly to the barons, and show what the state of the feudal system was at a time when its glories already seemed on the wane. Thus, we find the barons still enjoying the serious right of summoning their vassals together even against the king, whereas the king could not raise any troops on the domains of the barons.

The *Assises de Jérusalem* next claim our attention for a brief space. After the taking of

Jerusalem in 1099, the Crusaders established two courts of law: the superior one for the barons, presided over by the king, and the inferior one for the *bourgeoisie*, under the chairmanship of the viscount of the city. As the expedition to the Holy Land had been undertaken by men belonging to several nationalities, it was obviously indispensable that the legislative enactments should be adapted to them all; accordingly, Godefroy de Bouillon caused a compilation to be made of the principal customs belonging to these various nations, and gave them force of law. The *Assises de Jérusalem* differ from the other mediæval *coutumes*, inasmuch as they were from the beginning a written code; and although the part which we possess does not belong to the end of the eleventh century, as some persons will believe, it is anterior, nevertheless, by sixty years to the *coutumiers* of France, and is one of the most important authorities we possess on feudal usages.

The *Coutumes de Beauvoisis*, drawn up by Philippe de Beaumanoir (?–1296), are extremely useful as a source of information on the legislative ideas prevalent about the end of the thirteenth century in the *Pays de Langue d'Oïl*, because the learned author, not satisfied with collecting and annotating the customs of the province of Beauvoisis, had also consulted for purposes of comparison the usages of other districts, and brought together a mass of illustrative matter from various sources. The *Coutumes de Beauvoisis* throw considerable light, not only upon law, properly so called, but upon politics, and Philippe de Beaumanoir, agreeing with the *rédacteur* of the *Établissements de Saint Louis*, exalts the authority of the Crown at the expense of feudalism.

If we were to give the complete list of all the collections of feudal laws which have been published since Charles VII. first conceived the idea of having them arranged in methodical order, we should be taking up uselessly the time and attention of our readers; we prefer noticing briefly here two or three legists who, although not having composed *ex professo* treatises on legislature, took upon themselves to judge very freely the institutions and government under which they lived, and whose works are, therefore, of great value for the history of the Middle Ages. Pierre Dubois (fourteenth century,) Raoul de Presles (1316–1381), and Philippe de Maizières (1312–1405) show us the spirit of independence and of inquiry taking possession of the third estate, and leading them to discuss the origin of government, its conditions, and its obligations. The *Établissements* and the *Coutumes de Beauvoisis* expressed clearly the triumph of the kingship; in the *Songe du Verger* of Raoul de Presles, and the *Songe du vieil Pélerin* of Philippe de Maizières, we see the *bourgeoisie* preparing itself for the exercise of power by assuming the right of political discussion. Pierre Dubois composed a number of pamphlets, some in French, most in Latin. M. Renan, who has devoted to him two interesting notices in the *Revue des Deux Mondes*, gives us the highest idea of his political and administrative capacity. France was to have universal dominion, exercising it, of course, for the wisest purposes, and in the most unobjectionable manner. The power of the court of Rome is curtailed. Gallican maxims prevail in the relations between the king and the pope; a perpetual peace is established throughout Europe ; and the cessation of hostilities thus obtained in the west enables the various potentates to join together in a crusade, which ends in a definitive solution of the Eastern difficulty. Not only is Palestine wrested from the infidels, but European civilization is introduced into Constantinople. The explanation of this grand scheme gives the author an opportunity of stating his views on education, military tactics, etc.

The political views of Raoul de Presles are developed under the similitude of a dream in the *Songe du Verger*, or dialogue between a *clerc* and a knight; the former being a decided ultramontanist, whilst the latter stands up manfully against the pope, the ecclesiastical courts, the monastic orders, and the absorption of the temporal power by the successor of Saint Peter. It is amusing to see the *clerc* anticipating the unpatriotic theories of the *Ligueurs*, and attacking the throne on behalf of the Vatican. He openly pronounces against the

Salic law, and sides with the King of England and the Duke of Brittany, who were then threatening France. His hatred of the crown even goes so far as to transform him into a violent demagogue; he disputes the right of the king to raise the taxes, maintains to his antagonist that the aristocracy has no *raison d'être*, and that all men are equal. The only incontestable privilege which he grants to the monarch is that of fleecing the Jews, and expelling them from the kingdom.

The *Songe du Verger* is, our readers will see, a most important contribution to the historical literature of the Middle Ages; it describes in very vivid colours the state of society, and illustrates public opinion during the reigns of Charles V. and Charles VI. Philippe de Maizières, in his *Songe du vieil Pélerin*, develops exactly the same views, and makes himself the spokesman of the Gallican *bourgeoisie* against the ultramontanist tendencies of the day. Another semi-political work, containing, under the shape of an allegory, a kind of *programme* in favour of the crown, is the remarkable pamphlet entitled *Le Vray Régime et Gouvernement des Bergiers et Bergières*. It was composed in 1379, and the name Jean de Brie, given to the author, is evidently a pseudonym which the historians of French literature have not been able to identify. We thus find that in the fourteenth century the freedom of the press was beginning to assert its rights, and that the kings of France fully aware of the power of public opinion, were endeavouring with much shrewdness to obtain its support in the serious contest they were carrying on with the still respected and dreaded authority of the court of Rome. History is the best comment on legislative enactments; pamphlet literature, in its turn, perpetually illustrates history.

CHAPTER XIX.

CHRONICLES OF A LOCAL CHARACTER—"CHRONIQUE DES COMTES D'ANJOU"—"CHRONIQUE DES ÉGLISES D'ANJOU"—"CHRONIQUE DE SAINT MARTIAL DE LIMOGES"—SERMON LITERATURE—POLITICAL PREACHERS—ANECDOTES OF ETIENNE DE BOURBON.

IN addition to the histories or chronicles of a general character which have been brought to light at various epochs, we must not forget works of a more local description, bearing upon the annals of the country, and, at the same time, full of interest by the light they throw upon the laws, institutions, and customs of the various provinces of France. The volume published by the *Société de l'Histoire de France*, under the title of *Chroniques des Comtes d'Anjou*, is an excellent specimen of what we mean. It comprises five works, which we shall examine successively. In the first place, it appears that towards the end of the twelfth century there existed several histories of the Counts of Anjou, viz.: 1. An anonymous chronicle, beginning with the words, *De Consulibus Andegavorum*; 2. an abridged chronicle, ascribed to a certain Abbot Eudes; 3. a history of the Counts of Anjou, written by Thomas de Loches; 4. another history of the same counts, composed by Robin and Le Breton of Amboise; 5. a compilation, the author of which is John, a monk of the abbey of Marmoutiers. The first of these documents, and the oldest of all, concludes with the death of Geoffroi Martel (1107), son of Foulques le Réchin. It is far from being devoid of merit, and although it dwells too much in detail on the origin of the Counts of Anjou, yet it allows comparatively little room to the absurd legends with which most mediæval chronicles are full. When he comes to the accession of Foulques Nerra, especially, our author really takes up his position as a trustworthy historian, and his statements are amply confirmed by the official documents which time has handed down to us. The author of the second *rédaction* appears to have been Eudes, Abbot of Marmoutiers (1124), who died April 13, 1137. Thomas de Parcé (*de Paccio*), Prebendary of Loches (died April 27, 1168), adopted the text of Abbot Eudes, and modified it so considerably that it reads almost like a distinct and independent work. The passages he suppresses or abridges are numerous. On the other hand, he has introduced several additions, some of which would suffice to give him a distinguished rank amongst mediæval chroniclers; thus, the description of the battle fought at Alençon in 1118, between Foulques the Young and Henry I. King of England. The compilation of Robin and Le Breton of Amboise does not call for any distinct notice; it was prepared between 1160 and 1169. We come next to the fifth draft, that of the monk John, about whom all that we know is that he wrote his history of the Counts of Anjou about 1169 or 1170, and his biography of Geoffroy le Bel, Count of Anjou and Duke of Normandy, about the year 1180. This second work, full of valuable particulars, but composed without the slightest regard to method or style, forms part of the volume issued by the *Société de l'Histoire de France*. We are indebted to a monk of the abbey of Pont le Voy for two memoirs, bearing immediately upon the history of the castle of Amboise and of its lords, and incidentally illustrating the annals of the Counts of Anjou. The *Gesta Dominorum Ambaciensium* is an excellent work, whether we regard it from the historical or the literary point of view. The *Liber de Compositione Castri Ambaciæ*, on the other hand, borrowed by the Abbot of Pont le Voy chiefly from popular collections of legendary stories, such as the famous *Gesta Romanorum*, is comparatively valueless. To the same collection of documents on the history of Anjou belongs the *Historiæ Andegavensis Fragmentum, a Fulcone Comite Scriptum*. The author of this piece is Foulques le Réchin, and, in spite of the assertions of Dom

Luc d'Achéry, who published his work for the first
time, we cannot be expected to ascribe much
historical importance to a production full of ana-
chronisms and errors of every kind. Foulques
acknowledges himself that he knows nothing about
the early Counts of Anjou, such as Ingelger, Foulques le Roux, and Foulques le Bon; accordingly,
he omits them altogether. The life of Geoffroy
Grise-Gonelle is equally characterized by misstatements of a serious kind; thus, Foulques le Réchin
places to his credit two battles which he never
fought, which are mentioned by no other author,
and which the circumstances related must have
made utterly impossible. Even the biography of
Geoffroy Martel—the least imperfect portion of the
work—is often inaccurate in its details. Finally,
let us name a treatise composed by Hugues de
Cleres under the inspiration of English political
ideas, and in which he puts forth the pretended
claims of the Counts of Anjou to be hereditary
mayors and seneschals of France. This treatise
has absolutely no value, and it is mentioned here
only for the purpose of completing the series of
documents which we possess on the subject of the
Angevin chronicles. It is not our business to state
here the results which historians have deduced
from an attentive study of this important subject;
we shall only say that the supposed first Count of
Anjou, Ingelger, appears to have been a legendary
personage, destitute of all claims, even to existence,

and that Foulques le Roux must be regarded as really heading the list of these chieftains.

In close connection with the volume we have just described, must be named another one, comprising a set of historical documents taken from the most ancient monasteries, abbeys, and convents of Anjou. They are, for the most part, ecclesiastical annals, giving year by year the history of the monastery where they were compiled, and mentioning specially the nomination and decease of abbots or other distinguished members of the community, the promotion of bishops, the building and dedication of churches. We have already had to remark on the great historical importance of documents of this kind, and on the intimate connection which existed, during the Middle Ages, between religious and civil society. This connection is illustrated in the most interesting manner in the pieces which compose the *Chroniques des Églises d'Anjou*, and it is not too much to say that documents such as these form one of the most useful and solid foundations of local history, besides the importance they possess towards the accurate determination of chronological particulars.

The cathedral church of Anjou, the church of Saint Maurice, appears first, and the chronicle connected with it seems the oldest, in point of date, of the monuments before us. Like most annals, it begins in the far remote periods of ancient history, and is merely a compilation from the popular work of Orosius, till we come to the year 965, when it becomes of the highest value for the history of the province. The indications given are remarkable for their accuracy. Most of them seem borrowed from the obituaries or official records, preserved in the muniment-room of the chapter-house. The chronicle we are mentioning is generally designated as the *Chronique de Rainaud*, although this annalist is responsible only for the part concluded between 976 and 1075. Rainaud was successively Canon of Saint Maurice, Archdeacon of Angers about the year 1040, and then *écolâtre* of the chapter. He had studied under Fulbert, Bishop of Chartres. Baudry, Abbot of Bourgueil, praises his erudition and his eminent virtues. He died about the year 1076.

The abbey of Saint Aubin, founded during the sixth century at Angers, furnishes us with another set of annals, which had already attracted the notice of both Duchesne and Labbe on account of their general, as well as their local, importance. Begun towards the end of the tenth century, and continued to the thirteenth by contemporary writers, they deserve the fullest credence. Besides a number of ecclesiastical details referring to the abbey of Saint Aubin and to the see of Angers, they contain, on the political history of Anjou, a mass of information which no other chronicles give us with such minuteness. The first compilers had been satisfied with brief memoranda of facts and characters; but as we get into comparatively modern times, the narrative expands, the short phrases become long paragraphs, and when we reach the epoch of Henry II. and Richard Cœur de Lion, we find ourselves in possession of a narrative sketched with much vigour and picturesque talent. The statement of the dissensions between these two princes, and of their wars against the kings of France, is well worth studying.

It appears that the monks of Saint Aubin had to suffer considerable violence from the lords of Montreuil-Bellay, on account of a certain priory which they possessed at Méron, in Poitou. This incident has supplied materials for another brief chronicle, which reads almost like a sermon, but which will be found to illustrate, in the most curious and interesting manner, the social life of the Middle Ages and the habits of the barons, who recognized no law but their sword. This fragment gives us, likewise, a number of details on the siege of Montreuil-Bellay, by Count Geoffroy le Bel, in 1151.

Saint Sergius and Saint Bacq were the patrons of another abbey, founded in the seventh century by King Clovis II., at a short distance from Angers. The chronicle which bears their name is the work of several monks belonging to the abbey. It takes us down to the year 1180, and, important as it is for the history of the province, it seems in many places to have been borrowed from the annals of Saint Aubin.

We must next mention the document known as the *Chronique de Vendôme*, and which was successively continued, from 607 to 1251, by monks belonging to the priory of Evière, situated at Angers, but being an offshoot of the abbey of the Holy Trinity at Vendôme. The early part of this compilation is often a transcript of the Saint Maurice chronicle, some passages of which are copied *verbatim*. With the year 965, a greater attempt at originality is made, and the literary merit of the work goes on increasing till its end, which occurs in 1251. It is evident that two or three authors, at least, are responsible for the continuation of this chronicle. They were all, like the first compiler, monks of the priory of Evière, and belonged to the abbey of the Holy Trinity at Vendôme. With reference to the merits of the work as an historical document, we may say that the details it gives us on some of the events of the twelfth century are very trustworthy, and that it completes the chronicles of Saint Aubin and Saint Sergius.

The abbey of Saint Florent, at Saumur, contributes to the volume we are now examining a miscellaneous series of documents, the most notable of which are a *Breve Chronicon Monasterii S. Florentii Salmuriensis* and a prose work on the destruction of the monastery by Nomenoé, Duke of Brittany. The former of these pieces is important, especially from the chronological point of view. It describes the siege of Angers (873), the burning of that town, and the death of the Countess Elizabeth (999), the foundation of Saint Nicholas of Angers (1020), the taking of Saumur (1023), the burning of the monastery of Saint Martin of Tours (903), etc., etc. Several of the dates given by the writer enable us, besides, to determine somewhat accurately certain particulars which had remained obscure in the chronology of the Counts of Anjou.

For the mediæval history of Lower Poitou, at the time when the destinies of that province were closely connected with those of Anjou, the chronicle of Saint Maixent, or of Maillezais, is an excellent source of information. It includes numerous extracts from obituaries now lost, and entire transcripts of the annals of several abbeys—annals which have not reached us in their primitive form.

The abbey of Saint Martial of Limoges, like all important religious houses, boasted of its series of chronicles compiled by the monks of the community, who faithfully transmitted to one another the care of drawing up the annals of their *alma mater*, and of connecting them with the history both of France and of the world at large. Just as the annals of the Counts of Anjou, and those of the churches and monasteries of that province, are a fruitful source of information respecting the districts of France situated on the banks of the Lower Loire, so the chronicles of Saint Martial of Limoges are the history of Aquitaine during the busiest part of the Middle Ages. The oldest and most important of them was begun by Adhémar de Chabannais, who described the origin of the abbey, and continued its annals down to the year 1025; he subsequently took the cross, and died in the Holy Land in 1034. This compilation was continued in succession by several monks, and brought down as late as the fifteenth century. Of these continuators, the most remarkable was, no doubt, Bernard Itier, whose biography is given in detail by M. Duplès-Agier in his edition of the chronicles, and who was evidently one of the leading representatives of the French regular clergy during the later part of the twelfth century and the beginning of the thirteenth. Born in 1163, Bernard Itier became, at the age of fourteen, a novice in the monastery of Saint Martial, and soon rose to the important position of librarian, which he filled for a period of twenty-five years with equal assiduity and success. The original idea of Bernard Itier was, at first, merely to note down the most important events which had happened since the eleventh century, in connection especially with the history of the abbey. For this purpose he made use of the margins of an old church-service book, and, beginning with the year 1000, he entered his remarks on the *recto* of the pages till the end of the year 1224. Later on, his ideas expanded, and he attempted to put down a kind of historical summary for the time anterior to the epoch he had first selected as his starting point. The *recto* pages being already full, he utilized the *verso* ones; and by the time he had crowded with his notes the margins of the author's book, his work was complete. Written in the usual Latin of the thirteenth century—that is to say, rather incorrect and uncouth—the chronicle of Bernard Itier has, at all events, the merit of impartiality; and, although its statements are, in a great measure, confined to the events which affected the monastery, yet we find interspersed with them details of a more general character. The continuators of Bernard Itier, the various fragments added by M. Duplès-Agier in the appendix to his volumes, will be found full of interesting details on the history of Aquitaine. It is necessary sometimes to wade through many a page before we discover any incident worth our attention; but still the labour spent on such researches is not vain, and the sum total of facts collected in the course of this investigation tells, with considerable weight, in the history of Aquitaine and the general history of France.

There is another valuable source of historical information which we should not forget in this enumeration, although it does not belong to the class of memoirs or annals properly so called; we mean the sermons, discourses, and other works of edification which were so frequent during the Middle Ages. M. Lecoy de la Marche had already shown, in his volume entitled *La Chaire Française du Moyen Âge*, the great profit which historians might derive from an attentive study of the innumerable collections of sermons bequeathed to us by the Middle Ages.

The study of this subject is extremely interesting, for the preachers of those days made use of an amount of freedom to which we are not accustomed, and often stooped to personalities which make their sermons most *piquant*, however contrary such a mode of procedure may seem to all our notions of good taste and decorum. *Cum tangit prædicando, presbyter durus esse debet* was a precept laid down by Jacques de Vitry; and we must acknowledge that most of the pulpit orators of the Middle Ages, whether regulars or seculars, acted up to it in a really conscientious manner. The Church itself was not spared: and the sermons of Maurice de Sully and other celebrated preachers are full of allusions to the opulence, the immorality, the ignorance, and the laziness of the prelates, priests, and religious. The king comes next; and whilst Philip Augustus is rather roughly handled, Saint Louis, of course, is held up as a pattern of all the virtues which a monarch should possess. A rather amusing anecdote is related about the former, which, if true, shows a great amount of wit and of common sense. Philip Augustus, it is well known, was fond of the company of *trouvères*, minstrels, and jugglers, and bestowed upon them frequent marks of his partiality. One day a buffoon came boldly to him, asking for relief under the pretext that they were relatives. "On what side, and at what degree, are you my relative?" asked the king. "We are brethren on Adam's side," was the answer, "only the inheritance has been unequally divided between us." Philip told the man to come back the next day; and then, in the presence of all his courtiers, he gave him a penny. "I restore to thee," added he, "the legitimate share which belongs to thee by virtue of our relationship; and when I have paid the equivalent to all my other brethren, I shall not even have as much left for my own use." The barons, the knights, the military orders, the lawyers, the magistrates, the university, all deserve to be reproved; for the degeneracy is complete, and, unless the work of reformation begins speedily, society must soon perish. What is the lot of the poor? and how all the rules of Christian charity are forgotten by those whose duty it is, and whose highest privilege it should be, to render the circumstances of life easier for the disinherited and the miserable! Lords and barons are bad enough, but provosts (*præpositi*) and beadles (*bedelli*) are infinitely worse; they may be likened unto "crows from hell," watching greedily for the remains of the victims; and the serf has thus a multitude of lords, to whose will and good pleasure he is bound.

"Aspera sors populi: hic imperat, ille minatur."

They do not know what to invent for the purpose of wringing money out of the tax-payers, and, in their rapacity, they even manage to press the sun in their service. "My lord," said one day a certain bailiff to a count, "if you will trust me, I shall procure for you every year a splendid income; only allow me *to sell the sun* in your estates." "How?" "There are on your domains certain people who bleach and dry linen in the open air; by exacting twelve *deniers* for each piece of linen, you will realize a considerable sum." And thus it was done. But, on the other hand, examples are quoted of strange punishments inflicted upon these rapacious tyrants, and well calculated to make them reflect. "In the county of Mâcon, before that fief had been sold to the king (in 1239) by the Count John and his wife, there were continual disputes between the bishops, the clergy, and the citizens on one side, and the count, his knights, and his retainers on the other. Thanks to these quarrels, extortions of every kind abounded. A provost of the neighbourhood saw one day a cow which tempted him. 'Take that cow,' said he to one of his attendants. He had no sooner, however, uttered this phrase, than his tongue was struck with paralysis; and during the remainder of his life, the only words he could say were, 'Take that cow.'"

The sermons of the mediæval preachers are full of allusions which give us a curious insight into the framework of feudal society. Thus, Jacques de Vitry, describing the household of a rich man, divides it first into three classes: the varlets, the maid-servants, and the serfs. The serfs, in their turn, compose four categories: 1. the *servi hominis*, also called *ascripticii*; 2. the *servi glebæ*, attached to the land, and liable to be sold together with it; 3. the *servi originarii*, sprung from the *ascripticii* on the baron's estates; and 4. the *servi conducticii*, hired for a limited time, at the expiration of which they recover their liberty. All these *famuli* are represented by the preachers as plunged in ignorance and disorder; pride, blasphemy, and theft are their every-day vices. The servants (*garçones* = mod. Fr. *garçons*) who wait upon the students of the University of Paris are singled out for special denunciation (*omnes ferè latrunculi solent esse*), the carelessness of their masters unfortunately encouraging them in their nefarious habits. Books, clothes, articles of furniture—they seize indifferently all they can, fleecing the wretched young men out of their last penny, and making them pay for their board at the rate of four hundred per cent.!

Generalities, however, did not always satisfy the preachers, and they soon transformed the Church into political clubs, where the most violent denunciations, hurled against kings, queens, statesmen, and ministers, stirred up the animosity of party spirit and encouraged rebellion. What the Basochians and the *enfants sans soucy* attempted to do on the stage, the popular pulpit orators accomplished from the altar-steps, with this difference—that whereas the former stood out generally as the mouthpieces of the temporal power against the pretensions of the Church, the latter claimed to be expressly commissioned by the Church to denounce the wrong-doings and short-comings of the State. The sermons of Michel Menot (?–1518) and of Maillart (?–1502) are curious as pictures of society and as specimens of the most barbarous style, but the allusions they contain to politics and to government, are of a general nature; indeed, Louis XI. threatened Maillart with drowning if he was bold enough to venture upon any strong expressions of discontent at the condition of France; and the friar was wise enough to take the hint.

The period in the history of the French Middle Ages, when pulpit eloquence illustrates history with the greatest and most painful effect, is marked by the Hundred Years' War, and chiefly by the reign of the unfortunate Charles VI. During the second half of the fourteenth century, as M. Aubertin truly observes, sacred oratory, coming into contact with civil and religious disturbances, lost its character, and compromised its dignity. The preachers assumed the part of political orators, and made themselves the spokesmen of demagogues; they were seen in the assemblies of the States, at the Paris street-corners, in the public thoroughfares, exciting the passions of the mob, stimulating their hatred, and selling to the highest bidder their shameless eloquence. The "Malleteers," the "Flayers," the cut-throats of every kind, thought themselves thus justified, because they were backed by texts of Scripture and scholastic distinctions; the English invaders found champions amongst the members of the University of Paris, whilst the French cause had scarcely a man of talent to defend it from the pulpit.

If we wish to form some idea of the violence which characterized the representatives of the Gallican Church in those days, we must turn to the sermons of the Carmelite friar, Eustache de Pavilly; the master of arts, Benoit Gentien; and the Abbot of Moutiers, Saint Jean. Some of their addresses have been transmitted to us in substance by the *religieux de Saint Denis*, Monstrelet, Juvénal des Ursins, and other contemporary historians; and their style, their constant appeals to violence, their disregard of all the claims of logic and of fairness, remind us of what M. Thiers, M. Mortimer Ternaux, and M. Mignet tell us about the Reign of Terror in 1792 and 1793. "See these little truants, who were quite lately lawyers' clerks, men of nothing, and of small origin; now they are so befurred with sable and marten that no one can recognize them.... And you, chancellor, receiving two thousand livres of annual salary, besides four thousand five hundred gold francs for letters of remission, twenty-six thousand livres on the war subsidies, and two thousand livres for your wardrobe! ... you, attorney-generals, with a salary of six hundred livres ... councillors paid at the rate of three hundred livres ... all running about in quest of bribes, carrying on a bargain of sentences and decrees! ... and you, officers of the court, pluralists holding three or four posts to which you cannot attend, and of which you pocket the high and excessive wages; weeds and dangerous nettles of the royal garden, preventing the good seed from growing—we must clear you away, remove you, and have done with you, so that the rest may profit the more. We therefore require that you should be all taken, you and your property."

The result of such an outburst, pronounced from a window in the town hall, or from the top of a stone in the market-place, to an assembled multitude of three or four thousand armed men, can easily be imagined. We are told that after a speech delivered by Eustache de Pavilly, fifteen ladies belonging to the queen's household were locked up in the Conciergerie, besides a number of the king's officers. Amongst the manuscripts preserved in the Paris National Library, we find a *Relation Manuscrite de la Sédition et Émotion Populaire arrivée à Paris en l'An* 1413. It is preceded by a sermon which Pavilly pronounced, and which, no doubt, led to the riot. What the popular orators had advised, the mob immediately carried into execution.

We have thus enumerated the principal advisers on the side of the discontented. There is not the slightest doubt that during the conflict between the Burgundians and the Armagnacs, whilst the infamous Queen Isabel of Bavaria, the "she-wolf of France," was ruining the kingdom, and whilst the incapacity of Charles VI. and the wickedness of Charles the Bad, King of Navarre, combined, were helping on the work of destruction—there is no doubt, we say, that reforms were urgently needed; but appeals to brute force are seldom productive of any good, and the episode of Etienne Marcel shows, in the most conclusive manner, the folly of revolutionary measures. As a contrast to Eustache de Pavilly and his compeers, let us name Jean Chartier de Gerson (1363–1429), the celebrated chancellor of the University of Paris. Each of his speeches, says M. Aubertin, was a victory won by the party of order, of good sense, and of peace, over the worst demagogues that France ever saw. The evidence of historians is unanimous to prove that to his sound advice, his genuine eloquence, and his moderation, are due the measures which led gradually to the pacification of France under the reign of Charles VII. Another distinguished orator, the monk Augustin Legrand (fifteenth century), did much also for the cause of quiet and lawful reforms; and he would have deserved the gratitude of posterity, if the latter end of his life had not, to a certain extent, belied the promises of its beginning. We are told by the chronicler Guillebert of Metz that the whole of Paris flocked to Legrand's sermons. Preaching one day before the court, at a time when the officers who surrounded the king at the Louvre had the power in their own hands, he was bold enough to denounce openly the vices which dishonoured it, and which had nearly brought France to the verge of destruction. "If you do not believe me," he exclaimed, addressing Queen Isabel, "walk through the city in the disguise of a poor woman, and you will hear what every one says about you." He had hardly concluded his sermon when one of the courtiers said aloud, "If people believed me, this wretch should be pitched into the river."

That the generous indignation of Gerson and of Legrand produced the best possible results, there is no reason to doubt; that the sermons which have been handed down to us, as composed by them and by the other representatives of the French mediæval Church, throw the greatest light upon contemporary history, is equally certain.

The *recueil* of anecdotes compiled by the Dominican friar, Etienne de Bourbon, belongs also to sermon literature, and it is full of the most valuable information respecting the state of society during the thirteenth century—the political feeling, the intellectual tastes and pursuits; in one word, life considered in its broadest aspect. The name of the author is not given on the title-page of the work which M. Lecoy de la Marche has published. He was one of those who carried out in their life the maxim *ama nesciri;* and it is only from conjectures, based upon an attentive study of the text, that we have been able to ascertain with tolerable accuracy who he was, to what religious order he belonged, and what position he held in the Church. His work, entitled *Tractatus de Diversis Materiis Prædicabilibus,* is a collection of anecdotes, or facts, which might carefully be quoted by preachers in support of any point of doctrine they wished to enforce. Jacques de Vitry had already set the example of *analecta* of the kind; and, before him, Saint Dominic had indulged frequently in the habit of drawing for his sermons on the large stock of popular anecdotes and well-known tales, or legends, which were current in society during the Middle Ages. This system of preaching was not faultless, of course, and our readers will see at once how easily it could be turned aside from its proper channel, and made the vehicle of satire or scurrilous jokes; but, kept within proper bounds, it was extremely useful, and has preserved for us a number of curious historical facts. Etienne de Bourbon adopted the idea of Jacques de Vitry—he even developed it to a considerable extent—and the result of his labours as a pulpit orator is a volume where the practical application of all the Christian virtues is enforced through the medium of episodes borrowed from the most diverse quarters. The character of these episodes suggests a very natural and obvious division of Etienne de Bourbon's work into two parts of very unequal merit. The former is borrowed from old theological writings, *acta sanctorum*, legends, fables, poetry, etc., etc. The latter is the record of the author's own observations; it contains allusions to contemporary events, and to circumstances which had been related to him by eye-witnesses, when he had not been in a position to see them himself. The former portion, whilst it is of no value as bearing upon the history of the time, can still enable us to know what was the amount of erudition to be found in the University of Paris, and what works were read by the undergraduates. On the other hand, when we come to the anthology of historical extracts, and to the narrative of contemporary transactions, we find ourselves in possession of details which illustrate the reign of Saint Louis, and which deserve to be carefully noted. It would be absurd, of course, to claim for all these anecdotes, indiscriminately, the authenticity which we expect to find in the writings of professed historians. Etienne de Bourbon repeats a number of wonderful stories or idle rumours which would require close investigation; but in this respect he often compares favourably with mediæval annalists, and in many cases he relates things which he actually witnessed. Let us also note that he is always careful to quote his authorities; certain facts were told him by those who had taken a part in them, others belong to some local tradition which he had heard on the spot, a few are quoted on the evidence of a preacher. He carries so far his respect for truth, that whenever he is not absolutely certain of the faithfulness of his own memory or of that of his informers, he makes use of sentences such as "Sicut credo me vidisse; me audivisse credo, vel ab eodem, vel ab aliis; credo me interfuisse," etc. A man who displays so scrupulous a disposition can surely be believed, and the only circumstance in which he abstains from mentioning personages or families is when the narrative of some crime or scandalous transaction occurs as a caution to his hearers. Then he very properly declines to drag in a name which, although disgraced by one individual, might still be honourably borne by other members of the family. We should notice, likewise, that if he quotes some legend or miraculous story, he merely gives it as an apologue, without vouching for its authenticity — it is sufficient that it should contain a wholesome, moral lesson. Amongst the stories contained in the collection of anecdotes gathered together by Etienne de Bourbon, there are several which illustrate the character of Philip Augustus, Louis VII., Louis VIII., and of Saint Louis; and it is curious to remark how sometimes the appreciations given by the preacher differ from those which history has accustomed to consider as authentic. Thus, the father of Philip Augustus is generally described as a violent, headstrong prince; here, on the contrary, we find him a good, simple-minded monarch, a judicious and wiṣe arbitrator. "The Bishop of Paris (Peter Lombard) was dead, and the canons, before proceeding to the election of his successor, were anxious to consult Louis VII. 'Who,' said the king, 'are the best *clercs* in your Church?' They named two who completely outshone all the others by their learning and their general reputation; the one was Master Maurice, and the other Peter Comestor. The king inquired which of the two was the most zealous for the salvation of souls, the busiest in preaching, and the most anxious about the spiritual interests of the people. They answered that Maurice was distinguished chiefly as an earnest preacher, and as eager for the eternal welfare of the diocese; whereas Peter shone especially as a Biblical scholar and a divine. 'Well,' said the king, 'place the former at the head of the see, and appoint the latter to the direction of the schools.' It was thus done, and everybody was the better for the arrangement."

Philip Augustus, too, in the compilation of Etienne de Bourbon, is somewhat different from what history describes him to have been; he is facetious, fond of smart repartees, and the author places in his mouth a number of stale jokes, which are the current coin of the old *esprit Gaulois*. Consulted one day on a canonical election, he adopts a course which contrasts strangely with that related in the previous anecdote. The priests are all drawn up in a line; he reviews them, holding in his hand the pastoral staff, and discovering one of them more lean than the rest, he says to him, "Here, take this staff, in order that you may become as fat as your companions."

Of the really historical episodes quoted in the book of anecdotes, we shall name the following:—
1. The taking of Damietta by Saint Louis, in 1249. Here the author relates an incident, on the authority of one of the king's companions, which is not mentioned by other historians, although Matthew Paris, Joinville, and Lenain de Tillemont describe facts exactly similar in their general character. 2. The taking of Avignon by Louis VIII., on the 12th of September, 1226, when a certain number of houses were levelled with the ground, and two hundred hostages delivered into the power of the king. 3. The sacking of Déols by the *Coteraux*, during the wars between the French and the English, in 1187. Allusions to the Crusade against the Albigenses occur repeatedly, and the life of Saint Louis supplies Etienne de Bourbon with a number of anecdotes which are, to a great extent, undoubtedly authentic. It would be worth while comparing the *recueil* we are now describing with the voluminous collections of

sermons which the Middle Ages have transmitted to us; we should, no doubt, find an ample crop of materials to glean in confirmation of the details so diligently gathered by Etienne de Bourbon.

CHAPTER XX.

THE DRAMA CONSIDERED AS A SOURCE OF HISTORICAL INFORMATION.

IF there was any doubt respecting the importance of dramatic literature in connection with the subject of the present volume, we might refer our readers to M. Aubertin's *Histoire de la Langue et de la Littérature Françaises au Moyen Âge*, where a separate section is devoted to political comedy. The historians of the French nineteenth century in times to come will have to consult the productions of MM. Scribe, Bayard, Duveyrier, Emile Augier, and others, for allusions to political events, anecdotes, and satires; in like manner, M. Fournier's *Théâtre Français avant la Renaissance* and M. Jannet's *Ancien Théâtre Français* supply us with materials which could easily be expanded into a series of chapters. Leaving on one side the *confrères de la Passion*, who dealt with solemn subjects, and were supposed never to overstep the bounds of the strictest propriety, we find two companies of players enjoying the privilege of amusing the public: 1. a set of lawyers' clerks, known by the designation of *clercs de la Basoche;* the *Basoche* (basilica? βάζω, οἴκοι?) being the name given to the chief court of law in Paris. These young fellows acted dramatic satires, called *farces* or *pièces farcies*, from the *farsitæ epistolæ* in macaronic Latin, sung at church on certain solemn feast-days. A fine opportunity was thus given to them for denouncing the vices, foibles, and ridicules of their neighbours, and they availed themselves of it to the full, venturing even on the dangerous ground of politics, and expressing themselves rather freely on the blunders of the Government, Court intrigues, and international disputes. The Basochians, licensed by virtue of a charter of Philip the Fair, have left a voluminous *répertoire;* their best-known play being the famous *Farce de Patnelin*, which was translated into modern French by Bussy and Palaprat during the reign of Louis XIV., and has ever since retained its popularity. If, however, we place ourselves at the *historical* point of view, there is no doubt that one of the most curious specimens of the Basochian drama, if not the most notable in the whole collection, is the farce entitled *Mestier et Marchandise*, which M. Fournier has printed in his elegant volume already alluded to. It is anonymous; but everything leads us to believe that the author was a citizen of Paris, and that he expressed the general feeling of the *bourgeoisie* on the state of things in France at the time when Charles VII. occupied the throne. "Every subject which engaged the attention of the public," says M. Fournier, "is here mentioned: the rebellion of the barons and of the feudal lords, who were then (1440) organizing the war of the *Praguerie*, at the suggestion and under the leadership of the dauphin; the complaints of the working classes—tradesmen, mechanics, and husbandmen, whom these perpetual disturbances threw out of work; finally, the general hope which France placed in God's providence, first, and then in the wisdom of the king." Jacques Cœur, Jean Bureau, and several other distinguished patriots selected by Charles VII. from the third estate, were indeed endeavouring at that time to heal the wounds which their native country had received in consequence of the wars with England, the ambition of the nobles, and the wretched incapacity of the late monarch.

Next to the *clercs de la Basoche* we must notice another company of actors, known by the designation of the *enfants sans soucy*. It was an association of young men of good family, but not bound together by any similarity of trade or profession. Under the direction of a leader who assumed the ominous title of *prince des sots*, they acted a kind of plays called *soties*, the purpose of which, like that of the *farces*, was to hold up to ridicule the different orders of society, and to state with considerable freedom what the public thought of their rulers. Amongst the authors of *soties* we must mention Pierre Gringore, whom we have already alluded to in connection with the *Mystère de Saint Louis*, and who flourished during the fifteenth century. His proud motto was, *Tout par raison, raison par tout, par tout raison.* His play, *Le Jeu du Prince des Sots*, is the most remarkable of all his works.

It is no matter of surprise to find that the liberty enjoyed by the *clercs de la Basoche* and the *enfants sans soucy* soon degenerated into unbridled licentiousness. Besides overstepping very frequently the limits of decency and good taste, they were unsparing in their attacks upon those who exercised authority; and, as a necessary consequence, several edicts were fulminated against them. M. Aubertin remarks, very truly, that the power enjoyed by these dramatists was analogous to that which the newspaper press has at present, and that their audacity could be estimated from the more or less severity of the condemnations and interdictions which they incurred. In 1442 a few Basochians, of a hypercritical disposition, are locked up in prison, and fed upon bread and water. All the productions of the Basoche are, further, subjected to the examination of Government censors. On the 6th of May, 1475, a fresh edict is issued, prohibiting the acting of any new play without special permission. In 1476, the *clercs* of the

Parliament and of the Châtelet are visited with a preventive measure still more stringent in its character, for the bringing out and performance of any play *à convocation de peuple* is absolutely forbidden under penalty of banishment and confiscation. A *clerc* found guilty of asking leave to act in a *farce, sotie,* or *moralité,* is liable to have his name erased from the registers of the law courts. In 1486 Charles VIII. sends to prison, for twelve months, five Basochians who had indulged too freely in political allusions. Permissions to act are thus alternately granted and withdrawn; and finally, Henry III., the last of the Valois kings, pronounced a sentence of definitive suppression.

We see that the various kings of France who reigned from the thirteenth to the sixteenth century understood perfectly well the power exercised by the Basochians, and especially by the *enfants sans soucy;* nor can we wonder at their having, on more than one occasion, attempted to make use of that power for their own purposes. A certain poet, of the name of Jean Bouchet, who died about the year 1550, places this fact in the clearest light in a passage which we shall translate here, and which gives at the same time a correct definition of the term *sotie:*—

"Satire bears in France the name of *sotie,* because the *sots* exhibit in polished language on a stage the follies both of persons high in renown, and of the common people. This is allowed by princes and kings, in order that they may know the misdeeds of their advisers which no one dares bring plainly under their notice, and which they discover through the medium of satire. King Lous XII. desired that these *soties* should be represented in Paris; and he used to say that he thus became acquainted with many scandals which were otherwise too artfully concealed from him."[1]

Brantôme confirms this statement in his biography of Anne of Brittany, showing that Louis XII. was not afraid of seeing the stage-players indulge in political allusions:—

"The king honoured him (Gringore) so much that one day, when he had been told of the manner in which the *clercs* of the Palace Basoche and the Paris students had performed pieces containing allusions to his majesty, the court, and the nobility in general, he merely answered that they might employ their time in diverting themselves. He had no objection, therefore, to their speaking both of him and of his court, provided they kept within due bounds; especially they were not to mention the queen his wife in any manner whatsoever, under penalty of being all sent to the gallows."[2]

Pierre Gringore availed himself unscrupulously of the permission he had thus obtained; he undertook to interest the Parisian *badauds* in the

---

[1] *Epistres Morales et Familières du Traverseur.*
[2] *Brantôme*, M. Lalanne's edition, vii. 316.

quarrel which had broken out between Louis XII. and Pope Julius II., and it is not venturing too far to suppose that he was secretly encouraged by the king in his attempt to turn the Holy See into ridicule, and to represent the pontiff as an odious and absurd character. This curious and amusing specimen of satirical and historical comedy, entitled *Jeu et Sotie du Prince des Sots*, was "brought out," as we should say now, at the Paris marketplace during the carnival of 1511, in the presence of the king, the parliament, the town councillors, and the whole of the population. Gringore, like Molière, used to act in his own plays, and on the present occasion he took the part of *la Mère Sotte*. In giving our readers a brief account of this amusing contribution to the historical drama of the Middle Ages, we cannot do better than take as our guide M. Aubertin, to whose excellent work on mediæval French literature we have already alluded several times. The subject-matter, then, of the *Jeu du Prince des Sots*, is the opposition between the pope and the king, the temporal and the spiritual powers. Two characters appear as the antagonists, namely, the *Prince des Sots* (the king) and *la Mère Sotte* (the Church), each surrounded by his court. The great object for both of them is to secure the countenance and support of a third personage, *Sotte Commune;* that is to say, the nation, the commonalty of the realm. They are attached to the Church, as good catholics should be; means must be devised to alienate them from the pope, and win them over to the king. By way of preface, we have first a dialogue between two or three *sots*, who discourse freely about the events of the day: the French garrison has been driven out of Bologna; the English still occupy Calais; the Church encroaches upon the temporal power; the king is always "humane, just, and patient;" the Spaniards are "stretching their nets," and watching the opportunity of interfering and taking part either on one side or on the other. By degrees the stage begins to fill; the king and his court arrive, and the conversation turns upon the prelates, whose vices, ignorance, treachery, and fickleness are violently denounced. Finding that every one gives with all liberty his opinions on the state of the political world, *Sotte Commune* joins in: What careth it for all the wars, treaties, conquests, alliances, and treacheries which are made so much of? Of what consequence is it that the chair of St. Peter should be occupied by a fool or a wise man? All that the commonalty require is peace, the opportunity of earning an honest living, and the assurance of not being ruined by an edict which alters the currency. *Mère Sotte* then interferes, attempting first to win over by the most brilliant promises the dignitaries of the Gallican Church; having so far succeeded, she tries, but in vain, to secure the assistance of the lay lords for the cause of ultramontanism. Defeated in this instance, *Mère Sotte* draws the sword, becomes *gendarme*, and orders the prelates to fight manfully on the side of Rome. In the midst of the general confusion, *Sotte Commune* goes over to the king's party, being duly cautioned that *Mère Sotte* is not the Church, but a counterfeit power which, under the mask of religion, troubles consciences and endangers the peace of Christendom.

This very brief and incomplete sketch will show sufficiently, we hope, the drift of Gringore's *sotie*, and its great importance as illustrating the history of France during the reign of Louis XII. Viewed from the literary standpoint, it cannot be said to have any literary merit, but is a curious specimen of that Gallican animus which has characterized almost uniformly the policy of our neighbours on the other side of the Channel from the days of Philip the Fair to those of Bossuet and of Saint Cyran. Gringore was, to all intents and purposes, the court poet during the reign of Louis XII., and his *sotie* of the *Prince des Sots* had been preceded by attacks of equal violence directed against the court of Rome at the suggestion of the French Government: thus the pieces entitled *L'Entreprise des Vénitiens, La Chasse du Cerf des Cerfs* (allusion to the well-known phrase, *Servus servorum Domini*), *L'Espoir de la Paix*, etc. In a very exhaustive article published by M. Pico (*Romania*, April, 1878), twenty-six *soties* are described, all, or nearly all, full of political allusions, and deserving a mention here. Thus, in the play *Les Menus Propos*, composed, as it seems, by a Norman poet of the name of Cardinot, mention is made of Jeanne le Féron, an impostor who tried in 1460 to pass off as Joan of Arc, and was condemned in consequence during the following year. Thus again (*Farce des Gens Nouveaulx*), we have a notice of the edict of 1448, which instituted the body of *Francs-archers*, and was the first step towards the establishment of a regular army in France. The *Sots Nouveaulx Farcez* belong, probably, to the Rouen theatre. They tell us of Louis XII.'s expedition against the Venetians (1503); of the Pampeluna campaign (1512), where Francis I. made his first acquaintance with the vicissitudes of war; of the combined undertaking of Henry VIII. and the Emperor Maximilian against France (1513). André de la Vigne, who flourished in 1513, has also left a *sotie*, where a certain number of historical details can be easily discovered. "By Saint John! the king pays for this mess and for the pardon which it brings along with it." "It is the jubilee" (jubilee celebrated after the election of Leo X. to the papacy [March, 1513], and reconciliation of Louis XII. with the court of Rome [December, 1513]). "Oh, how deaf (ill-advised) the king was not to appoint to the chancellorship so . . . so great, so good, so holy a man, full of miracles such as might be worked in Rome! By my oath, it is no joke!" "Who is that Paris legate? Do you think he would take the office?" "'Sdeath! he thought he would lead the king astray by dissimulation." The chancellor whose place it was necessary to fill was Jean de Gannay, who died at Blois in 1512. Instead, however, of appointing a successor to him, the king entrusted the seals for a time to the Bishop of Paris, Etienne Poncher, who retained them till the accession of Francis I. The "so great, so good, and so holy man" whom the poet would have liked to see raised to the dignity of keeper of the seals was the well-known Briçonnet, one of the prelates assisting at the Council of Pisa. Julius II. had deprived him of the purple, but Leo X. restored him afterwards to his position in the Church. Pierre Gringore is also supposed to have been the author of the *Sotie Nouvelle des Croniqueurs*, which belongs to the reign of Francis I. This dramatic poem is nothing else but a series of political remarks, which would appear of the boldest character, says M. Picot, if we did not know that Francis I., as well as Louis XII., allowed the *enfants sans soucy* freedom of speech only on condition of their favouring the policy of the Government. The *Croniqueurs* from the very outset show plainly their hatred of the court of Rome: if France has suffered so many misfortunes during the last century, it is because the statesmen to whom the destinies of the kingdom were confided belonged to the clergy. They are particularly bitter against Cardinal la Balue.

"Louis XI. was led," they say, "to Liège by a cardinal, whence there nearly came great evil to his own person. . . . No priest ever did, or ever will do, good to France." The only dignitary of the Church who finds favour with the *Croniqueurs* is Briçonnet, "who died at Narbonne (1514) not long ago." All the favourites who formerly lived upon the substance of the people are severely called to account — Chastillon, Bourdillon, Bonneval. The *Croniqueurs* pass successively in review Louis XI., Charles VIII., Louis XII., Popes Julius II. and Leo X.; and they allude to the Italian expedition organized by Francis I. in May, 1515. This circumstance enables us to determine approximatively the date of the *sotie*, whilst the whole character, the style, and the introduction of a character named *la mère* (*sotte*) justifies us in ascribing it to Gringore.

If the States incur danger under ecclesiastical rule, it is equally desirable that power should not be placed within the hands of a woman. Such is the theme developed by the author of a *farce morale* entitled *Les Trois Pèlerins;* and the person selected for special censure is Louise de Savoie, whose want of principle drove the Constable of Bourbon to open revolt, and who was generally considered as responsible for all the misfortunes of the reign of Francis I. As early as the month of December, 1516, the king had caused three actors to be arrested and brought before him at

Amboise, to be tried on the charge of having turned the queen-mother publicly into ridicule on the stage by the name of *Mère Sotte*, accusing her of pillaging France, and of governing it according to her own whim. The sentence pronounced against Jacques the Basochian, Jean Serres, and Jean de Pont-Alais did not have the result which the king anticipated, for six years later the *farce morale* was performed to which we are now alluding.

We shall not continue our survey of historical dramatic literature any further. As our readers may have noticed, the last two specimens dealt with have landed us into modern history, and we must not forget that mediæval times mark the limits with which this volume is concerned.

CHAPTER XXI.

"LA GUERRE DE METZ"—BOURDIGNÉ—PARADIN —ALAIN BOUCHARD—CARTULARIES— POLITICAL SONGS—HISTORIANS—"CHRONIQUES MARTINIANES"—NICOLE GILLES—ROBERT GAGUIN.

THE poem published by M. de Bouteiller, on the war of Metz in 1324, is another proof of the increased interest lately taken in historical works of a merely local character, but which are nevertheless, more or less, connected with the general destinies of the country. The city of Metz, after having been, under the Merovingian *régime*, the metropolis of the kingdom of Austrasia, became the capital of Lorraine when the dismemberment of the empire of Charlemagne took place, and was ceded in 980, together with the whole province, by King Lothaire, to the Emperor Otho II. In a very short time the rule of these monarchs became purely nominal, so far as Metz was concerned, and the government of the city fell into the hands, first of the bishops, then of an oligarchy of *bourgeois*, known by the name of the *paraiges* (*i.e.* families—compare the Latin *cognationes, parentelæ*). At the time when the war of 1324 broke out, Metz had long been a kind of independent republic; enjoying, indeed, the title of imperial town, but in no wise contributing to the defence of the empire in time of war, and, by a kind of reciprocal arrangement, being left by the emperors of Germany, its nominal masters, perfectly at liberty to carry on its own private feuds, without any interference on their part. Political independence has its advantages, no doubt, but these are compensated by serious difficulties, and in 1324 Metz had to resist the combined efforts of no less than four neighbouring princes who had determined upon destroying it; viz. John, King of Bohemia and Count of Luxemburg, Baldwin, Archbishop of Trèves, Ferry IV., Duke of Lorraine, and Edward I., Count of Bar. The poem published by M. de Bouteiller is a real historical *chanson*, celebrating the exploits of the Messins during the siege; it is divided into two hundred and ninety-six stanzas of octosyllabic lines, and is equally interesting if we consider it as a literary monument, or an illustration of municipal laws and customs during the Middle Ages. The war, maintained with the utmost energy by the besieged citizens, ended in a more satisfactory manner than they had any reason to anticipate, and, although they were obliged to surrender, the conditions imposed upon them were of the easiest description possible. If we consult the evidence supplied by the historians of the fourteenth century, we are led to think that the inhabitants of Metz had partly brought upon themselves the evils which a siege must always entail. Rather overbearing by nature, and proud of the position which their beloved city enjoyed, both financially and politically, they did not always scrupulously pay the feudal dues and rights to the barons and lords on whose territories they purchased landed estates. On the other hand, two of the princes who had joined the league against Metz (the Count of Bar and the Duke of Lorraine) were over head and ears in debt, and as their creditors were the merchants of the imperial city, they thought that the opportunity of a war was excellent to enable them to cancel summarily the claims outstanding against them. The author of the poem on the siege of Metz is not known; M. de Bouteiller has endeavoured to identify him with a certain Lambelin who has composed a smaller work on the same subject, but it is even doubtful whether the name Lambelin is not a *nom de plume*.

Amongst the local chronicles which have obtained the greatest reputation, although they are not original works, but compilations borrowed from other sources, we must name the *Chroniques d'Anjou*, or, to give the real title, the *Histoire Agrégative des Annales et Chroniques d'Anjou, contenant le commencement et origine avecques partie des chevaleureux et marciaulx gestes des magnanimes princes, consulz, contes et ducs d'Anjou*. This work, printed for the first time in 1529, and then in 1533, had become extremely rare, when a new edition, in two vols. royal octavo, was published in 1842, by the care of a few learned and patriotic Angevins.

We possess no information respecting the life of Jean de Bourdigné, the author of the *Chroniques d'Anjou*. All we know about him is that he was born towards the end of the fifteenth century, and that he belonged to an ancient and noble family, possessing large estates in the province of Maine. Destined from his earliest infancy to the Church, he studied at the University of Angers, and took his degree of doctor of laws before he received ordination. It happened that, at the beginning of the year 1512, Roland de Bourdigné, the father of the young clerk, passed through Angers to take leave of his son. He was going to Italy, to join the army of Gaston de Foix, accompanied by a retinue of knights and squires of Anjou and Maine. Several months then elapsed before Jean received news of his father. One day, however, a herald, bearing the escutcheon of Jacques du Lude, high seneschal of the province, published through all the streets and public places of the city the glorious news of the great victory gained over the Spaniards by the French at Ravenna; and Jean was further informed that Sir Roland, after having distinguished

himself in the battle, had managed to escape safe
and sound. This welcome intelligence seems to
have inspired our young clerk with the desire of
becoming an historian, and, as his sacred character
did not allow him to take an active part in military
exploits, he formed the resolution of at least
recording them to the best of his ability. He
considered that "the deeds and glorious actions
of the noble and brave consuls, counts, and dukes
of Anjou had never yet been described, although
they existed in the shape of chronicles, and there
was great danger lest, in course of time, their high
renown might be forgotten." Moved by this idea,
Jean de Bourdigné set immediately to work. He
visited the monasteries, churches, and baronial
halls of the province, collecting traditions, examining records, charters, and title-deeds, and noting
down with the utmost care whatever details seemed
to him worthy of remembrance. The uncritical
spirit of those days accepted indiscriminately, as
equally true, the legends of the saints, the wonderful tales about Charlemagne and his twelve
peers, and the best authenticated facts of comparatively recent times. Nay, the more wonderful
the origins of a nation were, the better; and no
kingdom, dukedom, or principality was considered
as worth notice which could not trace back its
ancestry to some nephew or cousin of Æneas or
Turnus. Bourdigné's annals are compiled according
to that well-established and thoroughly orthodox

principle. They are divided into three parts, the first of which must be set aside as historically worthless, with the exception of a few geographical indications, the list of the Bishops of Angers, and some genealogical details on the houses of France and Anjou. To give an idea of the extravagances which Jean de Bourdigné seriously passes off as history, we may say that he traces down from Noah the list of the Kings of Gaul and the Counts of Anjou. He ascribes to a grandson of Japhet the foundation of the earliest universities, and he describes the colonization of Gaul by a band of fugitives from Troy, under the command of Francus, the son of Hector. In the fourteenth chapter we have the description of a terrible battle fought by King Arthur with a giant, whom, of course, he puts to death; and of another noteworthy encounter, where 460 Romans are killed by the Celtic king, and where perished the first Count of Anjou, Gayus, who had massacred the *King of Babylon!* The chapter following, although disfigured by a great many historical blunders, nevertheless contains a few well-authenticated facts; and, as we go on, accuracy increases, and fable makes way for truth.

Book I., beginning with the Flood, goes down to the baptism of Clovis; the next one describes the reign of the successors of Ingelger, whom Jean de Bourdigné considers as the founder of the second house of Anjou, and takes us down to the erection of the county of Anjou into a duchy on behalf of the second son of King John; the third ends with the year 1529, and the treachery of the Constable of Bourbon. In this division of the work we find ourselves treading safely on historic ground, and having to deal with realities, instead of legends and dreams more or less poetical. We are supplied with abundance of details on the princes of the third house of Anjou, good King René, and the general history of the period. As he goes on, our author describes the miseries under which the common people were groaning; the famines, inundations, plagues, and pestilences which at various times afflicted the country; the miracles performed by holy men of God, the foundation of monasteries and other religious establishments, the heresies and schisms which distracted the Church, and especially the deeds of valour performed by Angevin knights and squires. Jean de Bourdigné is a thorough Frenchman; he hates with equal intensity *le monstre Luthérique*, the Burgundians and the English. We may observe also that, whilst having no pretensions to be called a philosophic historian, such as Philippe de Commines, our Angevin chronicler has sometimes shrewdly perceived, and expressed accurately, the motives for certain political arrangements and international combinations. Thus, when he describes the expedition of Louis XII. into Italy, he appreciates perfectly well the policy of the French, the

Venetians, and the Mussulmans. The style of Jean de Bourdigné is very pleasant, even picturesque at times, and, without equalling in the slightest degree the brilliant language of Froissart, it carries the reader along through a variety of scenes and of political, civil, and ecclesiastical incidents. The Angevin barons played a prominent part in the history of Europe. Their province was the cradle of two of the greatest dynasties of kings; on the shores of the Mediterranean, at Jerusalem, in England, in Sicily, in Arragon, and in Hungary they left traces of their passage; and it is not much to be wondered at if the recollection of so many heroes inspired a patriotic scholar with the ambition of becoming their historian. The *Chronique d'Anjou* was dedicated by Bourdigné to the queen, Louise of Savoy, mother of Francis I.

Paradin de Cuiseaux and Alain Bouchard endeavoured to accomplish, respectively, for Burgundy and for Brittany, the task which Jean de Bourdigné had so successfully done for Anjou. Born about the year 1510 at Cuiseaux (Saône-et-Loire), the former of these compilers took orders, but devoted all his time to historical writing. The *Memoriæ nostri Temporis* (published in 1548, and translated into French two years afterwards), the *Chronique de Savoïe* (1552, 4°; 1602, folio), and an interesting journal extending from 1572 to 1573, are works which bear evidence, at any rate, of considerable industry; but the book which concerns us most here is the *Annales de Bourgogne*, published in 1566, in a folio volume. The preface, addressed to the most illustrious, high, and mighty prince, François de Bourbon, Dauphin of Auvergne, governor and lieutenant-general for the king, begins with an appeal to rulers and magistrates, founded upon the Scriptures and illustrated from the history of the Assyrians, Babylonians, etc. The author then declares his intention of committing to writing the annals of the people of Burgundy, being thereunto moved—first, by the spirit of patriotism, and, secondly, by the moral qualities of the Bourguignons and the natural advantages of the territory itself. The work is divided into three books: the first, beginning with the settlement of the Burgundians in Gaul, goes down to the destruction of the kingdom of Burgundy; the second describes the formation of the duchy, and traces the genealogy of the dukes to Hugh Capet—it terminates at the death of Philippe de Rouvre in 1361; the third comprises the history of the dukes belonging to the house of Valois. Paradin deserves a great deal of credit for his diligence and his enthusiasm in the cause of history; he travelled through part of France and the Netherlands in quest of materials, and contrived to find a kind appreciator of his merits in Charles, Cardinal of Lorraine, who introduced him to King Henry II. This monarch gave him assurances of his protection and good-will, speedily adding to these assurances a substantial proof, in the shape of a canonry attached to the chapter of Beaujeu. Unfortunately, with all his learning and industry, Paradin had not that critical spirit which we expect to find in historians, and his credulity is sometimes amusing. Saint Julien de Balleuse describes the *Annales de Bourgogne* as a "most excellent volume, so useful that he who possesses it need not trouble himself about Froissart, Monstrelet, Olivier de la Marche, or other such historiographers." This is somewhat exaggerated praise.

On the same rank as Paradin we can place Alain Bouchard, barrister at the Parliament of Rennes, and, chronologically speaking, the first professed historian of Brittany. The title of his work is *Grandes Chroniques de Bretaigne, parlans des très pieux, nobles et belliqueux rois, ducs, princes, barons, et autres gens nobles, tant de la Grand-Bretaigne, dite à présent Angleterre, que de notre Bretaigne de présent érigé en duché*, etc. ; it was published for the first time in 1514. The critic in M. Michaud's *Biographie Universelle* finds fault with Bouchard's style, which he describes as "aussi gothique que les caractères dont on s'est servi pour l'imprimer." The defect is a real one, no doubt, but it cannot be fairly made a cause of complaint against the annalist who, living in the sixteenth century, wrote like his contemporaries. The great drawback to the *Chroniques de Bretaigne* is their thoroughly unsound character, and the extreme credulity with which Bouchard admitted all the fables vulgarized by Geoffrey of Monmouth, the legends of the Round Table, and the facts contained in the chronicle of the pseudo-Turpin. Indeed, the fictitious element holds so important a place in the work in question, that Lenglet-Dufresnoy has included it in his *Bibliothèque des Romans*, and another bibliographer classes it under the heading *Romans de Chevalerie!*

Before bringing this chapter to a close, we must say a few words about another class of books, to which attention has been given in France only since a comparatively recent date, but which are of the utmost importance for the political, civil, and religious history of the Middle Ages; we mean the cartularies or records of monasteries or other ecclesiastical communities. At a very early time these establishments felt the necessity of preserving carefully the charters, letters, bulls, and other title-deeds which secured to them the enjoyment of their estates and their privileges; loose documents might easily be lost or mislaid, and, besides, the difficulty of deciphering the writing of various epochs was a serious one. Hence the custom of transcribing all these *pièces justificatives* in registers provided expressly for the purpose. The habit of keeping cartularies spread throughout Europe during the tenth and two following centuries; and, after having originated with monasteries and churches, it was adopted by kings, barons, and municipal corporations.

There are three kinds of cartularies: the first, which are, of course, the most valuable, contain the original documents themselves; the second give transcripts duly authenticated; the third consist of copies which may be perfectly trustworthy, but still have not been verified and examined by duly qualified persons. The instruments belonging to this last class cannot be appealed to in a court of justice, and yet they enjoy almost the same authority as the others, especially, 1. when they are of ancient date; 2. when they have been compiled before the custom had obtained of getting the cartularies collated by lawyers or magistrates; 3. when, belonging to a relatively recent date, they were compiled with the sanction or by the authority of trustworthy persons, and not for the purpose of sanctioning some act of usurpation. There are, moreover, other record-books or registers containing notices and quotations from charters, with explanatory notes and the narrative of historical facts. These cartularies, which thus may be almost classed amongst chronicles properly so called, have often been attacked by modern critics, but still they are valuable as a source of information.

The cartularies, under the various designations of *pastoral, livre admirable, livre d'or, livre noir, livre rouge*, etc., offer a great diversity in the order or classification of the documents which they contain. Some (*Le Petit Pastoral de Notre Dame de Paris*, for instance) are arranged in chapters, according as the pieces inserted have emanated from, 1. popes; 2. kings; 3. counts; 4. bishops; 5. abbots; 6. deans and chapters, etc. Others prefer to adopt a kind of geographical or topographical method, and classify the documents under names of localities. Others, again, simply adhere to the chronological system, inserting the charters and title-deeds just as they have been obtained; the cartulary becomes thus a kind of journal. In a very great number of record-books no order whatever is followed. Sometimes there is a considerable interruption in the series of entries; the last blank pages of the volume are used for the purpose of making considerable additions; in some cases the margins are turned into account for the insertion of notes or even small acts.

A few cartularies had been published in France before the Revolution of 1789, but it is only within the last forty years that an effort has been made to print as a collection these interesting monuments of mediæval history. The suggestion originated with M. Guizot, and one of the most competent antiquarians, the late M. Guérard, was appointed to superintend the undertaking, and to give it the benefit of his active co-operation. A certain number of cartularies have already appeared, forming part of the *Collection des Documents Inédits;* M. Guérard himself being responsible for those of Saint Père of Chartres, Notre Dame of Paris, Saint Rémi at Reims, besides the *Polyptyque* of the Abbot Irminon, which, together with its commentary, is so invaluable a source of information for the history of society during the Middle Ages.

The interesting collection of historical songs published by M. Leroux de Lincy is entitled to a very distinguished place in our notice of mediæval memoirs, for these short poems are certainly the record of important events and well-known historical characters, written by contemporaries; and if the *chansons de geste* often furnish us with trustworthy evidence, if the *Roman de Rou*, the *Roman de Brut*, and the poem on the Albigenses deserve to be taken into serious consideration by historians, the same remark applies to the *Recueil de Chants Historiques et Populaires*, for which we are indebted to M. Leroux de Lincy.

The habit which the French soldiers had of composing popular songs can be traced to the earliest times of the monarchy; under the Merovingian dynasty, they were written in Latin, and some specimens of these pieces have been preserved for us. Thus, in the *Bibliothèque de l'École des Chartes* we find a popular song composed in honour of King Childebert, and Lebeuf (*Dissertations sur l'Histoire Ecclésiastique et Civile de Paris*, vol. i. p. 426) has printed a Latin one, which celebrates the exploits of Eric, Duke of Friuli. We know that Charlemagne had collected together those which his soldiers were accustomed to repeat amongst themselves. Lebeuf (*Recueil de Divers Écrits*, vol. i. pp.

333-369) gives us a number of rough and patriotic lyrics referring to the reigns of Charlemagne's successors and of the early Capetians; some are in Latin, some in French. With the twelfth century begins an era of national literature for France; the idioms of Langue d'Oïl and Languedoc rise to the position of vulgar languages, and they are soon employed in celebrating the prowess of knights, barons, and soldiers who took part in the Crusades. *Troubadours* and *trouvères* vie with each other in composing the martial poems which served both as a record of ancient deeds and as an incentive to fresh exploits; and, during the period of time included between the accession of Philip Augustus and the death of Louis XI., we find a rich crop of historical songs, not possessing much merit, perhaps, if considered as literary compositions, but extremely valuable as *pièces justificatives* illustrating certain episodes in mediæval history. "The French soldiers," says Leroux de Lincy, "are often judges carried away by their passions, and they treat with undue severity the heroism spent upon causes which are either desperately lost or condemned by public opinion, but in most cases the judgment they pass is very fair, and has been ratified by the verdict of history." A great many of these compositions will be found in Raynouard's *Choix des Poésies Originales de Troubadours*, and in the *Romancero Français*, published by M. Paulin Paris. A few examples will serve to show the use of popular songs in illustrating historical facts of much importance. It is well known that, towards the beginning of the fifteenth century, the inhabitants of Liége having rebelled against the bishop, John of Bavaria, besieged him in Maestricht and ravaged the neighbourhood of that city. John, Duke of Burgundy, marched for the purpose of reducing the insurrection, and attacked them at Hasbain on the 23rd of September, 1408. This battle is one of the most noteworthy incidents in the military career of the Duke of Burgundy, who ran considerable danger, and obtained in consequence the surname of *Fearless* (*sans peur*), by which he has always been distinguished. Monstrelet, Pierre de Fénin, and the monk of Saint Denis have given a detailed account of this war, and of the severe chastisement inflicted upon the rebels by the Duke of Burgundy. It is curious to compare with these narratives the two *chansons* which form part of M. Leroux de Lincy's *recueil*, and to see how thoroughly the poet confirms all the particulars related by the chroniclers whom we have just been naming.

The war of the *public good* and the battle of Montlhéry occupy in the reign of Louis XI. so important a place, that we cannot wonder at their having been celebrated from various points of view by the popular minstrels of the fifteenth century. Some would take the part of the barons; others, on the contrary, extolling the political system of the wily monarch, would rejoice at the fresh effort made by him to strike down the tottering edifice of feudalism. Jacques de Clercq has inserted in his memoirs two ballads on the subject; four additional ones have been printed by M. Leroux de Lincy in the *Chants Historiques et Populaires*. One of these pieces alludes to an incident which the historians who have written on the reign of Louis XI. do not mention, and which is, however, one of the most curious episodes in the *League of the Public Good*. The anonymous poet says, addressing Louis XI.—

> " For those who have to rule the crown
> May perhaps deprive you of your power." [1]

Another poem, in like manner, contains the following suggestion :—

> ' The fourth wishes to obtain as much money
> As is worth the fine gold crown
> Of the new king or regent
> Appointed in France this year." [2]

Now, these two passages are a confirmation of the fact that the barons leagued in 1461 against Louis XI. had resolved upon dethroning him, and selecting from amongst themselves a regent or even a king, for the only direct heir to the crown

---

[1] " Car ceulx qui ont à régir la couronne
Te pouront bien l'oster de ta puissance."

[2] " Le quart souhaite autant d'argent
Que vault la belle couronne dorée
De ce nouveau roy ou régent
Mis sulz en Franche ceste année."

of France at that time was a girl three years old.
There can be no doubt whatever respecting the
design entertained by the confederates, for it was
plainly acknowledged by Crèvecœur in the examination he had to undergo after he had been
taken prisoner by the French troops.

The poems of Olivier Basselin and of Eustache
Deschamps deserve, to a certain extent, the name
of historical compositions, as they are full of allusions to the events which marked the occupation
of France by the English. We find, besides, in
Monstrelet, the *Journal d'un Bourgeois de Paris*,
and other contemporary memoirs, a number of
quotations from songs and ballads reported as
having been very popular, and intended to express
the feelings of the Burgundians and Armagnacs
respectively. For an account of these poetical
illustrations of history, we must refer our readers
to M. Charles Nisard's work, *Des Chansons Populaires, chez les Anciens et chez les Français*.

Materials had thus been accumulating for several
centuries, which professed historians might work
into something like artistic shape, and around which
they might throw the graces of literary composition; but the time had not come yet for such
results, and the earliest French historians, properly
so called, are distinguished by their credulity, their
pedantry, and the tedious, heavy style of their
writings. As we have already said, the *Chroniques
de France* may be considered as the first attempt

to produce a national history, but they still partook more of the nature of chronicles, being in most cases the record of what the successive authors had actually seen, and possessing, therefore, the merit of works composed at first hand. If we wish to come to an historian, we must name the compiler Martinus Polonus, thus called because he was a Pole by origin, and who, after having joined the Dominican order, went into Italy, became chaplain to Pope Clement IV., and was appointed by him, in 1278, to the archbishopric of Gnesnen; he died on the 29th of June of the same year, just one week after his nomination. The chronicle of Martinus Polonus (*Martini Poloni Chronica Summorum Pontificum Imperatorumque*, etc.) was published for the first time at Bâle in 1559, in folio. It was originally, as the title sufficiently shows, a mere collection of annals bearing upon the popes and the Emperors of Germany, extending from the apostolic times to the year 1277. Additions, however, were made to it at various times by Herold, Suffrid, and Fabricius; and Bernard Guidonis, Bishop of Lodève, entirely recast the work, adding a number of passages from authors which Martinus Polonus had neglected to consult, and bringing it down as late as the year 1328. After him, the next continuator we have to name is Father Echard Ververon, or Verneron, who wrote the history of the popes and of the empire as far as the death of Urban V., in 1378; and it was this compilation which Sebastian Mamerot translated into French under the title *La Chronique Martiniane de tous les Papes qui furent jamais, et finit au Pape Alexandre VI. dernier décédé*, printed about 1504, by Vérard, in folio. This curious work contains, amongst other things, a number of documents on the history of France, which were added on, as the Abbé Lebeuf supposes,[1] for the purpose of swelling the second volume, but which, at the same time, deserve the attention of students. We must do Mamerot the justice that, in his translation, he shows a judgment and a discrimination which are altogether wanting in the original work. The *Martini Poloni Chronica*, collected from all quarters, and containing extracts frequently from the most untrustworthy sources, is uncritical in the highest degree. Mamerot, on the other hand, suppressed a large number of passages which Bernard Guidonis and the latter continuators had inserted—passages of so absurd and childish a character, that they would have disfigured a work having the slightest pretensions to be called historical. The authors consulted by Mamerot in the preparation of his second volume are Jean de Montreuil and most of the chroniclers belonging to the fourteenth century; the part referring to the reign of Louis XI. is chiefly a transcript of the *Chronique Scan-*

---

[1] *Mémoires de l'Académie des Inscriptions et Belles-Lettres*, vol. xx. p. 224.

daleuse. Mamerot composed, in addition, a work describing the high deeds of Godefroy de Bouillon, Saint Louis, and other princes who took a part in the Crusades.

Nicole Gilles was a political personage, as well as an historian. Born in the fifteenth century, he held the offices of notary and secretary to King Louis XII., besides the post of secretary to the treasury; he died at Paris, in 1503. The *Annales et Chroniques de France . . . jusqu'au Roi Charles VIII.* may be regarded as the first attempt made to write the history of France as a distinct work, and a very tame attempt it is. Gilles merely satisfied himself with abridging the *Chroniques de Saint Denis* and the memoirs of Guillaume de Nangis, the only portion having the slightest claims to originality being that which treats of the reign of Louis XI. M. Augustin Thierry is rather severe in his appreciation of Nicole Gilles. It was absurd, of course, to repeat as facts the old legends about Francus, Marcomer, and the classical origin of the French nation; but we cannot much wonder at the uncritical statements of the old historian, when we see how Velly and even Anquetil have distorted facts and misrepresented characters.

On the same line as Gilles we must place Robert Gaguin, born in the province of Artois, about the year 1425, and who died in July, 1562, after a most useful and honourable career. He obtained, at an early age, great and, as it seems, deserved reputation as a lecturer on rhetoric, and the services he rendered to the University of Paris so far recommended him that he was elected general of the order of the Trinitarian friars. Three kings of France—Louis XI., Charles VIII., and Louis XII.—employed Gaguin upon negotiations of an extremely delicate nature, and on one occasion, in 1491, when he had been sent as ambassador to England, he pronounced a speech which must have been a masterpiece of tact and of genuine eloquence, if it was anything like the one given by Velly in his history of France. Robert Gaguin was entrusted, both by Charles VIII. and by Louis XII., with the keepership of the royal library, and the high esteem in which he was held at the Sorbonne enabled him both to render important services at the University of Paris, and to assist the Government with his advice on difficult occasions. The historical work which has entitled Gaguin to a place in this sketch is entitled *Compendium supra Francorum Gestis a Pharamundo.* The first edition goes down only to the year 1491; it was then continued as far as 1499, and a third edition, published in 1521, brought the narrative to the end of the reign of Louis XII. Robert Gaguin has been accused of flattery and of partiality, but the character he gives of Louis XI. should surely exonerate him in this respect. We think that, on the contrary, he is remarkable for the fairness of his appreciations, and Erasmus—no mean judge in literary matters—praises not only the method and accuracy of the *Compendium*, but the clearness and beauty of its style. We may add that the compilers of the *Chronique Martiniane* were under great obligations to our author. With him we come to the end of the subject. The historians who succeeded him belong to the period of the Renaissance, and when Pierre Pascal entered upon his duties as historiographer to King Henry II., mediævalism had long been a thing of the past.

BIOGRAPHICAL INDEX.

A.

Alcuin, ? 735-804.
Alexander III. (Roland Rainuce Bandinelli), pope, 1159.
Alexis I. Comnenus, 1048-1118; Emperor of Constantinople, 1081.
Amaury I., ? 1135 or 38-1173; King of Jerusalem, 1162.
Amaury de Montfort, 1192-1281, Constable of France.
Anastasius, librarian at the Vatican (ninth century).
Anne de Beaujeu, daughter of Louis XI., ? 1462-1522; Regent of France, 1483.
Ansegise, ?-833, Abbot of St. Wandrille.
Armagnac (Bernard VII., Count d'), 1391-1418.
Arteveld (Philip van), killed in 1382, at the battle of Roosebeke.
Arthur, King of England (sixth century).
Augustine (Saint), 354-430.

B.

Bajazet I. (surnamed *Ilderim = the Thunderbolt*), Sultan, 1389; died 1402.
Balue (Jean la), ? 1421-1491, cardinal, chaplain to Louis XI.
Baudouin I., Count of Boulogne, King of Jerusalem, 1100-1118.
Baudouin II., King of Jerusalem, 1118-1131.
Baudouin III., King of Jerusalem, 1144-1162.
Baudouin IV., King of Jerusalem, 1174-1185.
Baudouin IX., Count of Flanders, first Emperor of Constantinople, 1171-1206.
Bedford (John Pantagenet, Duke of), 1389-1435, youngest brother of Henry V. of England.
Benedict XIII. (Pedro di Luna), antipope, 1394-1424.

Berri (Jean, Duc de), 1340–1416, third son of Jean II., King of France.
Bohemond, Prince of Antioch, son of Robert Guiscard, died 1111.
Boniface III., Marquis of Montferrat from 1183 to 1207.
Boucicaut (Jean le Maingre, Sire de), 1364–1421; Marshal of France, 1389.
Bourbon (Charles, Duc de), better known as the *Constable of Bourbon*, 1489–1527.
Briçonnet (Guillaume), ? 1471–1533, Bishop of Meaux, ambassador of France at Rome.
Brosse (Pierre de la), died 1278, Prime Minister of Philip the Bold, King of France.

C.

Cauchon (Pierre), Bishop of Beauvais, died 1443.
Charlemagne, 742–814, King of the whole of France, 771; Emperor of the West, 800.
Charles Martel, 689–741; Duke of Austrasia, 714.
Charles the Bold, 1433–1477; Duke of Burgundy, 1467.
Charles the Bad, 1332–1387; King of Navarre, 1349.
Charles II. the Bald, 823–877.

KINGS OF FRANCE.

Charles III. the Simple, 879–929; King of France, 893.
Charles IV., 1294–1328; King of France, 1322.
Charles V., 1337–1380; King of France, 1364.
Charles VI., 1368–1422; King of France, 1380.
Charles VIII., 1470–1498; King of France, 1483.

Charles, Duke of Orléans, 1391–1466.
Charles, Count of Blois, died 1364.
Charles IV., emperor, 1376–1378.
Charles, Cardinal of Lorraine, 1525–1574.
Charles d'Anjou, Count of Maine, died 1472.
Chartier (Jean), died 1462.
Chartier (Alain), 1386–1458?
Childebert, King of Paris, 511; died 558.
Clément IV. (Guy de Foulque), 1200–1268; pope, 1265.
Clément V. (Bertrand de Got or Goth), pope, 1305; died 1314.
Cloatire I., ? 497–561; King of France, 558.
Clotaire II., King of Soissons, 584; of France, 613; died 628.

Clovis I., 465-511; king, 481.
Clovis II., King of Neustria and Burgundy, 638; died 656.
Cœur (Jacques), 1400-1456.

D.

Dagobert I., 604-638, King of Austrasia, 622; of France, 631.
Dandolo (Enrico), Doge of Venice in 1192; died 1202.
Deschamps (Eustache), 1325-1421.
Du Guesclin (Bertrand), 1314?-1380; Constable of France, 1370.

E.

Edward III., 1312-1377; King of England, 1327.
Edward IV., 1422-1483; King of England, 1461.
Eleanor of Guienne, 1122-1203.
Eudes, King of France; died 898.

F.

Ferry IV., Duke of Lorraine in 1312.
Foulques Nerra, Count of Anjou, 987; died 1040.
Foulques le Réchin, 1043-1109; Count of Anjou, 1060.
Foulques le Roux, Count of Anjou, 888; died 938.
François I., 1494-1547; King of France, 1515.
Frederic I. Barbarossa, 1121-1189; Emperor of Germany, 1152.
Frederic II., 1194-1250; Emperor of Germany, 1197.

G.

Gaston de Foix, 1489-1512.
Genseric, King of the Vandals from 428 to 477.
Geoffroy Martel, Count of Anjou from 1041 to 1060.
Geoffroy le Bel, Duke of Anjou, 1129; died 1150.
Geoffroy Grise-Gonelle, Count of Anjou, 958; died 987.
Gilbert de Montpensier, died 1496.
Godefroy de Bouillon, 1058-1100.
Gondebaud, fourth King of Burgundy, ?-516.
Gregory IX., pope in 1227, died 1241.
Gregory XI. (Pierre Roger de Beaufort), born 1332; pope, 1370; died 1378.
Guillaume au Court-nez, Duke of Aquitaine, died 812.

Guillaume Longue-Épée, Duke of Normandy, 927.
Guy de Châtillon, Count of Blois, died 1342.
Guy de Lusignan, King of Cyprus, 1192; died 1194 or 1195.

H.

Henri I., 1005–1060; King of France, 1031.
Henri II., 1518–1519; King of France, 1547.

KINGS OF ENGLAND.

Henry I., 1068–1135; king, 1100.
Henry II., 1133–1189; king, 1154.
Henry III., 1208–1272; king, 1216.
Henry IV., 1367–1413; king, 1399.
Henry V., 1388–1422; king, 1413.
Henry VI., 1422–1471; king, 1422.
Henry VII., 1458–1509; king, 1485.
Henry VIII., 1491–1547; king, 1509.

Hugues Capet, King of France, 987; died 996.

I.

Ingelberga, 1193–1236.
Innocent III. (Lothario Conti), pope from 1198 to 1216.
Innocent IV. (Sinibad be Fiesko), pope from 1243 to 1254.
Isaac Comnenus, Emperor of Constantinople from 1057 to 1059.

J.

Jacques de Vitry, ?–1240; Archbishop of Ptolemaïs, 1217.
James II., King of Scotland, 1430–1460; king, 1437.
Jean de Brienne, Emperor of Constantinople, 1231; died 1237.
Jean sans Peur, Duke of Burgundy, 1404; murdered, 1419.
Jean II., King of France, 1319–1364; king, 1350.
Jean de Montfort, claimant of the duchy of Brittany, died 1345.
Jeanne d'Arc, 1409–1431.
Jeanne de France, 1465–1505, daughter of Louis XI.
Jeanne de Navarre, died 1304, married Philip the Handsome, King of France.
John, King of Bohemia, king in 1310, died 1346.
Joinville (Geoffroy V. de), 1196–1205.
Julius II. (Giuliano della Rovere), 1443–1513; pope, 1503.

L.

La Trémouille (Louis II., Sire de), 1460-1525.
Leo X. (Giovanni de' Medici), 1475-1521 ; pope, 1513.
Lothaire, ? 795-855 ; King of France, 817 ; and Emperor of the West, 840.
Louis II. de Bourbon, 1337-1416.

KINGS OF FRANCE.

Louis III. the Stammerer, 846-879 ; king, 877.
Louis VI. the Fat, 1081-1137; king, 1223.
Louis VII., 1120-1180 ; king, 1137.
Louis VIII., 1187-1226 ; king, 1223.
Louis IX., 1215-1270 ; king, 1226.
Louis X., 1289-1316 ; king, 1314.
Louis XI., 1423-1483 ; king, 1461.
Louis XII., 1462-1515 ; king, 1498.

Louise de Savoie, 1476-1531, Regent of France.

M.

Manuel-Palæologus, Emperor of Constantinople, 1391 ; died 1477.
Marcel (Etienne), killed in 1358.
Margaret of Anjou, Queen of England, died 1472.
Margaret of Austria, 1480-1530, married to Philibert, Duke of Savoy.
Marguerite de Provence, Queen of France, 1221-1295.
Marie de France, thirteenth century.
Mary of Gueldres, wife of James II. of Scotland, died 1463.
Maurice de Sully, ? -1196 ; Bishop of Paris, 1160.
Maximilian I., 1459-1519 ; Emperor of Germany, 1493.

N.

Nicolas V. (Tommaso Parentucelli), pope from 1447 to 1555.
Nomenoé, died 851.

O.

Olivier Basselin, died 1500 ?
Olivier de Clisson, 1332-1407.
Otho II., 955-983 ; Emperor of Germany, 973.

Peter the Hermit, ? 1050-1115.
Peter II., King of Arragon, reigned from 1196 to 1213.

KINGS OF FRANCE.

Philip II. Augustus, 1165-1223; king, 1180.
Philip III. the Bold, 1245-1285; king, 1271.
Philip IV. the Fair, 1268-1314; king, 1285.
Philip V. the Long, 1229?-1332; king, 1317.

Philippe de Rouvre, Duke of Burgundy, 1345-1361.
Philip the Good, Duke of Burgundy, 1306-1467.

Q.

Quesnes de Béthune, died 1224.

R.

Raymond VI., Count of Toulouse, died 1222.
Raymond VII., 1197-1249, Count of Toulouse.
René I., 1408-1480; Count of Provence, 1431.
Richard I. Cœur de Lion, 1157-1199; King of England, 1189.
Richard I. the Fearless, Duke of Normandy, 935-996.
Richard II. the Good, Duke of Normandy in 996, died 1027.
Richard II., Prince of Capua in 1091.
Robert II., Count d'Artois, 1250-1302.
Robert Guiscard, ? 1015-1085.
Roger I., 1031-1101, Count of Sicily.
Roger II., 1097-1154, Count, then King of Sicily.
Roland, nephew of Charlemagne, king, 778.
Rollo, first Duke of Normandy, ? 860-932.

S.

Saintré (Jean de), 1320-1368.
Sancho VII., King of Navarre in 1194.
Simon de Montfort, ? 1160-1218.

T.

Talbot, first Earl of Shrewsbury, ? 1370-1453.
Tancred de Hauteville, died 1112.

Theodore Lascaris I., Emperor of Constantinople, 1206 ; died 1222.
Theodoric I., King of Austrasia, ? 486–534.
Thibaut II., Count of Champagne in 1125.
Thibaut IV., Count of Champagne, 1201–1253.
Thomas à Becket, 1117–1170; Archbishop of Canterbury in 1162.

V.

Valentine de Milan, Duchesse d'Orléans, ? 1370–1408.
Valentinian III., 419–455; emperor in 424.

W.

Walter the Penniless, eleventh century.
Wenceslaus of Luxemburg, Emperor of Germany from 1378 to 1400.
William Rufus, King of England, 1087 ; died 1100.

GEOGRAPHICAL INDEX.

A.

Agincourt, a village of France, in the department of Pas-de-Calais.
Agnadel, a small town in Lombardy (Lodi).
Aigues Mortes (L. *Aquæ Mortuæ*), a town of France, in the department of Gard.
Aire (L. *Aeria Atrebatum*), a town of France, in the department of Pas-de-Calais.
Aix (L. *Aquæ Sextiæ*), a town of France, in the department of Bouches-du-Rhône, formerly capital of Provence.
Alost, a town in Belgium (Eastern Flanders).
Amboise (L. *Ambacia*), a town of France, in the department of Indre-et-Loire (province of Touraine).
Amiens (L. *Samarobriva*, then *Ambiani*), chief town of the department of Somme, formerly capital of Picardy, in France.
Angers (L. *Juliomagus, Andes*, or *Andecavi*), chief town in the department of Maine-et-Loire, formerly capital of Anjou, in France.
Anjou (L. *Andecavi*), a province of France, situated between those of Poitou, Normandy, Maine, Touraine, and Brittany.
Antioch (L. *Antiochia ad Daphneri, Antakieh*), a town in Syria.
Aquitaine (L. *Aquitania*), one of the four great regions of Gaul.
Arcis-sur-Aube, a small French town, in the department of Aube.
Ardres, a small town in France (Pas-de-Calais).
Argenteuil, a village near Paris, in the department of Seine-et-Oise.
Argenton (L. *Argentomagus*), a town in the province of Berry (Indre), in France.

Arras (L. *Atrebates, Nemetacum*), formerly capital of the province of Artois, chief town of the department of Pas-de-Calais.

Artois, one of the provinces of Northern France; comprises nearly the district occupied by the Atrebates.

Auvergne, a province in the south-east of France.

Avenche (L. *Aventicum*), a town of Switzerland (Vaud).

Avesnes (L. *Avenæ*), a town in the department of the Nord (province of Artois).

Avignon (L. *Avenio*), a town in France, chief place of the department of Vauclure.

B.

Bar-sur-Aube (L. *Barrum-ad-Albulam*), a small but ancient town of Champagne (department of Aube).

Bayeux (L. *Augustodurus*), a city in the department of Calvados (Normandy).

Béarn, a province of France, comprising part of *Novempopulania*; capital, Pau.

Beauvais (L. *Cæsaromagus, Bellovaci*), capital of the department of Oise, in France.

Berry, a French province, corresponding to the territory of the *Bituriges*.

Biclar, an ancient town in the south of France, now destroyed.

Blaisois, or *Blésois*, formerly part of the province of Orléanais.

Blois (L. *Blesiæ, Blesa, Blesum*), formerly capital of Blaisois, now chief town of the department of Loir-et-Cher.

Bouillon (L. *Bullio*), capital of the old duchy of Bouillon, now part of Belgium.

Boulogne (L. *Gesoriacum, Bononia*), a seaport town in the department of Pas-de-Calais.

Boulonnais, a small district in the north of France, formerly part of Picardy; capital Boulogne.

Bourges (L. *Avaricum, Bituriges*), chief town of the department of Cher; formerly the capital of Berry.

Bourgueil, a small town in the department of Indre-et-Loire (province of Touraine).

Bouvines (L. *Boviniacum*), a village in the department of the Nord.

Brabant was formerly a duchy of the German empire, in the circle of Burgundy.

Brétigny, a hamlet in the department of Eure-et-Loir (Pays Chartrain).

Brie (L. *Brigensis Saltus*), an old province forming part of the governments both of Ile-de-France and of Champagne.

Brittany (L. *Britannia Major*, *Armorica*). This province, the capital of which was Rennes, now forms five departments.

Bruges, a town in Belgium, capital of Western Flanders.

C.

Caen (L. *Cadomus*), chief town of the department of Calvados, formerly capital of Lower Normandy.

Cahors (L. *Divona*, *Cadurci*), chief town of the department of Lot (province of Quercy).

Cambray (L. *Cameracum*), a town in the department of the Nord, France.

Canterbury (L. *Durovernum*, *Cantuaria*), chief town of the county of Kent.

Capua, a town of the old kingdom of Naples (*Terra di Lavoro*).

Carcassonne (L. *Carcaso*), capital of the department of Aude, in the south of France.

Castillon, a small town in the department of Gironde.

Châlons (L. *Catalauni*, *Duro Catalaunum*), chief town of the department of Marne (province of Champagne).

Cerdagne, a small district near the Pyrenees, part of which belongs to France (Pyrénées Orientales), and part to Spain.

Champagne, one of the most important provinces of ancient France; its capital was Troyes; forms four departments.

Chartres (L. *Autricum*, *Carnutes*), chief town of the department of Eure-et-Loir (province of Beauce).

Châteauneuf de Randon, a small town in the department of Lozère.

Chimay, a small town in Belgium (Hainaut).

Clermont (L. *Nemetum*, *Augustonemetum*), chief town of the department of Puy-de-Dôme, capital of Auvergne.

Cocherel, a village of Normandy (Eure).

Conflans, a small town near Paris, on the confluence of the Seine and the Marne; hence its name.

Corbie, a town in the department of the Somme (province of Picardy).

Crécy, a village of Picardy (Somme).

D.

Damietta, a seaport town in Lower Egypt.
Dijon (L. *Divio*), chief town of the department of the Côte-d'Or in France, capital of Burgundy.
Dol, a small town in the department of Ille-et-Vilaine (Brittany).
Dover (L. *Dubris*), a seaport town in Kent.
Dreux (L. *Durocasses*), a town in the department of Eure-et-Loir.

F.

Flanders. This vast province, extending over the *Belgica Secunda*, had *Ghent* for its capital.
Flavigny, a celebrated Benedictine abbey in the department of Côte-d'Or.
Fontenelle, an abbey in the department of La Vendrée.
Fornovo (L. *Forum Novum*), a small town in Italy (Parma).
Franche-Comté (*Maxima Sequanorum*), belongs to France since 1678.
Frascati, almost rebuilt by Pope Paul III. about 1550.
Friuli, a province in the north-east of Italy, on the Adriatic Sea.

G.

Gembloux, or *Gemblours*, a town in Belgium (Namur).
Genoa (L. *Genua*), a well-known town in Italy.
Gnesen, a town in Prussia (*Posnania*).
Grenoble (L. *Cularo, Gratianopolis*), capital of the department of Isère.
Guelders, a province of the kingdom of Holland.
Guines, a small town in the department of Pas-de-Calais.

H.

Ham (L. *Hametum*) a town in the department of the Somme (Picardy).
Hainaut (L. *Hanogovensis Comitatus*), a province of Belgium.

I.

Ile-de-France. This important province was so called because, being situated between the Seine, the Marne, the Aisne, the Ourcq, and the Oise, it formed nearly an island.

J.

Jumièges (L. *Gemeticum*), a village in the department of Seine-Inférieure (Normandy).

L.

Languedoc (including the greater part of *Septimania*) was so called because its inhabitants spoke the language in which *oc* is the sign of affirmation.

Laon (L. *Bibrax, Lugdunum Clavatum*), chief town in the department of Aisne.

Lauresheim, or *Lorsch* (L. *Lauriacum*), a town in Germany (Hesse-Darmstadt).

Liége (L. *Leodum, Leodicum*), a city in Belgium.

Limoges (L. *Augustoritum, Lemovices*), chief town in the department of Haute-Vienne, capital of Limousin.

Lisieux (L. *Lexovii, Noviomagus*), a town in the department of Calvados.

Loches (*Luccæ*), a town in the department of Indre-et-Loire (Touraine).

Lodève (L. *Luteva*), a town in the department of Hérault.

Louvain (L. *Lovanium*), a city in Belgium (Brabant).

Luxemburg, formerly a province of the Netherlands, now a private possession of the King of Holland.

M.

Mâcon (L. *Matisco*), chief town of the department of Saône-et-Loire (Burgundy).

Mailross or *Melrose*, a small town in Scotland (Roxburgh).

Maine. This French province forms now the departments of Sarthe and of Mayenne.

Marignano, a small town in Italy (Lombardy).

Marmoutiers (L. *Martini Monasterium*), a village near Tours (Indre-et-Loire); formerly the seat of a celebrated monastery.

Marseille (L. *Massilia*), an important French seaport town, capital of the department of Bouches-du-Rhône.

Metz (L. *Divodurum*, then *Mediomatrices*), a city in Lorraine.

Milan (L. *Mediolanum*), capital of Lombardy.

Mons-en-Puëlle, a French village in the department of Nord.

Montereau (L. *Condate Senonum*), a small town in the department of Seine-et-Marne.

Montferrat, in the north of Italy, was formerly a marquisate (tenth century), and then a duchy (1573).

Montlhéry (L. *Mons Letterici*), a French village in the department of Seine-et-Oise.

Montpellier (L. *Mons Puellarum*, *Mons Pessulanus*), capital of the department of Hérault, in France.

Montreuil-Bellay, a small French town in the department of Maine-et-Loire.

Moulins, capital of the department of Allier.

Muret, a small town in Languedoc (Haute-Garonne).

N.

Nangis, a town in the department of Seine-et-Marne.

Navarre was formerly an independent kingdom; belongs now to Spain.

Navas de Tolosa, a plain in Spain, near Jaen.

Nemours (L. *Nemus*, *Nemosium*), a town in the department of Seine-et-Marne.

Nevers (L. *Noviodunum*, *Nivernum*), chief town of the department of Nièvre (capital of the province of Nivernais).

Nicomedia (now *Isnikmid*), a town in Bithynia.

Nicopolis (now *Nicopoli*), a town in Turkey (Bulgaria).

Nogent (L. *Novigentum*), a small town in the department of Haute Marne.

Normandy. The capital of this important duchy was Rouen; it includes now four departments, and part of a fifth.

Northampton. Henry VI. and Margaret of Anjou were defeated there in 1460.

Novare, a fortified town of Northern Italy (Sardinian dominions).

O.

Orange (L. *Arausio*), a town in the department of Vaucluse.

Orbieux, a small river in the south of France.

Orléans (L. *Genabum*, *Aureliani*), chief town of the department of Loiret (Orléanais).

P.

Pampeluna (L. *Pompeiopolis*, *Pampelo*), a fortified town in Spain (Navarre).
Parcé, a small town in Touraine.
Patay, a small town in the department of Loiret (Orléanais).
Pavia, the chief town of a province in Northern Italy.
Péronne, a town in Picardy (department of the Somme).
Pisa, a city in Tuscany.
Poitiers (L. *Limonum*, *Pictavi*), chief town of the department of Vienne (capital of Poitou).
Pontigny, a village in the department of Yonne.
Pontlevoy, a small town in the department of Loir-et-Cher.
Pontorson (L. *Pons Ursonis*), a town in the department of Manche.
Pont Saint-Maxence (L. *Litanobriga*), a town in the department of Oise.
Ptolemaïs, or *Saint Jean d'Acre*, a town in Syria.
Puy, Le (L. *Civitas Vellavorum*), chief town of the department of Haute-Loire, capital of Velay.
Puy-Laurens (L. *Podium Laurentii*), a small town in the department of Tarn (Albigeois).

Q.

Quesnoy-le-Comte (L. *Quercitum*), a town in the department of the Nord.

R.

Reims (L. *Durocortorum*, *Remi*), a city in the department of Marne.
Roncevaux, a village in Spain (Pampeluna).
Roosebeke, or *Rosbecque*, a village of Belgium (Western Flanders).
Roussillon, an ancient province and government of Southern France.

S.

Saint Denis (L. *Dionysii fanum*), a small town near Paris, in the department of the Seine.
Saint Gall, a canton and town in Switzerland.

Saint James of Compostella, a town in Spain (Galicia).
Sainte-Maure, a small town of Touraine (Indre-et-Loire).
Saint-Pol, a small town of Artois (Pas-de-Calais).
Saint-Quentin (L. *Augusta Veromanduorum*), a town in the department of Aisne.
Salerno, a province and town of Southern Italy.
Salisbury, chief town of the county of Wilts, in England.
Satalieh, a town in Asiatic Turkey (Anatolia).
Saumur (L. ? *Segora* ; in modern Latin, *Salmurium*), a town in the department of Maine-et-Loire.
Sens (L. *Agendicum, Senones*), a large town in the department of Yonne.
Sivray, or *Civré*, an ancient town of Poitou (Vienne).
Sluys, a small town in Flanders.

T.

Tewkesbury, a town in Gloucestershire.
Tiberias (now *Tabarieh*), a town in Palestine.
Toulouse (L. *Tolosa*), chief town of the department of Haute-Garonne (capital of Languedoc).
Touraine. This province of Central France forms now the department of Indre-et-Loire.
Tours (L. *Cæsarodunum*, then *Turones*). capital of Touraine.
Trèves (L. *Treveri*), capital of *Belgica Prima* in the time of Julius Cæsar.
Troyes (L. *Augustobona, Tricasses*), chief town of the department of Aube.
Tyre, the capital of Phœnicia.

U.

Utrecht (L. *Trajectum ad Rhenum*), a city in Holland.

V.

Valenciennes, a large town in the department of the Nord.
Vaucouleurs (L. *Lorioum*), a small town in the department of the Meuse.
Vlaux-de-Cernay, a village in the department of Seine-et-Oise.

Velay (L. *Vellacum*), a small district in the province of Languedoc.
Vendôme (L. *Vendocinum*), a town in the department of Eure-et-Loir.
Villedaigne, a locality in the department of Aude (Languedoc).
Vitry-sur-Marne, a small town in the department of Marne.

W.

Waverley, a small town in Yorkshire.
Windsor. Charles, Duke of Orléans, was detained a prisoner there after the battle of Agincourt.

THE END.

PUBLICATIONS

OF THE

SOCIETY FOR PROMOTING CHRISTIAN KNOWLEDGE.

Most of these Works may be had in Ornamental Bindings, with Gilt Edges, at a small extra charge.

	s.	d.
A Brave Fight. Being a narrative of the many Trials of Master William Lee, Inventor. By the Rev. E. N. HOARE. With Three full-page Woodcuts. Crown 8vo. ....*Cloth boards*	2	0
A Dream of Reubens. By AUSTIN CLARE, author of "The Carved Cartoon," &c. With Three full-page Woodcuts. Crown 8vo. ....*Cloth boards*	1	6
An Innocent. By S. M. SITWELL, author of "Aunt Kezia's Will," &c. With Three page Woodcuts. Crown 8vo. *Cloth boards*	1	6
Baron's Head (The). By FRANCES VYVIAN. With Three page Woodcuts. Crown 8vo. ....*Cloth boards*	2	6
Bearing the Yoke. By HELEN SHIPTON, author of "Christopher," &c. With Three page Woodcuts. Crown 8vo. *Cloth boards*	2	0
Black Jack and Other Temperance Tales. By the Author of "Clary's Confirmation," &c. With Three page Woodcuts. Crown 8vo. ....*Cloth boards*	1	6
Bob Curtman's Wife. By the Author of "Clary's Confirmation," &c. With Three page Woodcuts. Crown 8vo. *Cloth boards* [Crown 8vo.	1	6

[12-8-85.]

PUBLICATIONS OF THE SOCIETY.

	s. d.
Captain Jewell's Wife. By the Author of "Our Valley." With Three page Woodcuts. Crown 8vo. ...*Cloth boards*	2 0
Carl Forrest's Faith. By MARY LINSKILL. With Three full-page Woodcuts. Crown 8vo. ....*Cloth boards*	1 6
Cuthbert Conningsby: A Sequel to "Maud Kinglake's Collect." By EVELYN E. GREEN. With Three page Woodcuts. Crown 8vo. ....*Cloth boards*	1 6
Crab Court. By M. SEELEY. With Three page Woodcuts. Crown 8vo. ....*Cloth boards*	1 6
Dick Darlington, at Home and Abroad. By A. H. ENGELBACH, Author of "Juanita," &c. With Three full-page Illustrations on toned paper. Crown 8vo. ....*Cloth boards*	2 0
Dresden Romance (A). By LAURA M. LANE. With Four page Woodcuts. Crown 8vo. ....*Cloth boards*	2 6
Good Copy (A) and Other Stories. By F. B. HARRISON. With Three page Woodcuts. Crown 8vo. *Cloth bds*	1 6
Great Captain (The): An Eventful Chapter in SPANISH HISTORY. By ULICK R. BURKE, M.A. With Two full-page Illustrations on toned paper. Crown 8vo. ...*Cloth boards*	2 0
Griffinhoof. By CRONA TEMPLE. With Four page Woodcuts. Crown 8vo. ....*Cloth boards*	3 6
Hide and Seek: A Story of the New Forest in 1647. By Mrs. FRANK COOPER. With Three full-page Illustrations on toned paper. Crown 8vo.............................*Cloth boards*	2 0
His First Offence: A True Tale of City Life. By RUTH LAMB, Author of "The Carpenter's Family," &c. With Three full-page Woodcuts. Crown 8vo. ....*Cloth boards*	1 6
Home and School: A Sequel to "the Snowball SOCIETY." By M. BRAMSTON. With Three full-page Woodcuts. Crown 8vo. ....*Cloth boards*	2 6
In His Courts. By MARGARET E. HAYES. With Three page Woodcuts. Crown 8vo. ....*Cloth boards*	2 6

		s.	d.

Isabeau's Hero: A Story of the Revolt of the Cevennes. By ESMÈ STUART, Author of "Mimi," &c. With Four full-page Woodcuts. Crown 8vo. ....*Cloth boards* **3 6**

Lapsed, not Lost: A Story of Roman Carthage. By the Author of "The Chronicles of the Schönberg-Cotta Family," &c. Crown 8vo. ....*Cloth boards* **2 6**

Lettice. By Mrs. MOLESWORTH, Author of "Carrots." With Three page Woodcuts. Crown 8vo. ....*Cloth boards* **2 0**

Magic Flute (The). By MARY LINSKILL. With Four page Woodcuts. Crown 8vo. .... *Cloth boards* **3 0**

Miles Lambert's Three Chances. By MARY E. PALGRAVE. With Three page Woodcuts. Crown 8vo. *Cloth bds.* **1 6**

Miscellanies of Animal Life. By ELIZABETH SPOONER. With Illustrations. Post 8vo. ....*Cloth boards* **2 0**

Muriel's Two Crosses; or, The Cross she rejected AND THE CROSS SHE CHOSE. By ANNETTE LYSTER. With Four page Woodcuts. Crown 8vo. ....*Cloth boards* **3 0**

Mutiny on the Albatross (The). By F. F. MOORE. With Four page Woodcuts. Crown 8vo.....................*Cloth boards* **3 6**

No Beauty. By H. L. CHILDE-PEMBERTON. With Three page Woodcuts. Crown 8vo. ....*Cloth boards* **2 6**

Not in Vain. By MARY E. PALGRAVE. With Three page Woodcuts. Crown 8vo. ....*Cloth boards* **2 6**

One Army (The). By S. M. SITWELL. With Three page Woodcuts. Crown 8vo.................................*Cloth boards* **2 0**

Out of the Shadows. By CRONA TEMPLE, Author of "Her Father's Inheritance," &c. With Three full-page Woodcuts. Crown 8vo. ....*Cloth boards* **2 0**

Paths in the Great Waters. A Tale wherein is comprised a record of Virginia's early troubles, together with the true history of the Bermudas or Somers Islands. By the Rev. E. N. HOARE. With Four full-page Woodcuts. Crown 8vo. *Cloth boards* **3 0**

PUBLICATIONS OF THE SOCIETY.

s. d.

Pirates' Creek (The). A Story of Treasure-quest. By S. W. SADLER, R.N., Author of "Slavers and Cruisers," &c. With Four full-page Woodcuts. Crown 8vo. ....*Cloth boards* 3 0

Pride of the Village (The). By A. EUBULE EVANS. With Three page Woodcuts. Crown 8vo. ....*Cloth boards* 2 6

Prisoner's Daughter (The): A Story of 1758. By ESMÉ STUART. With Four page Woodcuts. Crown 8vo. *Cloth boards* 3 6

Shadow and Shine. By MARY DAVISON, Author of "Lucile." With Three page Woodcuts. Crown 8vo. *Cloth bds.* 1 6

Sketches of Our Life at Sarawak. By HARRIETTE MCDOUGALL. With Map and Four full-page Woodcuts. Crown 8vo. ....*Cloth boards* 2 6

Three Sixteenth-Century Sketches. By SARAH BROOK. With Three page Woodcuts. Crown 8vo. *Cloth boards* 2 6

Turbulent Town (A); Or, the Story of the Arteveldts. By the Rev. E. N. HOARE. With Four page Woodcuts. Crown 8vo. ....*Cloth boards* 3 0

Una Crichton. By the Author of "Our Valley," &c. With Four full-page Woodcuts. Crown 8vo............ *Cloth boards* 3 6

Valley of Baca (The). By the Author of "Douglas Deane," &c. With Three page Woodcuts. Crown 8vo. *Cloth bds* 1 6

Wild Goose Chase (A). By F. S. POTTER. With Three page Woodcuts. Crown 8vo. ....*Cloth boards* 1 6

LONDON:
NORTHUMBERLAND AVENUE, CHARING CROSS, W.C.;
43, QUEEN VICTORIA STREET, E.C.; 26, ST. GEORGE'S PLACE, S.W.
BRIGHTON: 135, NORTH STREET.

www.ingramcontent.com/pod-product-compliance
Lightning Source LLC
Chambersburg PA
CBHW030342230426
43664CB00007BA/498